VISUAL QUICKSTART GUIDE

# Illustrator 7

## FOR MACINTOSH AND WINDOWS

**Elaine Weinmann**
**Peter Lourekas**

Peachpit Press

Visual QuickStart Guide
**Illustrator 7 for Macintosh and Windows**
Elaine Weinmann and Peter Lourekas

Peachpit Press
1249 Eighth Street
Berkeley, CA 94710
510/548-4393
800/283-9444
510/548-5991 (fax)

Find us on the World Wide Web at: http://www.peachpit.com

Peachpit Press is a division of Addison Wesley Longman

Cover design: The Visual Group
Interior design: Elaine Weinmann
Production: Elaine Weinmann and Peter Lourekas
Illustrations: Elaine Weinmann and Peter Lourekas, except as
noted

**Colophon**
This book was created with QuarkXPress 3.3 on a PowerTower
Pro 200 and a Power Macintosh 8500. The fonts used are
Sabon, Gill Sans, and NuevaMM from Adobe Systems Inc.

ISBN 0-201-69624-X
9 8 7 6 5 4

Printed and bound in the United States of America

This book is dedicated to

Martine

and

Danielle

# TABLE OF CONTENTS

Table of Contents

**Table of Contents**

Table of Contents

**Table of Contents**

Table of Contents

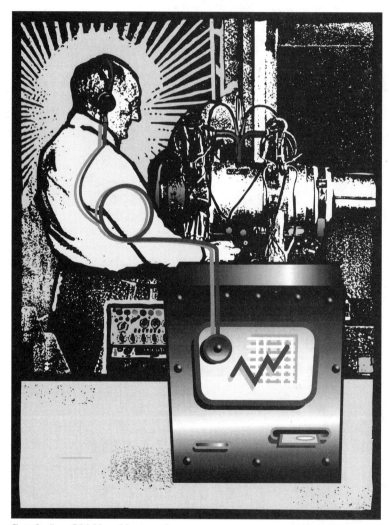

*Chris Spollen,* **Old Man Macintosh**

elcome to Illustrator 7, the electronic drawing kit from Adobe Systems Inc. Illustrator is a complete set of tools and commands for creating many different kinds of drawings, from corporate logos and symbols to children's book illustrations, from medical illustrations to party invitations.

If you're new to Illustrator, you might be terrified by your first glance at the 42 tools on the Toolbox and the 14 moveable palettes (Heavens!). Once you get rolling with this book in hand, though, you'll see that you can create hand-drawn shapes using an easy freehand style or create perfect geometric objects simply by clicking on your screen—bing. Once you learn how to create basic shapes, you will then learn how to select them, rearrange them, reshape them, and recolor them.

Your Illustrator masterpiece can be composed of objects, type, bitmap images, or all of the above. You can style type using an assortment of typesetting and word processing features or you can create your own letterforms by converting type into outlines and then reshaping the outlines like you would any other object. Using the Layers palette—Illustrator's indispensible stacking system—you can display/hide and organize individual drawing components. And when your illustration is completed, you can print it, color separate it, export it to another application, display it on the World Wide Web, or throw it in the Trash. As in our other *Visual QuickStart Guides,* the absolute read-me-first essentials are concentrated in the early chapters, whereas the latter chapters cover power tools like masks, compounds, and pathfinders, and precision tools like guides, grids, and the Align palette.

Is this a BIG, nasty upgrade? Sort of. What's big? The interface is different and lots of the keyboard shortcuts—a power user's best friend—are new or changed (sorry to break the news to you). If you got into a nice rhythm with the previous version of the application, and particularly if you were a

Michael Bartalos, **Technobabble,**
for Digital Equipment Corporation

virtuostic keyboard artist, these changes will be mildly to grossly irritating. The new shortcuts will start growing on you once you get over the annoying re-learning hump, and they'll save you time and energy in the long run. Use the list of frequently used shortcuts on the book's back flap for quick reference or refer to the complete shortcuts list in Appendix A. Many of the Illustrator shortcuts match those in Photoshop, so if you're a Photoshop 4 user, you'll have a head start. What's small? The new features list is, well, short. Whether that's a relief or a disappointment depends on what you were pining away for.

What's the same in this book? You'll find our trademark, reassuring, easy-to-follow, step-by-step instructions on almost every page, as always. And of course hundreds of screen captures of program features, and hundreds of images that were drawn in Illustrator, most of which were created expressly for this book. What's new? Lots of new illustrations, tips, and tricks, and keyboard shortcuts on almost every page. You'll be a flamboyant keyboard artist in no time (clickety-clickety-ping-ping...). ■

# THE BASICS

Chris Spollen

*This chapter is an introduction to Illustrator's tools, menus, and palettes.*

## The monitor

Color monitors display 8-bit, 16-bit, or 24-bit color, depending on the amount of Video RAM or the video card installed. With 8-bit color, 256 colors are available for on-screen color mixing. With a 24-bit color card or 2–4 megabytes of video RAM installed, 16.7 million colors are available, and every color can be represented exactly (gradients also look smoother). In order to have enough room to display your illustration in a workable size and also have several palettes open, you'll need at least a 17-inch monitor, preferably larger.

## Memory allocation

**Macintosh:** Allocating extra RAM to Illustrator is one way to make it run faster. To learn how much RAM you have available to allocate, launch Illustrator and any other applications that you want to have running at the same time, click in the Finder, then choose About This Macintosh from the Apple menu. Total Memory is the amount of hardware RAM installed, Largest Unused Block is the amount of available RAM. The applications you launched and their RAM allotments are also displayed. Ideally, you should allocate at least 12 to 18 megabytes (MB) of RAM to Illustrator. To do this, quit Illustrator, click the Illustrator application icon in the Finder, choose Get Info from the File menu, then enter the desired amount in the Preferred size field. To enter 12 MB, for example, type in "12000". Be sure to reserve enough RAM to run the System.

**Windows:** You cannot directly adjust the amount of application RAM allocated to Illustrator. Let Windows takes care of virtual memory and the RAM allotment.

## Hardware

*Macintosh:* Illustrator will run fastest on a Power Mac with 16 megabytes of application RAM (random access memory) allocated to the program, or on a Quadra with at least 12 megabytes of application RAM. The application also requires System 7.5.1 or later and at least 25 MB of available hard disk space. A Quadra must contain a math co-processor for certain Illustrator filters to be accessible and useable. For maximum speed, run Illustrator on a 200 megahertz or faster Power Mac with 20 MB of RAM allocated to Illustrator and 50 MB of available hard disk space.

*Windows:* Illustrator will run on an Intel 80486 or higher PC processor, Windows 95 or Windows NT 4.0 or later, a hard drive with at least 20 megabytes of available space after loading Illustrator's folder of data, and at least 16 megabytes of RAM (random access memory). You'll also need a CD-ROM drive to install the software. Illustrator will run faster on a Pentium or Pentium Pro with 32 megabytes of RAM and a large hard drive with at least 50 megabytes of available space. For optimal speed, we recommend an Intel MMX chipset running at 200 megahertz or higher, and a large, fast hard drive.

## Storage

Though most Illustrator files are small in storage size, an illustration that contains placed images can be quite large and require a large hard drive for storage. You'll also need a removable storage device—i.e. a SyJet, magneto-optical, or Iomega Zip or Jaz drive—to transport files to and from a service bureau or print shop.

## The Illustrator screen: Macintosh

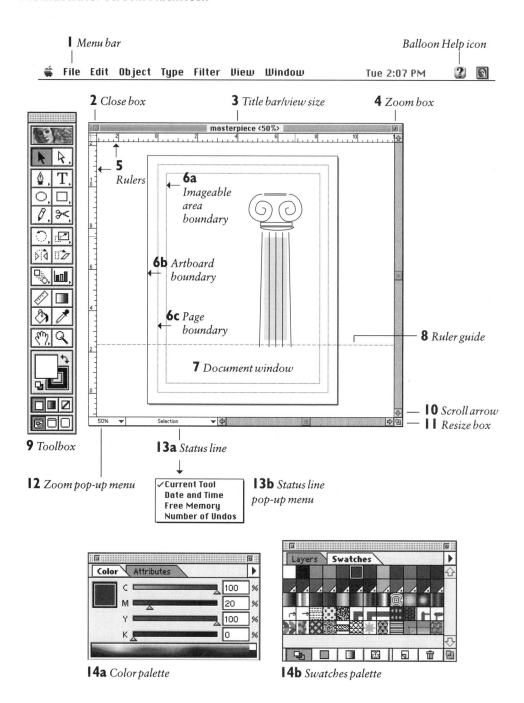

**1** *Menu bar*

*Balloon Help icon*

**2** *Close box*  **3** *Title bar/view size*  **4** *Zoom box*

**5** *Rulers*

**6a** *Imageable area boundary*

**6b** *Artboard boundary*

**6c** *Page boundary*

**7** *Document window*

**8** *Ruler guide*

**10** *Scroll arrow*
**11** *Resize box*

**9** *Toolbox*

**13a** *Status line*

**12** *Zoom pop-up menu*

**13b** *Status line pop-up menu*

**14a** *Color palette*  **14b** *Swatches palette*

## Key to the Illustrator screen: Macintosh

**1** *Menu bar*
Press a menu heading to access dialog boxes, submenus, and commands.

**2** *Close box*
To close a window or a palette, click its close box.

**3** *Title bar/view size*
Displays the illustration's title and view size.

**4** *Zoom box*
Click a document window zoom box to enlarge the window or shrink it to its previous size. Click a palette zoom box to shrink the palette or restore it to its previous size.

**5** *Rulers*
The current position of the pointer is indicated by a mark on the horizontal and vertical rulers. Ruler and dialog box increments can be displayed in any of five different units of measure.

**6a, b, c** *Imageable area, Artboard boundary, and Page boundary*
The Imageable area—within the margin guides—is the area that will print on the currently selected printer paper size. The Artboard is the user-defined work area and the largest possible printable area. The non-printing Page boundary corresponds to the paper size for the currently selected printer. Objects can be stored in the scratch area, but they won't print.

**7** *Document window*
The illustration window.

**8** *Ruler guide*
A non-printing guide used for aligning objects. Press and drag from either ruler to create a guide.

**9** *Toolbox palette*
The Toolbox contains 42 drawing and editing tools.

**10** *Scroll arrow*
Click the down arrow to move the illustration upward in the document window. Click the up arrow to move the illustration downward.

**11** *Resize box*
To resize a window, press and drag its resize box diagonally.

**12** *Zoom pop-up menu*
Displays the current zoom or view percentage. Press to choose a zoom percentage from a pop-up menu.

**13a, b** *Status line*
Displays the name of the currently selected tool, the current Date and Time from the Macintosh Control Panel, the amount of Free Memory (RAM) available for the currently open file, or the Number of Undos/Redos available, depending on which category you select from the pop-up menu. Hold down Option and press on the Status line pop-up menu to choose special information options (try it!).

**14a, b** *Palettes*
Swatches/Layers & Color/Attributes are four of 14 moveable palettes that open from the Window and Type menus.

Illustrrator Screen (Macintosh)

3

## The Illustrator screen: Windows

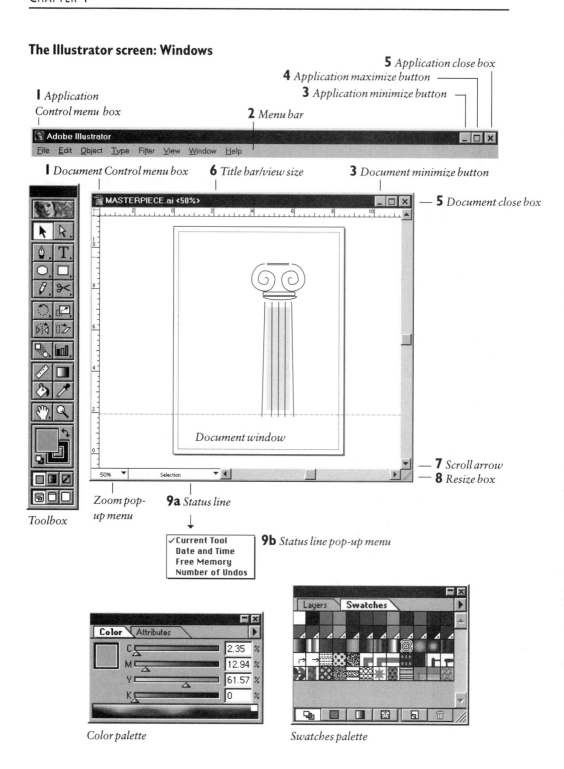

**5** *Application close box*

**4** *Application maximize button*

**3** *Application minimize button*

**2** *Menu bar*

**I** *Application Control menu box*

**I** *Document Control menu box*   **6** *Title bar/view size*   **3** *Document minimize button*

**5** *Document close box*

*Document window*

**7** *Scroll arrow*

**8** *Resize box*

*Zoom pop-up menu*

**9a** *Status line*

*Toolbox*

**9b** *Status line pop-up menu*

*Color palette*

*Swatches palette*

*Illustrator Screen (Windows)*

## Key to the Illustrator screen: Windows*

**1** *Application (or Document) Control menu box*
The Application Control menu box commands are Restore, Move, Size, Minimize, Maximize, and Close. The Document Control menu box commands are Restore, Move, Size, Minimize, Maximize, Close, and Next.

**2** *Menu bar*
Press a menu heading to access dialog boxes, submenus, and commands.

**3** *Application (or Document) minimize button*
Click the Application minimize button to shrink the document to an icon in the Taskbar. Click the icon on the Taskbar to restore the application window to its previous size.

Click the Document minimize button to shrink the document to an icon at the bottom left corner of the application window. Click the icon to restore the document window to its previous size.

**4** *Application (or Document) maximize/restore button*
Click the Application or Document Restore button to restore a window to its previous size. When a window is at the restored size,
the Restore button turns into the Maximize button. Click the Maximize button to enlarge the window.

**5** *Close box*
To close an image or a palette, click its close box.

**6** *Title bar/view size*
The image's title and view size.

**7** *Scroll arrow*
Click the down arrow to move the illustration upward in the document window. Click the up arrow to move the illustration downward.

**8** *Resize box*
To resize a window, press and drag its resize box diagonally.

**9a, b** *Status line*
Displays the name of the currently selected tool, the current Date and Time from the Windows Control Panel, the amount of Free Memory (RAM) available for the currently open file, or the Number of Undos/Redos available, depending on which category you choose from the pop-up menu. Hold down Alt and press on the Status line pop-up menu to choose special information options (try it!).

*The rulers, imageable area, artboard boundary, page boundary, document window, ruler guide, Toolbox, other palettes, and Zoom pop-up menu are described on page 3.

*Illustrator Screen (Windows)*

## The Toolbox

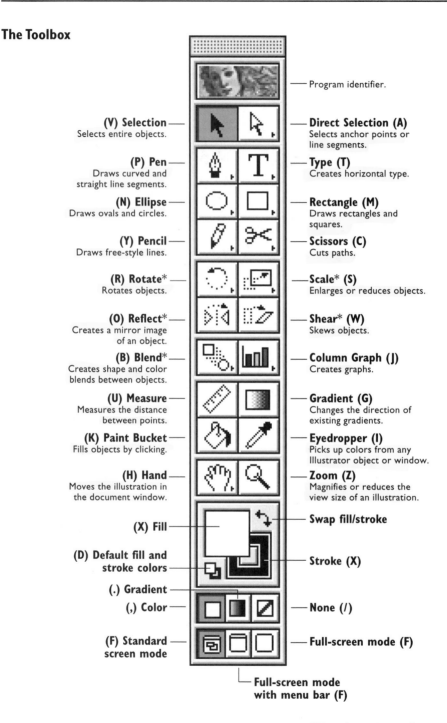

Program identifier.

**(V) Selection**
Selects entire objects.

**Direct Selection (A)**
Selects anchor points or line segments.

**(P) Pen**
Draws curved and straight line segments.

**Type (T)**
Creates horizontal type.

**(N) Ellipse**
Draws ovals and circles.

**Rectangle (M)**
Draws rectangles and squares.

**(Y) Pencil**
Draws free-style lines.

**Scissors (C)**
Cuts paths.

**(R) Rotate\***
Rotates objects.

**Scale\* (S)**
Enlarges or reduces objects.

**(O) Reflect\***
Creates a mirror image of an object.

**Shear\* (W)**
Skews objects.

**(B) Blend\***
Creates shape and color blends between objects.

**Column Graph (J)**
Creates graphs.

**(U) Measure**
Measures the distance between points.

**Gradient (G)**
Changes the direction of existing gradients.

**(K) Paint Bucket**
Fills objects by clicking.

**Eyedropper (I)**
Picks up colors from any Illustrator object or window.

**(H) Hand**
Moves the illustration in the document window.

**Zoom (Z)**
Magnifies or reduces the view size of an illustration.

**(X) Fill**

**Swap fill/stroke**

**(D) Default fill and stroke colors**

**Stroke (X)**

**(.) Gradient**

**(,) Color**

**None (/)**

**(F) Standard screen mode**

**Full-screen mode (F)**

**Full-screen mode with menu bar (F)**

*\*Transformation tools*

Toolbox

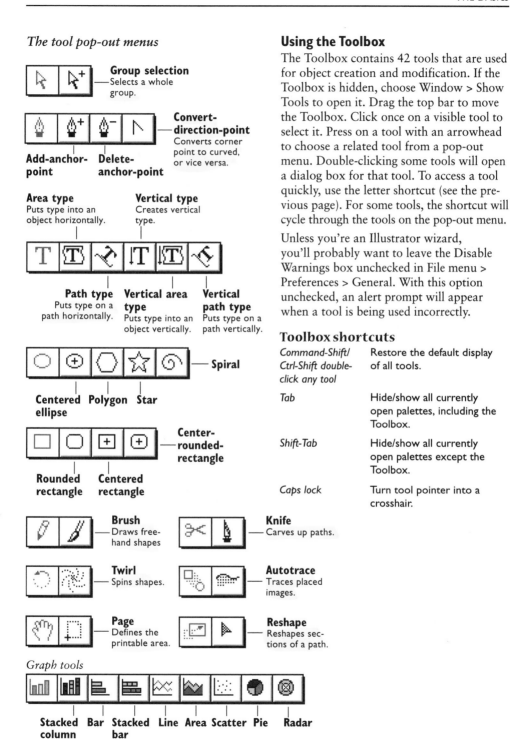

## The tool pop-out menus

**Group selection**
Selects a whole group.

**Convert-direction-point**
Converts corner point to curved, or vice versa.

**Add-anchor-point**

**Delete-anchor-point**

**Area type**
Puts type into an object horizontally.

**Vertical type**
Creates vertical type.

**Path type**
Puts type on a path horizontally.

**Vertical area type**
Puts type into an object vertically.

**Vertical path type**
Puts type on a path vertically.

**Spiral**

**Centered ellipse**  **Polygon**  **Star**

**Center-rounded-rectangle**

**Rounded rectangle**  **Centered rectangle**

**Brush**
Draws free-hand shapes

**Knife**
Carves up paths.

**Twirl**
Spins shapes.

**Autotrace**
Traces placed images.

**Page**
Defines the printable area.

**Reshape**
Reshapes sections of a path.

### Graph tools

**Stacked column**  **Bar**  **Stacked bar**  **Line**  **Area**  **Scatter**  **Pie**  **Radar**

## Using the Toolbox

The Toolbox contains 42 tools that are used for object creation and modification. If the Toolbox is hidden, choose Window > Show Tools to open it. Drag the top bar to move the Toolbox. Click once on a visible tool to select it. Press on a tool with an arrowhead to choose a related tool from a pop-out menu. Double-clicking some tools will open a dialog box for that tool. To access a tool quickly, use the letter shortcut (see the previous page). For some tools, the shortcut will cycle through the tools on the pop-out menu.

Unless you're an Illustrator wizard, you'll probably want to leave the Disable Warnings box unchecked in File menu > Preferences > General. With this option unchecked, an alert prompt will appear when a tool is being used incorrectly.

### Toolbox shortcuts

| | |
|---|---|
| *Command-Shift/ Ctrl-Shift double-click any tool* | Restore the default display of all tools. |
| *Tab* | Hide/show all currently open palettes, including the Toolbox. |
| *Shift-Tab* | Hide/show all currently open palettes except the Toolbox. |
| *Caps lock* | Turn tool pointer into a crosshair. |

**Toolbox**

**Mini-glossary**

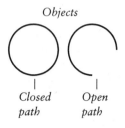

*Objects*

*Closed path*    *Open path*

**Object**  Any individual shape created in Illustrator.

**Path**  The edge of an object that defines its shape. Paths are composed of anchor points with direction lines which are joined by line segments. These elements can be modified to reshape the object. A path can be open or closed.

◆

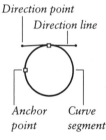

*Direction point*
*Direction line*

*Anchor point*    *Curve segment*

*Straight segment*

**Anchor point**  A corner point or a curve (smooth) point that joins two segments of a path.

**Curve segment**  The segment between two curve anchor points or a corner point and a curve anchor point.

**Straight segment**  The segment between two corner points.

**Direction line**  The control handle that defines the shape of a curved path segment. To reshape a segment, rotate, lengthen, or shorten a direction line by dragging its direction point.

◆

*Selected object*

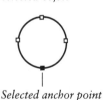

*Selected anchor point*

**Select**  Click on an object or group with the Selection or Group Selection tool to select the whole object or group. All anchor points and segments will be highlighted.

**Direct select**  Click on an anchor point or segment with the Direct Selection tool to select only that anchor point or segment.

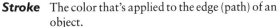

*Fill*

*Stroke*

*Linear     Radial*
*Gradient  Gradient*

*Transparent*

*Original  Compound*
*objects      Path*

*Original*
*objects*

*Mask      Mask*
*(Preview  (Artwork*
*view)      view)*

**Stroke** The color that's applied to the edge (path) of an object.

**Fill** A color, pattern or gradient that's applied to the inside of an object.

**Gradient fill** A graduated blend between two or more colors. A Gradient fill can be linear (side to side) or radial (radiating outward from a center point of your choice).

**Stack** The positioning of objects on top of one another within a layer. The most recently created object is placed at the top of the stack.

**Layer** The positioning of a stack of objects relative to other stacks. An illustration can contain multiple layers, which can be reordered.

**Compound path** Two or more objects that are combined into a larger, single object. Areas where the original objects overlapped become transparent.

**Mask** An object that trims ("clips") away parts of other objects that extend beyond its border. Only parts of objects that are within the confines of the mask object will display and print.

**Group** Individual objects that are combined so they can be moved or modified as a unit. When objects are grouped, they are moved to the layer of the topmost object.

**Mini-glossary**

## Units of measure

You can enter numbers in dialog boxes or on palettes in any of the units of measure used in Illustrator, regardless of the default ruler units. You can choose a default unit of measure for the application *(see page 266)* or for a particular document *(see page 256)*. If you enter a number in a unit of measure other than the default unit, the number will be translated into the default unit when you press Tab or Return/Enter. If you enter the symbol for subtraction (-), addition (+), multiplication (*), or division (/) in any entry field, the program will do the math for you automatically.

**TIP** To enter a combination of picas and points, separate the two numbers by a "p." For example, 4p2 equals four picas plus 2 points, or 50 pts.). Be sure to highlight the entire entry field first.

## Our new writing format

If you're familiar with the previous edition of this book, you may notice that we changed our writing format slightly. We did this to make more room for tips, keyboard shortcuts, and other helpful information. Where you see a configuration like this: View menu > Artwork, its just a less wordy way of saying "Choose Artwork from the View menu." And if you see a configuration like this: Filter menu > Colors > Saturate, it means you should choose Saturate from the Colors submenu under the Filter menu. So this is the basic format:

**Menu > command** *or*
**Menu > submenu > command**

And, because this is a hybrid Macintosh/Windows book, you'll notice we're using a new format for writing keyboard shortcuts. Here's an example: Command-S/Ctrl-S. If you're a Macintosh user, train yourself to always look to the left of the slash for your shortcut; Windows users, look to the right of the slash.

**Macintosh shortcut/Windows shortcut**

## Division the easy way

Select an object. In the W or H field on the Transform palette, click to the right of the current entry, type an asterisk, then type a percentage. For example, enter "*50%" to reduce the current value by half (i.e., 4p becomes 2p). Or type *75% to reduce the W or H to three-quarters of it's current value (i.e., 4p becomes 3p). Press Tab to apply the division and advance to another field or press Return/Enter to exit the palette. If you highlight the whole field, you only need to type in the percentage ("50%"), without the asterisk (*).

## Symbols you can use

| Unit | Symbol | |
|---|---|---|
| Picas | p | |
| Points | pt | |
| Inches | " *or* in | *12 pts = 1 pica* |
| Millimeters | mm | *6 picas = 1 inch* |
| Centimeters | cm | |

## The Illustrator menus

### The File menu

File menu commands are used to create, open, close, save, print, or color separate an illustration; place (import) art or text from another application; choose document, printer or separation specifications; set application and document preferences; choose color settings; and quit/exit Illustrator.

### The Edit menu

Edit menu commands include Undo and Redo, the Clipboard commands Cut, Copy, and Paste, the Select commands, the Paste In Front/ Paste In Back commands, which place the current Clipboard contents in front of or behind the currently selected object, Define Pattern, for creating custom patterns, and the Select commands.

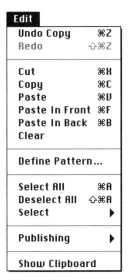

| File | |
|---|---|
| New | ⌘N |
| Open... | ⌘O |
| Close | ⌘W |
| Save | ⌘S |
| Save As... | ⇧⌘S |
| Save a Copy... | ⌥⌘S |
| Revert | |
| Place... | |
| Export... | |
| Selection Info... | |
| Separation Setup... | ⌥⌘P |
| Document Setup... | ⇧⌘P |
| Print... | ⌘P |
| Preferences ▶ | |
| Color Settings... | |
| Quit | ⌘Q |

| Edit | |
|---|---|
| Undo Copy | ⌘Z |
| Redo | ⇧⌘Z |
| Cut | ⌘H |
| Copy | ⌘C |
| Paste | ⌘U |
| Paste In Front | ⌘F |
| Paste In Back | ⌘B |
| Clear | |
| Define Pattern... | |
| Select All | ⌘A |
| Deselect All | ⇧⌘A |
| Select ▶ | |
| Publishing ▶ | |
| Show Clipboard | |

### About the Undo command

To undo an operation, choose Edit > Undo (Command-Z/Ctrl-Z). To undo the second-to-last operation, choose Edit > Undo again, and so on. To reverse an undo, choose Edit > Redo (Command-Shift-Z/Ctrl-Shift-Z). You can undo after saving your document, but not if you close and then reopen it.

The minimum number of undos that you can perform depends on the Undo Levels setting in the Units & Undo Preferences dialog box (File menu). You can undo up to 200 operations, depending on currently available memory. If Illustrator requires additional RAM to perform illustration edits, it will reduce the specified number of undos to the minimum.

### The Object menu

Under the Object menu are many essential commands for styling and shaping objects. The Transform commands augment or modify the shape of an object. The Transform Again command repeats the last transformation. The Arrange commands reposition an object or objects within a stack. Other Object menu commands can be used to group, lock, hide, or rasterize an object (turn it into a bitmap). The Path commands join line segments, average anchor points, or slice objects into smaller shapes. The Pathfinder commands combine, divide, and color-mix overlapping objects. Separate chapters in this book are devoted to masks, compound paths, and graphs, which are also created via Object menu commands.

### The Type menu

Use the Font submenu to choose fonts that are currently installed and available in your System. Type specifications are applied via the Character, Paragraph, MM Design, or Tab Ruler palette, all of which are opened from this menu. Other Type menu features control text flow by linking type blocks, wrapping type around objects, and creating text rows and columns. The Smart Punctuation command produces professional typesetting marks, and the Create Outlines command converts type characters into graphic objects. Word processing features under this menu include Check Spelling, Find/Change, and Find Font. The Type Orientation command changes horizontal type into vertical type, or vice versa.

### The Filter menu

The various Illustrator filters recolor, create, distort, and stylize objects. The Ink Pen filters create a hand-drawn fill effect. Commands in the lower part of the menu apply artistic effects only to rasterized objects or placed bitmap images.

### The View menu

View menu commands affect document display. You can choose the full-color Preview view or wire frame Artwork view, enlarge or reduce the view size, show or hide rulers, tiling, edges, guides and the grid, enable objects to snap to the grid, and create and choose custom view settings via View menu commands.

| View | |
|---|---|
| Artwork | ⌘Y |
| Preview Selection | ⇧⌘Y |
| Zoom In | ⌘+ |
| Zoom Out | ⌘- |
| Fit In Window | ⌘0 |
| Actual Size | ⌘1 |
| Hide Edges | ⌘H |
| Hide Page Tiling | |
| Show Rulers | ⌘R |
| Hide Guides | ⌘; |
| Lock Guides | ⌥⌘; |
| Make Guides | ⌘5 |
| Release Guides | ⌥⌘5 |
| Show Grid | ⌘" |
| Snap To Grid | ⇧⌘" |
| New View... | |
| Edit Views... | |

Filter Menu; View Menu

### The Window menu

Window menu commands create new or activate open illustration windows and hide and show most of the palettes. Windows users can cascade or tile open document windows using Window menu commands. Other Swatch Libraries from other color systems like PANTONE or other Illustrator documents are imported via this menu.

### The Help menu

The Help menu commands provide access to on-screen support. Macintosh users: Choose Adobe Illustrator Help Contents from the System's Balloon Help menu (the ? icon). Windows users: Choose from the Help menu. Plug-in information can also be accessed from this menu. On either platform, choose How to Use Help to learn about on-screen Help.

If you are connected to the World Wide Web, you can access the Adobe Illustrator Web Site from either platform.

Macintosh Help menu

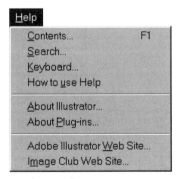

Windows Help menu

## Dialog boxes

Dialog boxes are like fill-in forms with multiple choices. The various ways to indicate choices are shown in the figure below.

To open a dialog box, choose any menu item followed by an ellipsis (...) or use the corresponding keyboard shortcut.

Some modifications are made by entering a number in an entry field. Press **Tab** to highlight the next field in a dialog box. Hold down **Shift** and press **Tab** to highlight the previous field. Press on a drop-down menu to choose from more options.

Click **OK** or press **Return/Enter** to accept modifications and exit a dialog box. To cancel a dialog box, use the Command-**.** (period) shortcut or press Esc.

Many Illustrator dialog boxes now have a **Preview** option, which, when turned on, will apply the effect while the dialog box is open. Take advantage of this great time-saver. In a dialog box that has sliders, you can hold down Option/Alt and click Reset to restore the last used settings to the dialog box.

Illustrator dialog boxes, like all the other features in the program, function the same way in Macintosh and Windows. The differences in appearance are due to the graphic interface inherent in each operating system.

*A **Windows** dialog box.*

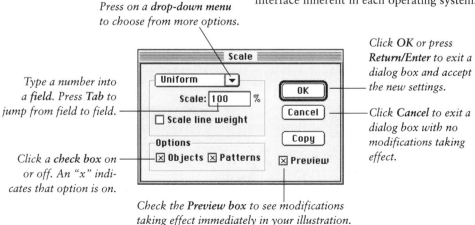

*Press on a **drop-down menu** to choose from more options.*

*Type a number into a field. Press **Tab** to jump from field to field.*

*Click a **check box** on or off. An "x" indicates that option is on.*

*Check the **Preview box** to see modifications taking effect immediately in your illustration.*

*Click **OK** or press **Return/Enter** to exit a dialog box and accept the new settings.*

*Click **Cancel** to exit a dialog box with no modifications taking effect.*

*A **Macintosh** dialog box.*

## The palettes

### How to use the palettes

There are 14 moveable palettes that are used for creating artwork. To save screen space, the palettes are joined into groups: Color/Attributes, Stroke/Gradient, Layers/Swatches, Character/Paragraph/ MM Design, Info/Transform/Align, Tab Ruler, and Toolbox, but you can compose your own groups.

To **separate** a palette from its group, drag its tab (palette name) away from the group **1**–**2**. To **add** a palette to any group, drag the tab over the group. When you release the mouse it will be the frontmost palette in the group. The Layers/Swatches group window can be widened, so if you want to gather more palettes together, use this one as your home base so the tabs (palette names) will be readable across the top.

To **dock** (hook up) a palette to the bottom of another palette or palette group, drag the

tab name to the bottom of another palette, and release the mouse when the thick, black line appears **3**. To un-dock, drag the palette tab name away from the dock group.

**Open** the Character, Paragraph, Tab Ruler, or MM Design palette from the Type menu. Open all the other palettes from the Window menu. The palette name you choose will appear in front in its group.

To **display** an open palette at the front of its group, click its tab (palette name).

Press Tab to **hide/show** all currently open palettes, including the Toolbox. Press Shift-Tab to hide/show all open palettes except the Toolbox. Palettes that are open when you quit/exit Illustrator will appear in their same location when you re-launch.

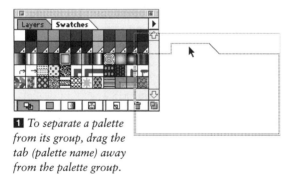

**1** *To separate a palette from its group, drag the tab (palette name) away from the palette group.*

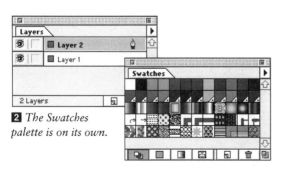

**2** *The Swatches palette is on its own.*

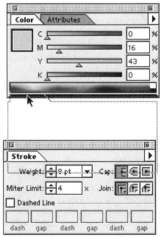

**3** *To dock palettes together, drag the tab name of one palette to the bottom of another palette, and release the mouse when the thick, black line appears.*

*Double-click a tab to cycle through the palette configurations: Tab name only, one option panel, or two option panels.*

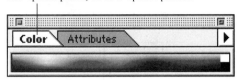

*To collapse a palette or group of palettes, click the zoom box (Macintosh) or the minimize/ maximize box (Windows). Click again to restore a palette to its last open size.*

### Macintosh users
You can shrink your palettes using the Macintosh WindowShade feature. Choose WindowShade from the Control Panels submenu under the Apple menu. With WindowShade on at a setting of two clicks ◼, you can double-click any window or palette move bar to shrink the palette to its name only. Double-click it again to enlarge the palette. *Note:* The Tools palette requires three clicks.

In OS8, the new Macintosh operating system, the WindowShade feature will be accessed via a box in the upper right corner of every window.

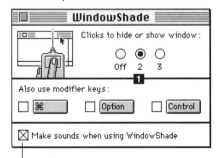

*Check this box if you like sound effects ("Whoosh").*

## Free up screen space
To **shrink** a palette, double-click its tab. Double-click a tab again to enlarge the palette. Or click the palette zoom box (Macintosh) or the minimize/maximize box (Windows) (both in the upper right corner) to reduce a palette to just the tab names. Click again to restore the last size of the palette.

All the palettes except Info/Transform/Align have two panels. To display the full palette, choose Show Options from the pop-up menu at the palette's upper right.

**The Toolbox, Color, and Stroke palettes**
The current fill and stroke colors display in color squares on the Toolbox **1**, and on the Color palette **2**. The Color palette displays the color model and breakdown of the fill or stroke in the currently selected object or objects, and is used to mix process colors or adjust spot color tints. The Stroke palette displays the weight and style of the stroke in the currently selected object or objects, and can be used to change those attributes. If no object is selected, then changes made on the Color or Stroke palette will apply to newly drawn objects.

*Whichever box (Fill or Stroke) is currently active (is on top) will be affected by changes on the Color palette.*

*Swap Fill and Stroke colors*

**1** *Fill color*

*Stroke color*

*Default Fill and Stroke colors*

*Color*

*None (no color)*

*Gradient*

## Color palette
The Color palette is used for mixing and choosing fill and stroke colors. Choose a color model for the current color from the palette pop-up menu. You can quick-select a color or black or white from the color bar on the bottom of the palette.

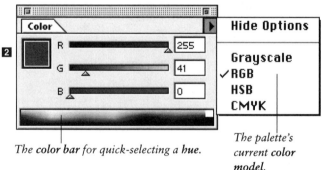

*The color bar for quick-selecting a hue.*

*The palette's current color model.*

## Stroke palette
The Stroke palette is used for editing the stroke weight and style on the currently selected object, and for creating dashed lines.

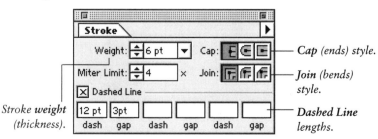

*Cap (ends) style.*

*Join (bends) style.*

*Stroke weight (thickness).*

*Dashed Line lengths.*

## The Swatches palette

Click on a swatch to make that color the current fill or stroke color, depending on which of those color boxes on the Toolbox is currently active. Drag from the current Fill or Stroke color box on the Toolbox or the Color palette or from an object in your illustration to the Swatches palette to save a swatch of that color in the current file.

*A **selected** swatch*

*Choose commands for viewing and editing swatches from this pop-up menu.*

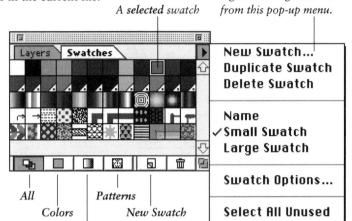

*Swatch display icons*

*All*

*Colors*

*Patterns*

*Gradients*

*New Swatch*

## The Gradient palette

Use the Gradient palette to edit an existing gradient or create a new gradient. Move a color by dragging its square, or click a square and use the Color palette to choose a different color, or click below the color bar to add a new color.

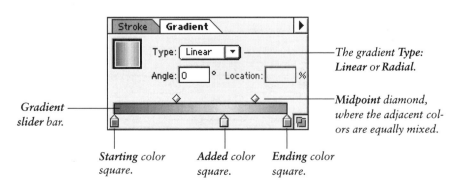

*The gradient **Type**: Linear or **Radial**.*

*Gradient slider bar.*

*Midpoint diamond, where the adjacent colors are equally mixed.*

*Starting color square.*

*Added color square.*

*Ending color square.*

## The Character palette

The Character palette is used to apply type attributes: Font, size, leading, baseline shift, vertical scale, horizontal scale, tracking, and kerning. To apply an attribute to currently highlighted text, choose a value from the drop-down menu, or click the up or down arrow, or enter a value in the field and press Return/Enter. The palette is also used for choosing foreign language options.

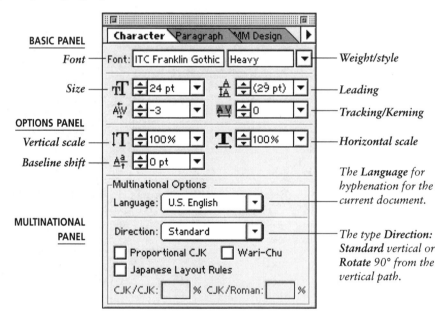

BASIC PANEL
Font
Weight/style
Size
Leading
Tracking/Kerning
OPTIONS PANEL
Vertical scale
Horizontal scale
Baseline shift

*The **Language** for hyphenation for the current document.*

MULTINATIONAL PANEL

*The type **Direction**: **Standard** vertical or **Rotate** 90° from the vertical path.*

## Multiple Masters Design palette

The Multiple Masters Design palette is used to edit variables for multiple master fonts. Each edited multiple master font is called an instance. Instances are saved with the document in which they are created.

*Font name*

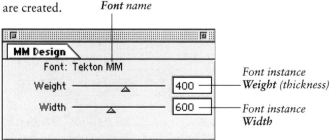

*Font instance **Weight** (thickness)*

*Font instance **Width***

## The Paragraph palette

The Paragraph palette is used to apply para-graph-wide specifications, including horizon-tal alignment, indentation, inter-paragraph spacing, word spacing, and letter spacing.

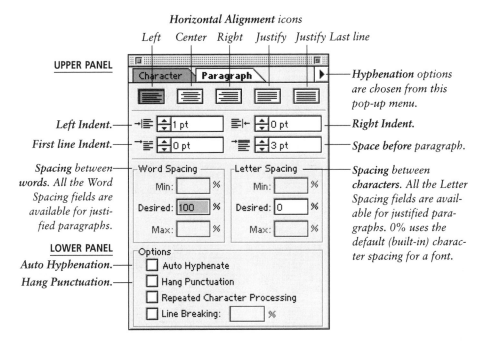

*Horizontal Alignment* icons

Left    Center    Right    Justify    Justify Last line

UPPER PANEL

*Hyphenation* options are chosen from this pop-up menu.

*Left Indent.*

*First line Indent.*

*Right Indent.*

*Space before* paragraph.

*Spacing between words. All the Word Spacing fields are available for justified paragraphs.*

*Spacing between characters. All the Letter Spacing fields are available for justified paragraphs. 0% uses the default (built-in) character spacing for a font.*

LOWER PANEL

*Auto Hyphenation.*

*Hang Punctuation.*

## The Tab Ruler palette

The Tab Ruler palette is used to insert or reposition custom tab markers, which are used to align columns of text.

*The **Left-, Center-, Right-,** or **Decimal-Justified** button.*

*Check the **Snap** box to have a tab marker snap to the nearest ruler tic mark as you insert it or drag it. Or, to temporarily turn on the Snap fea-ture when the Snap box is unchecked, hold down **Command/Ctrl** as you drag a marker. Ruler increments will display in the currently chosen Ruler units (Document Setup or Preferences).*

*Click the **Alignment** box to align the Tab Ruler with the left edge of the currently selected text.*

*A **left-justified tab marker.** To move a tab stop, drag the marker to the left or the right.*

*A selected **center-justified tab marker.***

*Drag the **Extend Tab ruler** box to the right to widen the ruler.*

**Paragraph Palette; Tab Ruler Palette**

### The Layers palette

The Layers palette is used to add, delete, hide/show, and restack layers in an illustration. You can also use this palette to control which layers are editable or printable, or to move an object to a different layer.

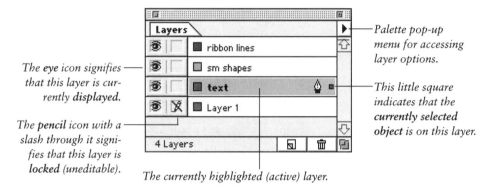

*The eye icon signifies that this layer is currently displayed.*

*The pencil icon with a slash through it signifies that this layer is locked (uneditable).*

*Palette pop-up menu for accessing layer options.*

*This little square indicates that the currently selected object is on this layer.*

*The currently highlighted (active) layer.*

### The Info palette

If no object is selected in the current document, the Info palette shows the horizontal and vertical location of the pointer on the illustration, as in the palette illustrated at right. If an object is selected, the palette displays the location of the object on the page and the object's width and height. If a type tool and type are selected, the palette displays type specifications. The Info palette automatically opens when the Measure tool is used, and displays the distance and angle calculated by that tool.

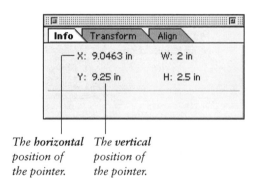

*The **horizontal** position of the pointer.*

*The **vertical** position of the pointer.*

### The Attributes palette

The Attributes palette is really a miscellaneous palette. Use it to specify overprint options, show or hide an object's center point, reverse an object's fill in a compound path, or change an object's output resolution.

In the URL field, you can enter a Web address for an object when designating it as an imagemap. Click Launch Browser to launch an installed Web browser.

*Reverse Path Direction On and Reverse Path Direction Off icons to reverse a shape's fill to transparency in a compound path.*

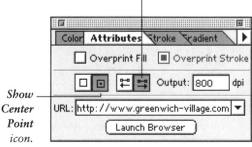

*Show Center Point icon.*

## The Align palette

The Align palette is used to align two or more objects along their centers or along their top, left, or bottom edges, or to equalize (distribute) the space between three or more objects.

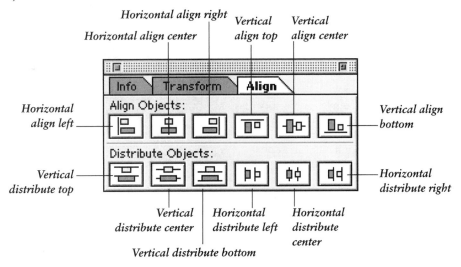

Horizontal align right
Horizontal align center
Vertical align top
Vertical align center

Horizontal align left

Vertical align bottom

Horizontal distribute right

Vertical distribute top

Vertical distribute center
Horizontal distribute left
Horizontal distribute center

Vertical distribute bottom

## The Transform palette

The Transform palette displays location, width, and height information for a selected object, and the palette can be used to move, resize, rotate, or shear a selected object or objects.

*The **Reference Point Options** icon (the part of the object from which the Transform palette amounts are calculated).*

*The **x** and **y** axes location of the currently selected object. Enter new values to move the object.*

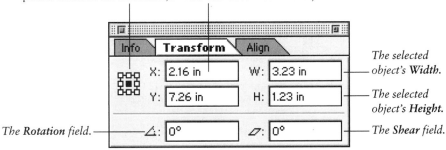

*The selected object's **Width.***

*The selected object's **Height.***

*The **Rotation** field.*

*The **Shear** field.*

## Context-sensitive menus

To choose a command from an on-screen menu without having to mouse to the menu bar or a palette, hold down Control and press the mouse button (Macintosh) or click the right mouse button (Windows).

*Note:* Some of the commands that appear on a context-sensitive menu may not be applicable to the currently selected objects.

## On-Screen help

An extensive on-screen help directory that functions like a digital stand-in for the Illustrator User Guide is supplied with the application. To open it, choose Adobe Illustrator Help Contents from the balloon help menu (Macintosh) or the Help menu (Windows).

You can access a topic in one of these three ways:

■ Click the Contents tab, double-click a book name, then double-click a topic.

■ Click the Index tab, scroll through and double-click a name on the list or type in the name of the feature you are looking for to locate it on the list.

■ Click the Find folder tab, type in a word or phrase to search for, then click Search.

You can quit the QuickHelp application or you can close the Help windows without quitting/exiting the Help application. If you don't quit QuickHelp, you can click in an open Illustrator window to get back into Illustrator.

*The Adobe Illustrator Help Contents window. Each tab offers a different method for locating information.*

## On-screen list of shortcuts

Macintosh users: Choose Keyboard from the balloon help menu. Windows users: Choose Keyboard from the Help menu. Click a category on the Shortcuts scroll list, then click the Windows or Macintosh tab or click Changed to see which shortcuts are new in Illustrator 7.

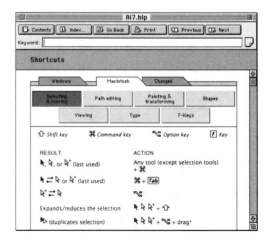

# HOW ILLUSTRATOR WORKS | 2

*In this chapter you will learn the basic differences between object-oriented and bitmap applications and you'll get a broad overview of how objects are created and modified in Illustrator.*

*bitmaps are raster-based*

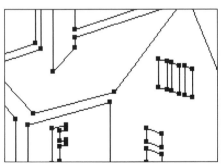

**1** *An object-oriented graphic.*

**2** *Closeup of the same object-oriented graphic in Artwork view, showing selected line segments and anchor points.*

## Illustrator is primarily an object-oriented program

*vector based*

There are two main types of picture-making applications on Macintosh or Windows: bitmap and object-oriented, and it's important to know their strengths and weaknesses. (The fancier terms "raster-based" and "vector-based" are sometimes also used.) Bitmap programs are great for creating soft, painterly effects; object-oriented programs are great for creating sharp, smooth-edged layered images, like logos, and for creating typographic designs.

Some of the latest versions of bitmap applications—like Painter—also have some built-in vector capabilities. In Illustrator, you can **rasterize** a vector image (convert an object-oriented image into a bitmap image). And you can also place or open a bitmap image into an Illustrator document.

Drawings created in an **object-oriented** program like Adobe Illustrator or Macromedia FreeHand are composed of separate, distinct objects that are positioned on one or more **layers**. Objects are drawn using free-style or precise drawing tools, and are mathematically defined. An object drawn in Illustrator can be recolored, resized, and reshaped without diminishing its sharpness or smoothness, and it can be moved easily without disturbing any other objects. An object in an object-oriented drawing will look smooth and sharp regardless of the size at which it is displayed or printed **1**–**2**.

Object-oriented files are usually relatively small in storage size, so you can save multiple versions of a file without filling up valuable hard drive space. And object-oriented drawings are resolution independent, which means the higher the resolution of the printer, the sharper and finer the printed image will be.

An image created in a **bitmap** program, like Photoshop, on the other hand, is composed of a single layer of tiny squares on a grid, called pixels. If you paint on a bitmap image, you'll recolor just that area of pixels, not whole, independent shapes. If you zoom in on a bitmap image, you'll see a checkerboard of tiny squares. Bitmap files tend to be quite large, and the printout quality of a bitmap image is dependent on the resolution of the image. On the other hand, bitmap programs are ideal for creating subtle color gradations, digital paintings or montages, photorealistic images, and for editing continuous-tone images **1**–**2**.

### How objects are made

The key building blocks that you will be using to compose an illustration are Bézier objects, type, and placed bitmap images. Bézier objects are composed of **anchor points** connected by **curved** or **straight segments** **3**. The edge of an object is called its **path**. A path can be open (with two end-points) or closed and continuous, and you can close an open path by joining its end-points or open a closed path using the Scissors tool.

Some Illustrator tools—like the Rectangle, Ellipse, Polygon, and Star—produce complete, closed paths simply by clicking on your screen. The number and position of the anchor points on these paths is determined automatically.

Other tools—like the Pencil and Pen—produce open *or* closed paths. To use these tools, you'll be clicking or dragging with the mouse. The **Pencil** tool creates open or closed freeform lines. The Paintbrush tool creates closed, ribbon-like brush stroke shapes. If you want to use a scanned image

**1** *A bitmap graphic.*

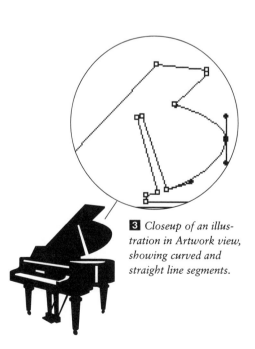

**2** *Extreme closeup of a bitmap, showing the individual pixels that make up the image.*

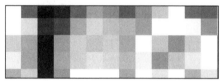

**3** *Closeup of an illustration in Artwork view, showing curved and straight line segments.*

as a starting point, you can place it into an Illustrator file and then trace it manually, or trace it automatically using the **Auto Trace** tool. And using Illustrator's most versatile tool of all—the **Pen**—you can create as many corner or curve anchor points as you need to form any shaped object.

### Type

Illustrator has six tools for creating PostScript **type**, and a smorgasbord of features with which type can be styled and formatted. Type can be free floating (point type), it can conform to the edge of an object (path type), or it can fill the inside of any shape object (area type). Depending on which tool is used to create it, path type or area type can flow and read vertically or horizontally. It can be repositioned, edited, restyled, recolored, or transformed. If your text is too long to fit inside its object, it can be linked so it flows into another object.

And finally, you can convert type characters into graphic objects, called **outlines**, which can be reshaped or modified like any other Illustrator object **1**–**2**. This is the way to personalize your letter shapes.

### How objects are modified

An object must be **selected** before it can be modified, and there are three tools that do the job: Selection, Direct Selection, and Group Selection.

An object can be modified using a variety of features, including filters and other menu commands, dialog boxes, palettes, and tools. There are 42 (yes, 42) tools and fourteen movable palettes (Tools, Color, Attributes, Stroke, Gradient, Character, Paragraph, MM Design, Tab Ruler, Layers, Swatches, Info, Transform, and Align). For fast access, leave most of them open while you work, but to save screen space, you can dock them together in groups and shrink down the ones you use infrequently.

An object's path can be reshaped by moving its anchor points or segments or by

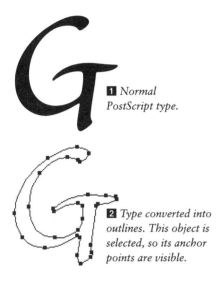

**1** *Normal PostScript type.*

**2** *Type converted into outlines. This object is selected, so its anchor points are visible.*

converting its curve anchor points into corner anchor points (or vice versa). A curve segment can be reshaped by rotating, lengthening, or shortening its direction lines. Because a path can be reshaped easily, you can draw a simple shape first and then develop it into a more complicated form later on **1**. We'll show you how to do this.

Some tools are specifically designed for modifying paths, such as the **Add-anchor-point** tool, which adds points to a path; the **Delete-anchor-point** tool, which deletes points from a path; the **Scissors** tool, which splits a path; the **Convert-direction-point** tool, which converts points from corner to curved (or vice versa); and the **Knife** tool, which carves out sections of an object like—well, a knife. The **Reshape** tool reshapes all or a portion of a path in one fell swoop.

Illustrator's **filters** modify a placed bitmap image or a vector object in one or two easy steps. They randomly distort an object's shape, modify its color, or add artistic, painterly touches or textures to a rasterized object or a placed bitmap image.

The **Pathfinder** commands combine overlapping objects, divide areas where objects overlap into separate objects, or apply color to areas where objects overlap—and produce a new object in the process.

Other modifications can be made using the **transformation** tools. The **Scale** tool enlarges or reduces an object's size; the **Rotate** tool rotates an object; the **Reflect** tool creates a mirror image of an object; the **Shear** tool slants an object; and the **Blend** tool transforms one object into another object by creating a series of transitional shapes. Multiple transformations can be performed at once using the Transform Each command or the Transform palette.

Still other Illustrator commands combine individual objects into more complex configurations. The **Compound Path** command, for example, "cuts" a hole through an

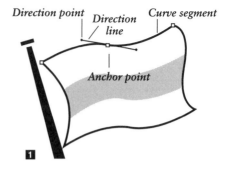

*Direction point*  *Direction line*  *Curve segment*

*Anchor point*

**1**

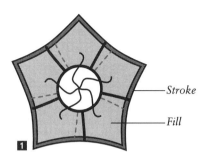

Stroke

Fill

object to reveal underlying shapes. Or you can use an object as a **mask** to hide parts of other objects that extend beyond its edges.

## Coloring

You can **fill** the inside of an object or **stroke** the edge of an object . A fill can be a flat color, a gradient (a smooth gradation of two or more colors), or a **pattern** of repeating shapes. You can create your own patterns and gradients right in Illustrator. A stroke can be solid or dashed.

A stroke or fill color can be a color from a matching system, like Pantone, or a CMYK, HSB, or RGB color that you mix yourself. In Illustrator, you can mix, apply, and save colors in a true RGB or CMYK color mode. This means that color will be consistent for its model—whether it's an RGB color being color managed for color separation, a CMYK color being color managed for displayed on screen, or a spot color being converted to a process color. For any illustration that is created for on-screen display (not print output) you can use the RGB color mode, the color mode for your computer screen.

## On the screen

You can draw an illustration by eye or you can use any of Illustrator's precision tools to help you work more exactly: **Rulers, guides, grids**, the **Measure** tool, the **Move** dialog box, and the **Align** palette.

You can change the **view size** of an illustration as you work to facilitate editing and reduce eyestrain. You can **Zoom in** to work on a small detail or **Zoom out** to see how the drawing looks as a whole. Or you can move the illustration in the document window using the **Hand** tool.

An illustration can be displayed and edited in **Preview** view 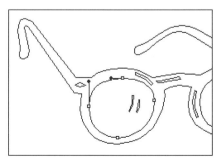, in which all the fill and stroke colors are displayed. To speed up editing and screen redraw and to make it easier to select anchor points, you can display your illustration in **Artwork** view **3**,

**2** *Preview view.*

**3** *Artwork view.*

**How Illustrator Works**

**29**

where objects are displayed as "wire frame" outlines. Or, you can selectively preview individual objects in **Preview Selection** view.

You may already be familiar with **tool tips**, the on-screen prompter, which you can use to remind yourself of a tool name or shortcut. And there are two other on-screen helpers. You can read the user guide on screen (Help menu) and you can choose some commands from a **context-sensitive menu** while you're working.

## When your illustration is finished

You have many options for outputting your artwork from Illustrator **1**. You can **color separate** it right from Illustrator and print it on any PostScript output device, like a laser printer or imagesetter.

If you want to **export** an Illustrator file to a page layout application, like PageMaker or QuarkXPress, or to an image editing application, like Photoshop, you can choose from many commonly used file formats, including EPS, TIFF, PICT, and WMF.

And finally, for **on-screen** output, you can use an Illustrator file in a multimedia project; you can save it in the GIF or JPEG file format and display it on a World Wide Web page; or you can assign a URL to an Illustrator object to create an imagemap GIF and export the file to use as an element on a Web page.

## How to use this book

If Illustrator is brand new to you, we recommend that you read Chapter 1 to familiarize yourself with the basic application features (if you snuck past it, go back now). Read Chapter 3 to learn how to open and save documents, and read Chapter 4 to learn how to navigate around your document. Then proceed to Chapter 5, where you'll learn how to draw basic shapes, and so on, up to the power and precision tool features in the later chapters.

Happy illustrating!

*Illustrator image*

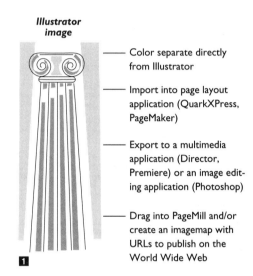

Color separate directly from Illustrator

Import into page layout application (QuarkXPress, PageMaker)

Export to a multimedia application (Director, Premiere) or an image editing application (Photoshop)

Drag into PageMill and/or create an imagemap with URLs to publish on the World Wide Web

**1**

# STARTUP 3

*In this chapter you will learn how to launch Illustrator, create a new illustration, define the working and printable areas of a document, save an illustration in any of the three Illustrator file formats, open an existing illustration, place a file from another application into Illustrator, close an illustration, and quit/exit Illustrator.*

**1** *Click the Illustrator application icon on the Launcher.*

## To launch Illustrator (Macintosh):

Double-click the Adobe Illustrator folder on the desktop, then double-click the square Illustrator application icon.
*or*
Click the Illustrator application icon on the Launcher. **1**
*or*
Double-click an Illustrator file icon. **2**

**TIP** If you launch Illustrator by clicking the application icon, a new untitled document window will appear automatically.

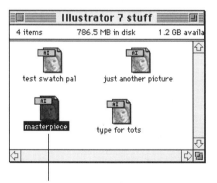

**2** *Or double-click an Illustrator file icon.*

## To launch Illustrator (Windows):

Open the Adobe Illustrator folder in My Computer, then double-click the Illustrator application icon.

*or*

Double-click an Illustrator file icon **1**.

*or*

Click the Start button on the Taskbar, choose Programs, choose Adobe, choose Illustrator 7.0, then click Adobe Illustrator 7.0 **2**.

**TIP** If you launch Illustrator by choosing or clicking the application icon, a new untitled document window will appear automatically.

**1** *Double-click an Illustrator file icon.*

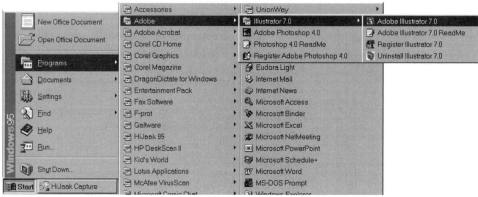

**2** *Click the Start button, then locate and click the application.*

## To create a new document:

When you launch Illustrator using any method other than by clicking an existing file icon, a new document window will open automatically. If Illustrator is already open and you want to create a new document, choose File menu > New (Command-N/Ctrl-N) **3**.

**TIP** If you want to trace over a bitmap image at any time, use File menu > Place to import a TIFF, PICT or EPS from another application, then use the Pen or Auto Trace tool to draw path shapes over the placed image (see page 90).

**3** *Choose New from the File menu.*

In the center of every Illustrator document is a non-movable artboard work area that represents the maximum printable size of the illustration. The default artboard area is 8½ inches wide by 11 inches high. You can specify whether the artboard will contain one printable page or facing printable pages. Or you can tile (subdivide) an over-sized illustration into a grid so it can be printed in sections on standard size paper. The size of the printable page is specified in the Page Setup/Print Setup dialog box.

## To change the artboard dimensions:

1. Choose File menu > Document Setup (Command-Shift-P/Ctrl-Shift-P).

2. Choose a preset size from the Artboard: Size drop-down menu ■.
   *or*
   Enter numbers in the Width and Height fields. The maximum work area is 120 by 120 inches.
   *or*
   Check the Use Page Setup/Use Print Setup box to have the Artboard dimensions conform to the Paper size currently selected in the Page Setup/Print Setup dialog box. Click Page Setup/ Print Setup to view those settings.

3. Click OK or press Return/Enter.

**TIP** Objects placed outside the artboard will be saved with the illustration, but they won't print.

**TIP** If the Page Setup/Print Setup Reduce or Enlarge percentage is other than 100%, the illustration will print proportionately smaller or larger. If the Use Page Setup/Use Print Setup box is unchecked in the Document Setup dialog box, the artboard won't be affected by this Setup output percentage, but the Page boundary will. If Use Page Setup/Use Print Setup *is* checked, the artboard dimensions will match the custom printout size. Either way, the illustration will print at the size specified in Page Setup/ Print Setup.

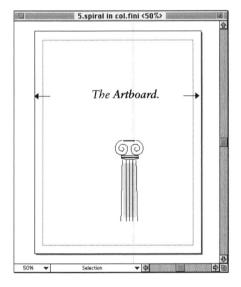

*The Artboard.*

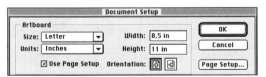

**■** *In the **Document Setup** dialog box, choose a preset **Artboard Size**, or enter custom **Width and Height** values, or check the **Use Page Setup/Use Print Setup** box to use the paper size currently selected in the Page Setup/Print Setup dialog box.*

Change the Artboard Dimensions

You can switch the printable area of an illustration from a vertical (portrait) to a landscape orientation. Then you'll need to make the artboard conform to the new orientation.

### To create a landscape page:

1. Choose File menu > Document Setup (Command-Shift-P/Ctrl-Shift-P).
2. Click Page Setup/Print Setup. Macintosh users: Choose Page Attributes from the drop-down menu. Windows users: Click Properties.
3. Click the landscape Orientation icon **1**.
4. Click OK or press Return/Enter.
5. Click OK again to close the Document Setup dialog box **2**.

**TIP** Press and drag with the Page tool **3** if you want to reposition the printable area within the artboard.

**TIP** Double-click the Hand tool to display the entire artboard.

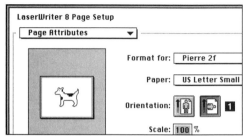

*Click the **landscape Orientation** icon in the Page **Setup** dialog box (Macintosh).*

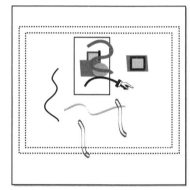

**2** *The **printable page** in landscape Orientation.*

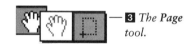
**3** *The Page tool.*

### To create a landscape artboard:

1. Choose File menu > Document Setup.
2. Click the landscape Orientation icon, if it isn't already highlighted.
3. Click OK or press Return/Enter **4**. *(See the tips above).*
4. If the entire page isn't visible on the artboard, reopen Document Setup and enter new Width and Height values to enlarge the artboard to accommodate the new orientation. And remember, objects outside the artboard area won't print.

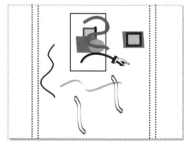

**4** *The **artboard** in landscape Orientation. The printable page doesn't extend beyond the artboard.*

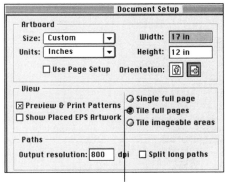

**1** *Click the **Tile full pages** button in the* ***Document Setup*** *dialog box.*

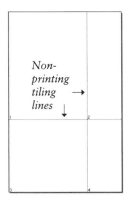

**2** *The* ***Page*** *tool.*

*Parts of objects that fall within this "gutter" area will not print.*

**3** *The* ***artboard*** *divided into two pages.*

*Non-printing tiling lines* →
↓

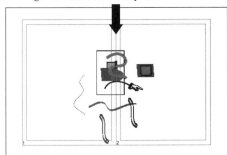

**4** *An oversized illustration tiled into sections for printing (see page 272)*

By default, a new document contains a single page, but you can turn it into a multi-page document. If you turn on the Tile full pages option, as many full page borders as can fit in the current size of the artboard will be drawn. Changing the artboard size will then increase or decrease the number of page borders.

### To divide the artboard into multiple pages:

1. Choose View menu > Fit in Window (Command-0/Ctrl-0).

2. Choose File menu > Document Setup.

3. Enter a new Width value that's at least double the existing, single page width.

4. Click the View: "Tile full pages" button **1**.

5. Click OK or press Return/Enter.

6. *Optional:* Choose the Page tool (press "H" to toggle between the Hand and Page tools) **2**, then click near the left edge of the artboard. New page borders will be drawn **3**. (If the tile lines aren't displayed, choose View menu > Show Page Tiling.)

**TIP** You can also tile full pages in landscape mode by clicking the landscape Orientation icon in the Document Setup dialog box, and choosing Size: Tabloid. Then, if necessary, click with the Page tool near the top or bottom of the artboard to cause the new page borders to be drawn **4**.

**Divide the Artboard**

A file saved in the native Illustrator format will be smaller in file size than the same file saved in the EPS format. However, if you want to open an Illustrator file in another application other than Photoshop, you must save it in the Illustrator EPS format (instructions on the next page) or in another file format that your target application can read (see pages 278–282).

### To save a new illustration in the native Illustrator format:

1. Choose File menu > Save (Command-S/Ctrl-S).

2. Enter a name in the "Save this document as" field **1**.

3. Click Desktop.

4. Highlight a drive, then click Open.

5. Highlight a folder in which to save the file, then click Open. Or, to create a new folder, choose a location in which to save the new folder, click New, enter a name for the folder, then click Create.

6. Leave the Format (Macintosh) or Save as Type (Windows) as Illustrator, and click Save or press Return/Enter.

7. Click a Compatibility option **2**. If you choose an earlier version, some elements of your illustration may be altered if it's reopened in Illustrator 7.

8. *Optional:* Check the Include Placed Files box to save a copy of any placed files within the illustration.

9. Click OK or press Return/Enter.

**1** *Enter a name in the* **Save this document as** *field, click* **Desktop***, open a drive and a folder, then click* **Save***.*

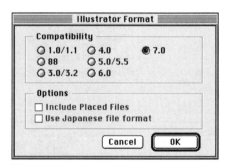

**2** *Click a* **Compatibility** *option (Illustrator version) and other* **Options***, if applicable, in the* **Illustrator Format** *dialog box.*

The prior version of a file is overwritten when the Save command is executed. Don't be shy—save frequently!

### To save an existing file:

Choose File menu > Save (Command-S/Ctrl-S).

A file in the native Illustrator format has no preview option, and it can only be opened and modified in Illustrator or Photoshop. To import an Illustrator file into a page layout, word processing, or other drawing application, save it in the Illustrator EPS format. Other file formats for other applications are discussed on pages 278–282.

## To save an illustration as an EPS:

1. Follow steps 1–5 on the previous page. If the file has already been saved, choose File menu > Save As or Save a Copy for Step 1.

2. Choose Format (Macintosh) or Save as Type (Windows) Illustrator EPS **1**.

3. Click Save or press Return/Enter.

4. Click a Compatibility option **2**. If you choose an earlier version, some elements of your illustration may be altered when reopened in Illustrator 7.

5. Click a Preview option:
   None to save the illustration with no preview. The EPS won't display on screen in any other application, but it will print.

   1-bit IBM PC or 1-bit Macintosh to save the illustration with a black-and-white preview.

   8-bit IBM PC or 8-bit Macintosh to save the illustration with a color preview. This option produces the largest file storage size.

   *Note:* Regardless of which preview option you choose, color information will be saved with the file and the illustration will print normally from Illustrator or any other application.

6. *Optional steps:*
   Check the Include Placed Files box to save a copy of any placed files with the illustration.

   Check the Include Document Thumbnails box to save a thumbnail with the file for previewing in Illustrator's

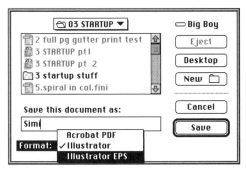

**1** *Choose* **Format: Illustrator EPS** *in the Save or Save As dialog box.*

**2** *Click a Compatibility option (Illustrator version), a* **Preview** *option, and other* **Options,** *if applicable, in the* **EPS Format** *dialog box.*

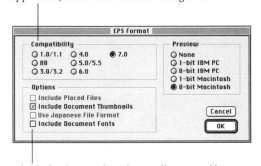

*Check this box or die: If your Illustrator file contains type and you're going to import it into a layout application, check the* **Include Document Fonts** *box, or the file probably won't print properly.*

*An EPS file icon.*

*(Continued on the following page)*

Open dialog box (QuickTime must be installed in the Macintosh system).

Check the Include Document Fonts box to save any fonts used in the document as a part of the document. Only individual characters used in the font are saved, not the whole character set. Included fonts will show and print on any system, even where they aren't installed.

7. Click OK or press Return/Enter.

### To revert to the last saved version:

1. Choose File menu > Revert.

2. Click Revert.

### Acrobat PDF

Use the PDF format to transfer your Illustrator file to another application or another computer platform that reads PostScript-based Acrobat PDF files. Or use the Acrobat format to save your Illustrator file for display on the World Wide Web. The PDF format preserves groups, text, and layering information, and saves RGB colors as RGB and CMYK colors as CMYK. Currently, vertical type displays correctly in Acrobat Reader 3, but will be reoriented into horizontal type if you open the PDF file in Illustrator. A file in PDF format can also be viewed in Acrobat Reader or edited with Acrobat Exchange.

In Illustrator, you can open one page of a multi-page PDF file, edit any vector graphics or bitmap images on the page, and then resave the page in PDF format.

### To save a file as an Acrobat PDF:

1. Choose File menu > Save, Save As, or Save a Copy.

2. Enter a name in the "Save this document as" field, and choose a location in which to save the file.

3. Choose Acrobat PDF from the Format (Macintosh) or Save as Type (Windows) drop-down menu.

4. Click Save or press Return/Enter.

### Save As or Save a Copy?

You can use the Save, Save As, or Save a Copy command to save an existing illustration in the Illustrator, Illustrator EPS or Acrobat PDF file format or to convert it to an earlier Illustrator version. Use Save As to save the illustration under a new name and continue working on this new version while preserving the original on disk. Use Save a Copy to do just the opposite—save the current version as a new file to disk and continue working on the original.

*Note:* If you save an illustration in an earlier version, but it was created using features that are not present in that earlier version, the illustration may be altered or information may be deleted from it to make it compatible with the earlier version. For example, a gradient fill may be converted into a blend, or vertical type will become horizontal type. The earlier the Illustrator version, the more the illustration may change.

## A note regarding resolution

A TIFF that you drag-and-drop or a PICT that you drag-and-drop, open, or place into Illustrator will downsample to 72 ppi, which is an acceptable resolution for a multimedia or Web project, but not for printing. To acquire a high resolution image for a print project, use Illustrator's Place command to place an EPS or TIFF, or use the Open command.

## Formats you can Open or Place

*Native formats:* Illustrator versions 1.0 through 7.0 (.ai), EPS (.eps), Acrobat PDF (.pdf).

*Raster (bitmap) formats:* EPS, Amiga IFF, BMP, GIF89a, JPEG, PCX, Photoshop (layers are flattened!), PICT, Pixar, Targa, and TIFF.

*Import only formats:* Filmstrip, Kodak PhotoCD, MacPaint, and PixelPaint.

*Graphics (vector) formats:* FreeHand 4/5, CorelDRAW 5/6, CMX, CGM, WMF, and Macintosh PICT (from DeltaGraph or a CAD program).

*Text file formats:* Plain text (ASCII), MS RTF, MS Word, and WordPerfect DOS or Windows.

## Painter to Illustrator

A Fractal Design Painter 4 file can be opened or placed into Illustrator if it is saved in a file format Illustrator can read. For example, you can place or open a Painter EPS, TIFF, or PICT; it will appear as a raster image. You can apply some color filters and the raster filters to an embedded (non-linked) image. Illustrator can't read Painter's native RIFF format.

You can open or place an image in Painter's Photoshop 3 file format into Illustrator, but the image will import at a larger scale and lower resolution than the original, so you'll need to scale it down.

To export Painter shapes into Illustrator 7 to use as vector objects, use Painter 4.0's File menu > Export command. In Illustrator, choose File menu > Open. You may need to increase Illustrator's RAM allotment first.

## Acquiring images in Illustrator

You can use Illustrator to open or import an illustration from a variety of file formats. This means that in Illustrator, you can work with imagery that was originally created in another application. And you can export your Illustrator file to another application or platform. Methods for acquiring an image from other application include the Open command, the Place command, and the drag-and-drop method. The method you choose to use depends on which formats the original application can save to and how you intend to use the imagery in Illustrator.

When you open a document from another object-oriented application using the **Open** command, a new Illustrator file is created, and the acquired objects can be manipulated using any Illustrator tool, command, or filter. If you open a document from a bitmap-based program like Photoshop or Painter using the Open command, the image won't convert into workable paths; it will stay in an outlined box. (*Note:* You can open a FreeHand or CorelDRAW file in Illustrator but see the Illustrator ReadMe file to learn about some of the limitations.)

The **Place** command inserts imagery or text into an existing Illustrator document. EPS and TIFF are particularly good formats for saving a file for placing into Illustrator. In these formats, the the color, detail, and resolution of the original image are preserved. You can dim any placed image in Illustrator if you're planning to trace it.

And, finally, you can **drag-and-drop** a Photoshop 4 selection or layer into Illustrator, where it will appear in an outlined box.

A bitmap image that is acquired in Illustrator via the Place or drag-and-drop method can be moved, placed on a different layer, masked, or modified using any transformation tool or any raster (bitmap) filter.

A list of file formats that can be opened in Illustrator appears on the previous page.

### To open an illustration from within Illustrator:

1. Choose File menu > Open (Command-O/Ctrl-O).

2. Check the Show Preview box to display a preview of the illustration, if the file contains a preview that Illustrator can display.

3. *Macintosh users:* Check the Show All Files box to see all files. Otherwise, only files in the formats Illustrator can read will appear on the list.

   *Windows users:* Filter out files by choosing from the Format drop-down list, or choose All to display files of all formats. The default setting is *.ai.

4. Locate and highlight a file name, then click Open ■.
   *or*
   Double-click a file name.

**TIP** If you open an EPS file that contains a mask or a clipping path, select the outlined box using the Selection tool to select both the image box and the mask or use the Direct Selection tool to select only the mask or the image box.

**TIP** A new untitled document opens when you launch Illustrator. It will close and be deleted automatically if you haven't created any artwork in it and you then open another document.

### To open an illustration from the Macintosh Finder or Windows Explorer:

Double-click an Illustrator file icon in the window. Illustrator will launch if it is not already open ■.

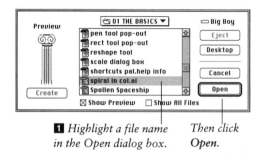

■ *Highlight a file name in the Open dialog box.*   Then click **Open**.

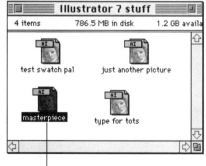

■ *Double-clicking an existing Illustrator file icon will launch the application, if it isn't already launched.*

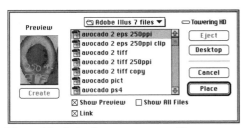

**1** *Double-click a bitmap or vector file.*

### Watch your links

If the actual linked image is moved from its original location after the file it was placed in was last saved, you will be prompted to re-link the image when you reopen the Illustrator file. Click Replace **2**, relocate the file or a different file, then click Replace.

If you click Ignore, the linked image will not display, though its bounding box will still be present in the Illustrator file (in Artwork view). Delete this box and save the file to completely break the link and prevent any alert prompts from appearing. You'll never need to re-link a Macintosh PICT file, because these types of files are always embedded.

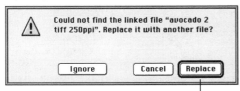

**2** *Click Replace, then locate the file, to reestablish the link for a placed image that was moved.*

A placed picture can be moved, placed on a different layer, masked, or modified using any transformation tool or raster filter. A list of file formats that can be placed into Illustrator is on page 39.

### To place a file from another application into an Illustrator document:

1. Open an Illustrator file.
2. Choose File menu > Place.
3. Locate and highlight the name of the file that you want to place, then click Place.
   *or*
   Double-click a file name **1**.
4. Check the Link box to place only a screen version of an image into Illustrator. The actual, original image will remain separate from the Illustrator file at its original resolution. If you modify and resave the image in its original program, it will automatically update in your Illustrator document.

   Uncheck the Link box to embed (parse) the actual image into the Illustrator file. This can dramatically increase the file's storage size.
5. Click Place or press Return/Enter.

**TIP** See the first tip on page 40.

**TIP** Fonts used in a placed EPS that are not installed in your system will print in Courier.

**TIP** If you place an EPS file with a clipping path into Illustrator, the area around the image will be transparent, and it will remain transparent even if you move, scale, reflect, rotate, shear, or apply a bitmap filter to it.

### If you replace one placed image with another of the same format…

After you click Place, a warning prompt will appear. Click Replace. Any transformations made to the original placed image will be applied automatically to the newly placed one. (Click Don't replace if you change your mind and want to place the new image in its own outlined box or click Cancel to cancel the place command altogether.) The prompt will appear if you replace a PICT with a TIFF, replace a TIFF with a (non-linked) TIFF, or an EPS with an EPS 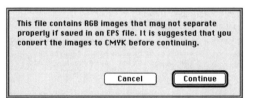.

### If you place a TIFF image...

...the TIFF Color Management Options dialog box will open 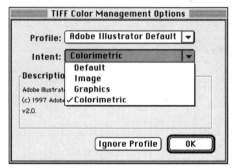. (*Note:* You must first set up the Color Settings preferences to include TIFF profiles. See page 288.) Choose a monitor Profile from the drop-down menu, and also choose from the Intent drop-down menu. The Description box will display Adobe's definition of the chosen Intent.

Click OK to accept. If you use a profile to place a TIFF, you'll have the option to embed the profile if you then export the artwork as TIFF. Click Ignore Profile to place the image with no color management and no referenced profile applied to the image.

### RGB warning

A warning prompt will appear if you save artwork in the Illustrator EPS format if the file contains an RGB image 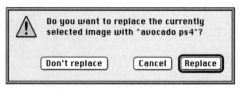. Dragging an image from Photoshop to Illustrator creates an RGB image. To prevent a mode change, create the file in Photoshop in CMYK Color mode and save it as TIFF or EPS, then place it into Illustrator. RGB color objects will be saved as RGB in an Illustrator EPS file and will separate correctly from Illustrator.

If you then import the file into PageMaker, that application will report an error when the EPS file is placed. Ignore the error and choose to replace the color.

QuarkXPress will automatically convert the colors to CMYK equivalents. To retain RGB spot colors in XPress, convert the colors to CMYK spot colors before creating the EPS file.

**1** *This warning prompt will appear if you use the **Place** command while an existing placed image is selected.*

**2** *The **TIFF Color Management Options** dialog box will open if you Place a TIFF image.*

**3** *This warning prompt will appear if you save an Illustrator file as an EPS that contains an RGB image.*

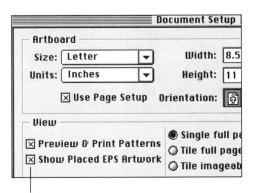

**1** *Check the Show Placed EPS Artwork box in the Document Setup dialog box.*

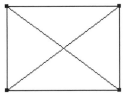

**2** *Placed EPS, Artwork view.*

**3** *Placed EPS, Artwork view, "Show Placed EPS Artwork" checked.*

**4** *Linked placed EPS selected, Preview view. Notice the "X" across the outline box, designating this image as a linked EPS.*

If it was saved in its original application with an EPS preview that Illustrator recognizes, a placed EPS image will render fully in Preview view, regardless of the "Show placed images" setting in the Document Setup dialog box. If you place an EPS that does not contain a preview that Illustrator recognizes, the image will display as an empty outlined box with an "x" through it in either view. Follow these instructions to display a black-and-white version of the image in the outlined box in Artwork view.

## To display a placed EPS in Artwork view:

1. Choose File menu > Document Setup.
2. Check the "Show Placed EPS Artwork" box **1**–**4**.
3. Click OK or press Return/Enter.

If the Include Placed Files option is turned off when you save your file, linked placed images will not be saved within the Illustrator file into which it is placed. A screen version of the image(s) will save with the file, with a reference to the actual image file(s) for printing. Turn Include Placed Files on if you want to to save a copy of any linked placed image files with your illustration, but keep in mind that this can greatly increase the storage size of your file.

## To save a copy of a linked placed image file with an illustration:

1. With the Illustrator document that contains the linked placed image open, choose File menu > Save As.
2. Choose Format (Macintosh) or Save as Type (Windows) Illustrator EPS.
3. Click Save.
4. Check the "Include Placed Files" box **5**.
5. Click OK or press Return/Enter. The image(s) is now embedded in the file.

**5** *Check the Include Placed Files box in the EPS Format dialog box.*

## To locate the actual placed image file:

1. Choose a selection tool.
2. Click on the placed image.
3. Choose File menu > Selection Info.
4. Choose Info: Linked Images. The drive and folder location of the actual placed image file will be listed.
5. Click Done or press Return/Enter or Esc.

**TIP** To display a list of all the placed files in an illustration, make sure no objects are selected, choose File menu > Document Info, then choose Info: Linked Images. For a list of embedded images, choose Embedded Images.

To save the Document info as a text file, click Save, choose a location in which to save the file, click Save, then click Done. Open the file in a word processing or text editing application.

## To close an illustration:

*Macintosh:* Click the close box in the upper left corner of the document window (Command-W).

*Windows:* Click the close box in the upper right corner of the document window (Ctrl-W).

If you attempt to close a picture that was modified since it was last saved, a warning prompt will appear **1**. You can close the file without saving, save the file, or cancel the close operation.

**TIP** Hold down Option/Alt and choose Close (or Option/Alt click the close box) to close all open files.

## To quit/exit Illustrator:

*Macintosh:* Choose File menu > Quit (Command-Q).

*Windows:* Choose File menu > Exit (Ctrl-Q).

All open Illustrator files will close. If changes were made to an open file since it was last saved, a warning prompt will appear. Save the file or quit/exit without saving it.

## Automatic picture update

Hold down Option/Alt and double-click a placed image to launch the application in which it was created, if the application is available on your system. If you then modify the original placed image and save it, the placed image in the Illustrator document will update automatically. *Macintosh users:* If the original application is available but it doesn't open, try rebuilding the Desktop first.

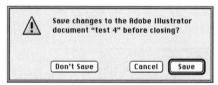

**1** *If you try to close a picture that was modified since it was last saved, this prompt will appear.*

# DISPLAY 4

*In this chapter you will learn how to change view sizes, change views (Preview or Artwork), create custom view settings, change screen display modes, move an illustration in its window, and display the same illustration in two windows.*

| View | |
|---|---|
| Artwork | ⌘Y |
| Preview Selection | ⇧⌘Y |
| **Zoom In** | **⌘+** |
| Zoom Out | ⌘- |
| Fit In Window | ⌘0 |
| Actual Size | ⌘1 |
| Hide Edges | ⌘H |
| Hide Page Tiling | |
| Show Rulers | ⌘R |
| Hide Guides | ⌘; |
| ✓Lock Guides | ⌥⌘; |
| Make Guides | ⌘5 |
| Release Guides | ⌥⌘5 |
| Show Grid | ⌘" |
| Snap To Grid | ⇧⌘" |
| New View... | |
| Edit Views... | |

**1** *Choose **Zoom In** or **Zoom Out** from the **View** menu.*

*The current view size.*

Brush by Diane Margolin

**2** *The current view size on the **Zoom** pop-up menu.*

Within the document window, you can display the entire artboard or an enlarged detail of an illustration, or any preset view size in between. The display size is indicated as a percentage on the title bar, and can range from 6.25% to 1600%. 100% is actual size. The display size does not affect the printout size.

## To choose a preset view size:

Choose View menu > Zoom In (Command-+/Ctrl-+) **1**. Repeat to magnify further.
*or*
Choose View menu > Zoom Out (Command--/Ctrl--). Repeat, if desired.
*or*
Choose a preset view percentage level from the Zoom pop-up menu in the lower left corner of the document window **2**.

**TIP** Choose View menu > Fit in Window (Command-0/Ctrl-0) or double-click the Hand tool to display the entire artboard in the document window.

**45**

## To change the view size using the Zoom tool:

1. Choose the Zoom tool (Z) **1**.

**1** *the Zoom tool.*

2. Click on the illustration in the center of the area that you want to enlarge or drag a marquee across an area to magnify that area **2**–**3**. The smaller the marquee, the greater the level of magnification.
   *or*
   Hold down Option/Alt and click on the illustration to reduce the display size.
   *or*
   Drag a marquee, then, without releasing the mouse, press and hold down Space bar, move the marquee over the area you want to magnify, then release the mouse.

**TIP** Double-click the Zoom tool to display an illustration at Actual Size (100%). Or, choose View menu > Actual Size (Command-1/Ctrl-1).

If you double-click the Zoom tool when your illustration is in a small display size, the white area around the Artboard may appear in the document window, instead of the illustration. Hold down Space bar and drag to reposition the illustration in the document window.

**TIP** You can click to change the view size while the screen is redrawing.

**2** *Press and drag with the Zoom tool.*

This is the method to master for speedy picture editing.

## To change the view size using the keyboard:

To magnify the illustration with any tool other than Zoom selected, hold down Command/Ctrl and Space bar and click or drag in the document window.

To reduce the display size, hold down Command-Option-Space bar/Ctrl-Alt-Space bar and click.

**3** *The view enlarged.*

An illustration can be displayed and edited in three different views: Preview, Artwork, or Preview Selection. In all three views, the other View menu commands—Hide/Show Page Tiling, Edges, Guides and Grid— are accessible, and any selection tool can be used.

## To change the view:

From the View menu, toggle between...

**Preview** (Command-Y/Ctrl-Y) to display all the objects with their fill and stroke colors and all placed images –.
*or*
**Artwork** (Command-Y/Ctrl-Y) to display all the objects as wire frames with no fill or stroke colors 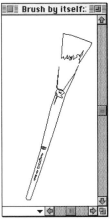. Editing is faster in Artwork view.

Choose **Preview Selection** Command-Shift-Y/ Ctrl-Shift-Y to display any currently selected object or objects in Preview view, and all other objects in Artwork view **4**. To preview an object, click on it with any selection tool. To turn this option off, choose Artwork view.

**TIP** Use the Layers palette to choose a view for an individual layer *(see page 161)*.

**TIP** The display of placed EPS images is discussed on page 43. The display of patterns is discussed on page 142.

**1** *Toggle between* **Preview** *and* **Artwork,** *or choose* **Preview Selection** *from the View menu.*

**2** *Preview view.*

**3** *Artwork view.*

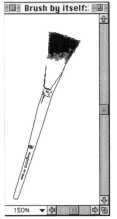

**4** *Preview Selection view.*

Change the View (Artwork or Preview)

You can define and save up to 25 custom view settings that you can switch to quickly using an assigned shortcut, and you can specify whether your illustration will be in Preview view or Artwork view for each setting that you define.

### To define a custom view setting:

1. Follow the instructions on page 45 or page 46 to display your illustration at the desired view size, and choose scroll bar positions.

2. Choose View menu > Preview or Artwork.

3. Choose View menu > New View **1**.

4. Enter a name for the new view in the Name field **2**.

5. Click OK or press Return/Enter.

**1** *Choose New View from the View menu.*

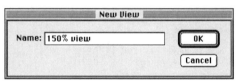

**2** *Enter a* **Name** *for the view setting in the* **New View** *dialog box.*

### To choose a custom view setting:

Choose the view name from the bottom of the View menu **3**.
*or*
Hold down Command-Option-Shift/ Ctrl-Alt-Shift and press the number that was automatically assigned to the view setting. The shortcut will be listed next to the view name under the View menu.

**TIP** You can switch views at any time. For example, if you choose a custom view setting for which you chose Artwork view, but you want to display your illustration in Preview view, choose View menu > Preview.

**3** *Choose a custom view setting from the View menu.*

*Custom View Settings*

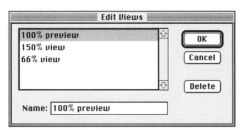

**1** *In the* **Edit Views** *dialog box, highlight a view, then change the* **Name** *or click* **Delete.**

**2** *Hand tool.*

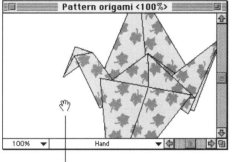

**3** *Hold down Space bar and drag in the document window to move the illustration.*

**4** *Standard Screen Mode.*

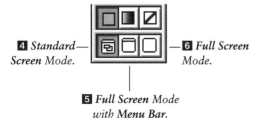

**6** *Full Screen Mode.*

**5** *Full Screen Mode with Menu Bar.*

## To rename or delete a custom view setting:

1. Choose View menu > Edit Views.
2. Click on the name of the view you want to alter **1**.
3. Type a new name in the Name field.
   *or*
   Click Delete to delete the view setting.
4. Click OK or press Return/Enter. The View menu will update to reflect your changes.

## To move an illustration in its window:

Click the up or down scroll arrow.
*or*
Choose the Hand tool **2** (or hold down Space bar to turn any other tool into the Hand tool temporarily), then drag the illustration to the desired position **3**.

**TIP** Double-click the Hand tool to fit the entire Artboard in the document window.

## To change the screen display mode:

Click the Standard Screen Mode button **4** at the bottom of the Toolbox to display the image, menu bar, and scroll bars in the document window. This is the default mode.
*or*
Click the Full Screen Mode with Menu Bar (second) button **5** to display the image and menu bar, but no scroll bars. The area around the image will be white.
*or*
Click the Full Screen Mode button **6** to display the image, but no menu bar or scroll bars. The area around the image will be white.

**TIP** Press "F" to cycle through the three modes.

**TIP** Press Tab to hide (or show) all currently open palettes, including the Toolbox; press Shift-Tab to hide (or show) all the palettes except the Toolbox.

Move an Illustration in its Window; Screen Modes

The number of Illustrator documents that can be open at a time is limited only by the amount of RAM (Random Access Memory) currently available to Illustrator. Open windows are listed under and can be activated via the Window menu 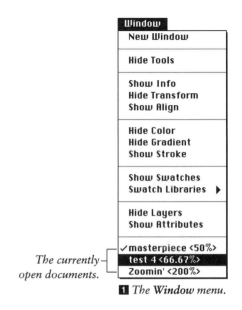.

You can open the same illustration in two windows, one in a large display size, such as 200%, to edit small details, and the other in a smaller view size so you can see the whole illustration. In one window you could hide individual layers or display individual layers in Artwork view and in another window you could Preview all the layers together.

*Note:* The illustration in the window for which Preview view is selected will redraw each time you modify the illustration in the window for which Artwork view is selected, which means you won't save processing or redraw time when you work in the Artwork window.

*The currently open documents.*

**1** *The* **Window** *menu.*

### To display an illustration in two windows:

1. Open an illustration.

2. Choose Window menu > New Window. A new window of the same size will appear on top of the first window, and with the same title followed by ":2" **2**.

3. Reposition the new window by dragging its title bar so the original and new windows are side by side, and resize one or both windows.

   If you close and reopen the file, both windows will display again.

TIP Windows users: Choose Window menu > Cascade to arrange the currently open illustrations in a stair-stepped configuration. Or choose Window menu > Tile to tile open windows side by side.

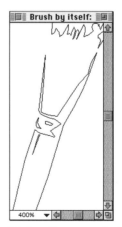

**2** *One illustration displayed in two windows.*

# CREATE OBJECTS 5

An object is a shape that is composed of anchor points connected by straight and/or curved line segments. An object can be open or closed. A path is the edge of an object that defines its shape. Rectangles and ovals are closed paths because they have no endpoints. A line is an open path.

In this chapter you will learn how to use the creation tools to draw rectangles and ovals. How to round the corners of any existing object. How to delete an object. How to use the Paintbrush tool to create filled shapes that look like brush strokes. How to use the Pencil tool to create hand-drawn lines. How to use the Polygon, Spiral, and Star tools to create geometric shapes. And finally, how to turn an Illustrator object into a bitmap image using the Rasterize command.

(The Pen tool, which produces curved and straight line segments, is covered in Chapter 8.)

*Daniel Pelavin,* **Anchor**

## To create a rectangle or oval by dragging:

1. Choose the Rectangle (M) or Ellipse tool (N) .

2. Press and drag diagonally **2**. As you drag, you'll see a wire frame representation of the rectangle or oval. When you release the mouse, the rectangle or oval will be selected and colored with the current fill and stroke settings (Preview view).

**TIP** Hold down Option/Alt while dragging to draw a rectangle or oval from the center.

**TIP** Hold down Shift while dragging to draw a square with the Rectangle tool or a circle with the Ellipse tool.

*Ellipse tool.* — 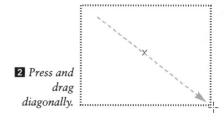 —*Rectangle tool.*

**2** *Press and drag diagonally.*

## To create a rectangle or oval by specifying dimensions:

1. Choose Rectangle (M) or Ellipse tool (N).

2. Click on the Artboard where you want the object to appear.

3. In the Rectangle or Ellipse dialog box, enter dimensions in the Width and Height fields **3**. To create a circle or a square, enter a number in the Width field, then click the word Height to copy the width value into the Height field.

4. *Optional:* To create a rectangle with rounded corners, enter a value greater than 0 in the Corner radius field. If the radius is equal to or greater than the height or width, an ellipse will be created.

5. Click OK or press Return/Enter.

**TIP** Values in dialog boxes are displayed in the unit of measure that is currently selected in the File menu > Preferences > Units & Undo dialog box. The Units field setting in the Document Setup dialog box supercedes the Units & Undo setting.

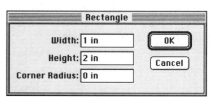

**3** *Enter **Width** and **Height** dimensions in the **Rectangle** (or Ellipse) dialog box. The dimensions of the last drawn object will display when the dialog box opens.*

*Chris Spollen*

**Create a Rectangle or Oval**

**1** *Rounded Rectangle tool.*

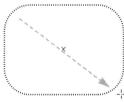

**2** *Press and drag diagonally.*

**3** *The rectangle is automatically painted with the current fill and stroke settings.*

## To create a rounded rectangle:

1. Choose the Rounded Rectangle tool **1**.

2. Press and drag diagonally. As you drag, you'll see a wireframe representation of the rounded rectangle **2**. When you release the mouse, the rounded rectangle will be selected and colored with the current fill and stroke settings (Preview view) **3**.

**TIP** You can also create a rounded rectangle using the Rectangle dialog box. Choose the Rounded Rectangle tool, click on the Artboard, then enter values in the Width, Height, and Corner radius fields.

**TIP** The current Corner radius value in the Preferences > General dialog box, which determines how rounded the corners of the rectangle will be, is entered automatically in the Corner radius field in the Rectangle dialog box, and vice versa.

**4** *Top row: the original objects; second row: after applying the Round Corners filter (30pt).*

## To round the corners of an existing object:

1. Select the object.

2. Choose Filter menu > Stylize > Round Corners.

3. Enter a Radius value (the radius of the curve, in points).

4. Click OK or press Return/Enter **4**.

## To delete an object:

1. Select the object.

2. If all the anchor points on the object are selected, press Delete once or choose Edit menu > Clear.
   *or*
   If only some of the object's points are selected, press Delete twice.

*Create a Rounded Rectangle; Delete an Object*

You can use the Paintbrush tool to produce hard-edged brush strokes in a uniform thickness if you're using a mouse, or variable thicknesses if you're using a stylus and pressure sensitive tablet (the harder you press on the tablet, the wider the shape). You can also use the Paintbrush tool to create calligraphic strokes (see the next page). A stroke created with the Paintbrush tool is actually a closed path with stroke and fill attributes, as opposed to a line, which is an open path with endpoints and a stroke color, but no fill.

## To use the Paintbrush tool:

1. Double-click the Paintbrush tool **1**.
2. Enter the desired stroke thickness in the Width field. If you're using a stylus and a pressure-sensitive tablet, click Variable and enter a Minimum and Maximum stroke Width **2**.
3. Click the round or square-cornered Caps button for the shape of the stroke ends.
4. Click the smooth or square-cornered Joins button for the bends in the stroke shape.
5. Click OK or press Return/Enter.
6. Press and drag to draw a stroke. When you release the mouse, the stroke will be painted with the current fill and stroke settings **3**–**4**.

**1** *Paintbrush tool.*

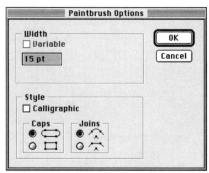

**2** *Enter a Width in the Paintbrush Options dialog box.*

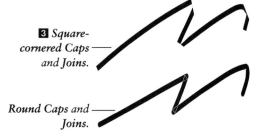

**3** *Square-cornered Caps and Joins.*

*Round Caps and Joins.*

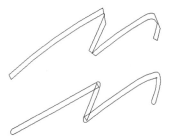

**4** *The same strokes in Artwork view. The strokes are actually closed paths.*

DIANE MARGOLIN

The Paintbrush tool can be used to create calligraphic "strokes" that vary in thickness as you draw, like those produced by traditional drawing tools.

### To create a calligraphic brush stroke:

1. Double-click the Paintbrush tool.

2. Check the Calligraphic angle box **1**.

3. Enter a number in the Calligraphic angle field. The Calligraphic angle controls the thickness of the horizontal and vertical directions of the stroke relative to each other. A 0° angle will produce a thin horizontal stroke and a thick vertical stroke. A 90° angle will produce the opposite effect. Other angles will produce different effects.

4. Click OK or press Return/Enter.

5. Press and drag to draw a stroke. The stroke will preview as you drag, and will be painted with the current fill and stroke settings when you release the mouse **2**–**3**.

**TIP** To make a line calligraphic *after* it's created rather than as it's drawn, apply the Calligraphy filter (Filter menu > Stylize > Calligraphy) *(see page 233)*.

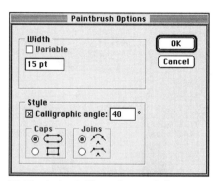

**1** Check the **Calligraphic angle** box in the Paintbrush Options dialog box.

**2** A calligraphic stroke in Preview view...

**3** ...and in Artwork view.

**Create a Calligraphic Brush Stroke**

Lines drawn with the Pencil tool look hand drawn or quickly sketched.

*Note:* The Pencil tool tends to create bumpy curves, and it doesn't create straight lines—that's not what it was designed for. Use the Pen tool to create straight lines and smooth curves.

### To draw a line using the Pencil tool:

1. Choose the Pencil tool (Y toggles between the Paintbrush and Pencil tools) .

2. Click the Stroke color box on the Toolbox, and choose a stroke color and attributes from the Stroke palette.

3. Click the Fill Color box and the None button on the Toolbox so the curves on the path won't fill in.

4. Press and drag to draw a line. A dotted line will appear as you draw. When you release the mouse, the line will be colored with the current fill and stroke settings and its anchor points will be selected (Preview view) **2**. In Artwork view, you'll see only a wire frame representation of the line **3**.

TIP See the info about Curve Fitting Tolerance on the next page.

### To erase part of a line as you draw with the Pencil tool:

1. Keep the mouse button down, then hold down Command/Ctrl and drag with the erasure pointer over any section of the dotted line preview that you want to eliminate.

2. Release Command/Ctrl, position the point of the pencil right on the dotted line, and continue to draw.

 **1** *Pencil tool.*

**2** *Blue-footed booby, drawn with the Pencil tool.*

**3** *The booby in Artwork view.*

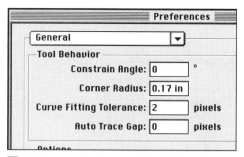

Enter a number between 0 and 10 in the *Curve Fitting Tolerance* field.

The number of anchor points the Pencil tool produces is determined by the Curve Fitting Tolerance setting in the General Preferences dialog box. The fewer the anchor points, the smoother the line. If you change this setting, only subsequently drawn lines will be affected, not existing lines.

### To increase or decrease the number of points the Pencil tool produces:

1. Choose File menu > Preferences > General (Command-K/Ctrl-K).

2. Enter a number between 0 and 10 in the Curve Fitting Tolerance field **1**. A Curve Fitting Tolerance of 0 will produce many anchor points **2**. A higher Curve Fitting Tolerance will produce anchor points only at sharp line direction changes **3**.

3. Click OK or press Return/Enter.

**TIP** You can remove anchor points from a line using the Delete-anchor-point tool, and reposition points on a line using the Direct Selection tool.

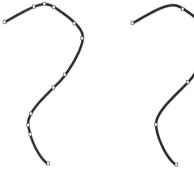

**2** *A line drawn with a Curve Fitting tolerance of 2.*

**3** *A line drawn with a Curve Fitting tolerance of 8.*

DIANE MARGOLIN

**Curve Fitting Tolerance**

## To add to a line:

1. Choose the Pencil tool.

2. Position the pencil pointer directly over either end of the line. The pencil icon will change to a white point with a black eraser tip when it is positioned over an endpoint **1**–**2**.

3. Press and drag the mouse to add to the line. When you release the mouse, the completed line path and its anchor points will be selected and the addition will be connected to the existing line.

**TIP** If the new and existing lines did not connect, delete the new line and try again or use the Join command to join the two lines *(see page 83)*.

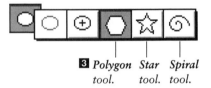

**1** *Continue-a-line pointer.*    **2** *Start-a-separate-line pointer.*

Using the **Polygon, Spiral,** or **Star** tool, you can easily create geometric objects with sides of equal length without having to draw with the mouse. The current fill and stroke settings are automatically applied to objects produced using these tools.

## To create a polygon by clicking:

1. Choose the Polygon tool from the pop-out menu on the Ellipse tool **3**.

2. Click where you want the center of the polygon to be.

3. Enter a value in the Radius field (the distance in the current Ruler units from the center of the object to the corner points) **4**.

4. Choose a number of sides for the polygon by clicking the up or down arrow or entering a number between 3 and 1000. The sides will be of equal length.

5. Click OK or press Return/Enter **5**.

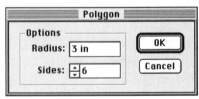

**3** *Polygon   Star   Spiral*
*tool.    tool.   tool.*

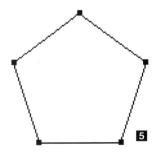

**4** *In the* **Polygon** *dialog box, choose a* **Radius** *distance and a number of* **Sides**.

*Add to a Line; Create a Polygon*

**1** *The Polygon tool.*

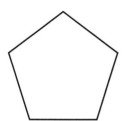 **2** *The polygon used as a starting point for figure* **3**.

*Diane Margolin*

**3** *To refine the large shape, a curve anchor point was added between each pair of existing points and then dragged inward. The Reshape tool could also have been used to add a point and drag the curve in one move.*

## To create a polygon by dragging:

1. Choose the Polygon tool from the pop-out menu on the Ellipse tool **1**.

2. Press and drag, starting from where you want the center of the polygon to be **2**.

   While dragging, use any of the following options:

   Drag away from or towards the center to increase or decrease the size of the polygon, respectively.

   Drag in a circular fashion to rotate the polygon.

   Hold down Shift while dragging to constrain the bottom side to the horizontal axis.

   With the mouse still held down, press the up or down arrow key to add or delete sides from the polygon.

   Hold down Space bar while dragging to move the polygon.

3. When you release the mouse, the polygon will be selected and colored with the current fill and stroke settings.

**Create a Polygon**

### To create a spiral by clicking:

1. Choose the Spiral tool from the pop-out menu on the Ellipse tool .

2. Click where you want the center of the spiral to be.

3. Enter a number in the Radius field (the distance in the current Ruler units from the center of the spiral to the outermost point) .

4. Enter a percentage between 5 and 150 in the Decay field to specify how tightly the spiral will wind.

5. Choose a number of Segments for the spiral (the number of quarter revolutions around the center point) by clicking the up or down arrow or by entering a number.

6. Click a Style button (the direction the spiral will wind from the center point).

7. Click OK or press Return/Enter .

8. Apply a stroke color to the spiral *(see pages 115–117).*

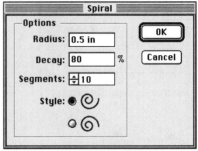

**1** *The Spiral tool.*

*In the Spiral dialog box, enter numbers in the **Radius** and **Decay** fields, choose a number of **Segments**, and click a **Style** button.*

*A spiral.*

## To create a spiral by dragging:

1. Choose the Spiral tool from the pop-out menu on the Ellipse tool.

2. Press and drag, starting from where you want the center of the spiral to be.

3. While dragging, use any of the following options:

   Drag away from or towards the center to increase or decrease the size of the spiral, respectively.

   Hold down Option/Alt while dragging to add or delete segments from the center of the spiral as you change its size.

   Drag in a circular fashion to rotate the spiral.

   Hold down Shift while dragging to constrain the rotation of the entire spiral to 45° increments.

   With the mouse still held down, press the up or down arrow key to add to or delete segments from the center of the spiral.

   Hold down Space bar while dragging to move the spiral.

   Hold down Command/Ctrl and drag away from/towards the center to control how tightly the spiral winds. (The Command/Ctrl key affects the Decay value.)

4. When you release the mouse, the object will be selected and colored with the current fill and stroke colors.

**TIP** If you hold down Command/Ctrl while dragging and manage to end up with a very low Decay value and only one segment, release the mouse and delete the spiral. Click with the Spiral tool and enter a higher Decay value.

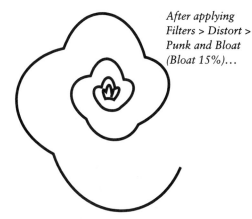

*After applying Filters > Distort > Punk and Bloat (Bloat 15%)...*

*...and reversing the fill and stroke colors.*

## To create a star by clicking:

1. Choose the Star tool from the pop-out menu on the Ellipse tool .

2. Click where you want the center of the star to be.

3. Enter a number in the Radius 1 field (the distance from the center of the object to the outer points in the current Ruler units) **2**.

4. Enter a number in the Radius 2 field (the distance from the center of the object to the inner points, where the segments bend inward).

5. Choose a number of Points for the star by clicking the up or down arrow or entering a number between 3 and 1000.

6. Click OK or press Return/Enter **3**–**4**.

**TIP** The distance from the center to the outer points of the star shape will always be the larger of the two Radius values, regardless of which field contains the larger value.

**TIP** The greater the difference between the Radius 1 and Radius 2 values, the longer will be the arms of the star.

**TIP** You can use the Rotate tool to rotate the completed star.

**1** The *Star* tool.

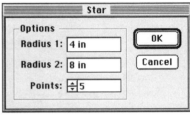

**2** In the *Star* dialog box, enter numbers in the **Radius 1** and **Radius 2** fields, and choose a number of **Points**.

**3**

**4** Stars created using the *Star* tool, with different numbers of points and Radius amounts.

**Create a Star**

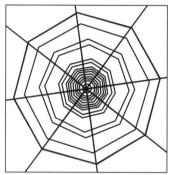

**2** *Multiple polygons drawn with the Polygon tool with "~" held down.*

**3** *Stars created by dragging with the Star tool with "~" held down, and then twirled using the Twirl filter.*

## To create a star by dragging:

1. Choose the Star tool from the pop-out menu on the Ellipse tool.

2. Press and drag, starting from where you want the center of the star to be.

   While dragging, use any of the following options:

   Drag away from or towards the center to increase or decrease the size of the star, respectively.

   Drag in a circular fashion to rotate the star.

   Hold down Shift while dragging to constrain one or two points to the horizontal axis.

   With the mouse still held down, press the up or down arrow key to add or delete sides from the star.

   Hold down Space bar while dragging to move the star.

   Hold down Option/Alt to make shoulders (opposite segments) parallel **1**.

   Hold down Command/Ctrl and drag away from/towards the center to increase/decrease the difference between the two radii of the star, making the arms of the star appear to be longer or shorter.

3. When you release the mouse, the object will be selected and colored with the current fill and stroke settings.

**TIP** Hold down "~" while dragging with the Star or Polygon tool to create progressively larger copies of the shape **2**. Drag quickly. Apply a stroke color to distinguish the different shapes. Use the Twirl tool to twirl the shapes around their center **3**.

**Create a Star**

63

Using the Rasterize command, you can convert a vector-based path object into pixel-based image right in Illustrator. Then you can apply any raster (bitmap) filter to it.

### To convert a path object into a pixel image:

1. Select an object.

2. Choose Object menu > Rasterize.

3. Choose a Color Model for the image: RGB for video or on-screen display (all raster filters available); CMYK for print output (only the Pixelate raster filters available); Grayscale for shades of black and white (all raster filters available); or Bitmap for only black-and-white (no raster filters available) 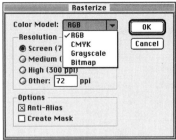.

4. Click a Resolution setting or enter a resolution value in the Other field.

5. *Optional:* Check the Anti-Alias box to have Illustrator softly fade the edge of the rasterized shape.

6. *Optional:* Check the Create Mask box to include a mask with the image that follows the contours of the object.

7. Click OK or press Return/Enter. A bounding box will surround the path object. If the Create Mask option was unchecked, the background of the box will be opaque white **2**–**5**.

**TIP** If you rasterize an object containing a pattern fill, the pattern color and line weight may change somewhat (especially if anti-aliasing is turned on). If the object had a pattern fill with a transparent background, the transparent background will turn solid white (except for the Bitmap Color Model). Rasterizing an object containing a pattern fill using the Bitmap Color Model can produce interesting results. You can also apply a fill color to an object rasterized using the Bitmap Color Model.

**1** *Choose a **Color Model** and **Resolution** in the **Rasterize** dialog box.*

**2** *A rasterized object with a mask after applying the Glass filter. The mask limits the effect to the object shape.*

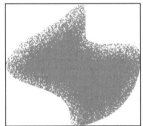

**3** *A rasterized object without a mask after applying the Glass filter. The effect extends beyond the object's original edge.*

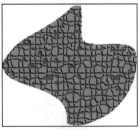

**4** *A rasterized object with a mask after applying the Mosaic Tile filter. The mask limits the effect to the object shape.*

**5** *A rasterized object without a mask after applying the Mosaic Tile filter. The effect extends beyond the object's original edge.*

# SELECT/MOVE 6

In Chapter 5 you learned how to create various objects. In later chapters you will learn many methods for modifying objects, such as reshaping, recoloring, and transforming. An object must be selected before it can be modified, however, so selecting objects is an essential Illustrator skill to learn. In this chapter you will learn how to use the selection tools and commands to highlight objects for modification. You'll also learn how to hide an object's anchor points and direction lines, how to hide, lock, or deselect whole objects, and how to copy or move objects within the same file or between files.

If you like to move or position objects by entering values or measuring distances, after you learn the fundamental techniques in this chapter, read Chapter 21, Precision Tools.

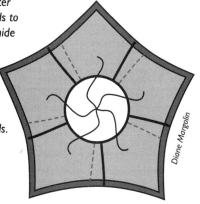

Diane Margolin

## The three selection tools

The **Selection** tool is used to select all the anchor points on an object or path. If you click on the edge or the fill of an object with the Selection tool, you will select all the points on that object.

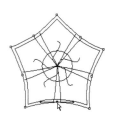

The **Direct Selection** tool is used to select one or more individual anchor points or segments of a path. If you click on the edge of an object with the Direct Selection tool, you will select only that segment, and the segment's direction lines and anchor points will become visible. (Straight line segments don't have direction lines—they only have anchor points.) If you click on the fill of an object in Preview view using this tool, you will select all the points on the object.

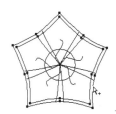

The **Group Selection** tool can be used to select all the anchor points on a path, but its primary use is to select groups within a group in the order in which they were added to the larger group. Click once to select an object; click twice to select that object's group; click three times to select the next group that was added to the larger group, and so on.

## To select an object or objects:

1. Choose the Selection tool (V) or Group Selection tool (press "A" to toggle between the Direct Selection and Group Selection tools) –, then click on the object's path **3**.
   *or*
   If your illustration is in Preview view and the Area Select option is on *(see the sidebar at right),* click on the object's fill.
   *or*
   Position the pointer outside the object or objects you want to select, then drag the pointer diagonally across them (a dotted marquee will define the area as you drag over it). The whole object or objects will be selected, even if only a portion of the object is marqueed **4**.

2. *Optional:* Shift-click to select additional objects or deselect any selected objects individually.

**TIP** Hold down Option/Alt to use the Group Selection tool while the Direct Selection tool is chosen, and vice versa.

### Area select

If the Area Select box is checked in the General Preferences dialog box (File menu > Preferences > General), you can click on an object's fill when your illustration is in Preview view to select the object's entire path. If the Area Select box is unchecked or the object has no fill, you must click on the edge of the object to select it. If your illustration is in Preview Selection view, you must click on the edge of an object to select it, regardless of the Area Select setting. ("Fill" and "stroke" are defined in Chapter 9.)

 **1** *Selection tool.*

**2** *Group Selection tool.*

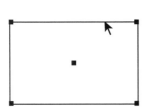

**3** *A path and all its anchor points being selected with the Selection tool.*

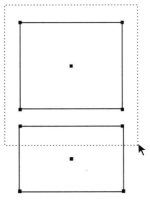

**4** *Selecting two objects by marqueeing them with the Selection tool.*

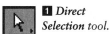 **1** *Direct
Selection tool.*

*Selected anchor
points are **solid**
little squares.*

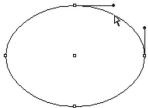

*Unselected
anchor points are
**hollow** squares.*

**2** *One anchor point selected
with the **Direct Selection** tool
(Artwork view).*

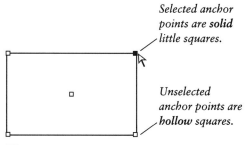

**3** *A segment selected with the
**Direct Selection** tool.*

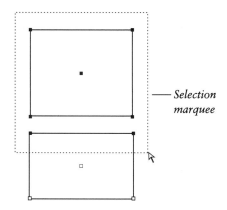

— *Selection
marquee*

**4** *A marquee selection being
made with the **Direct Selection**
tool. Only anchor points within
the marquee are selected.*

## To select anchor points or segments:

1. Choose the Direct Selection tool (press "A" to toggle between the Direct Selection and Group Selection tools) **1**.

2. Click on the anchor point(s) or segment(s) **2**–**3**.
   *or*
   Position the pointer outside the object or objects you want to select, then drag the pointer diagonally across them (a dotted marquee will define the area as you drag over it). Only the anchor points or segments you marquee will be selected **4**.

3. *Optional:* Shift-click to select additional anchor points or segments or deselect selected anchor points or segments individually.

   **TIP** Hold down Command/Ctrl to use the last highlighted selection tool while a non-selection tool is highlighted. With Command/Ctrl held down, you can click to select or deselect an object.

   **TIP** If you select or move curve segments without moving their corresponding anchor points, you will reshape the curves and the anchor points will remain stationary (more about reshaping curves in the next chapter).

**Select Anchor Points or Segments**

## To select all the objects in an illustration:

Choose Edit menu > Select All (Command-A/Ctrl-A) . All unlocked objects in your illustration will be selected, wherever they are—on the artboard or the scratch area. Any objects on a hidden layer (eye icon turned off) will not be selected.

**1** *Choose Select All from the Edit menu.*

Use the **Select** commands to select objects with similar characteristics to a currently selected object. Each command is named for the attributes it searches for.

## To select using a command:

1. Choose any selection tool.

2. Click on an object that contains the characteristics you want to search for in other objects.

3. Choose from the Select submenu under the Edit menu **2**:

   **Same Paint Style** (fill and stroke color and stroke weight) to search for all paint attributes.

   **Same Fill Color** to search for Fill attributes only.

   **Same Stroke Color** to search for stroke attributes only.

   **Same Stroke Weight** to search for strokes of the same weight.

   **Masks** to select masking objects. This command is useful because the edges of a masking object display in Preview view only when the object is selected.

   **Stray Points** to select single points that are not part of any paths, so they can be deleted easily.

   **Inverse** to select currently deselected objects and deselect currently selected objects.

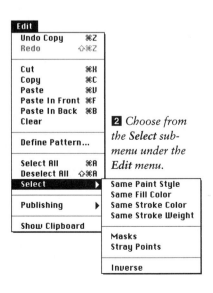

**2** *Choose from the Select submenu under the Edit menu.*

To prevent an object from being modified, it must be deselected.

**To deselect an object or objects:**

1. Choose a selection tool.

2. Click outside the selected object or objects.
   *or*
   Choose Edit menu > Deselect All (Command-Shift-A/Ctrl-Shift-A).

**TIP** To deselect an individual object within a multiple selection, hold down Shift and click on it or press and drag over it.

**TIP** To deselect all selected objects and select all unselected objects, choose Edit menu > Select > Inverse.

Choose the Hide Edges command to hide an object's anchor points and direction lines while still keeping the object selected and editable. Use this command if you want to see how different stroke colors or widths look on an object in Preview view, or to hide distracting points when you're working in Artwork view.

**To hide the anchor points and segments of an object or objects:**

1. Select the object or objects.

2. Choose View menu > Hide Edges (Command-H/Ctrl-H).

**TIP** To redisplay the anchor points and segments, choose View menu > Show Edges.

**TIP** To display or hide a selected object's center point, open the Attributes palette, expand the palette to show the palette options, if they're not visible, then click on the Don't Show Center or Show Center icon ■.

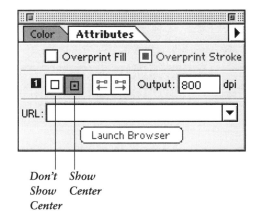

*Don't    Show*
*Show    Center*
*Center*

Hide Objects; Lock Objects

The Hide Selection command can help you isolate objects to work on. If your illustration is complex, you'll find this command to be particularly useful both for selecting the objects you *do* want to work on more easily and to speed up screen redraw. A hidden object will be invisible in both Artwork and Preview views, and will not print. If you close and reopen the file, hidden objects will redisplay.

### To hide an object:

1. Select the object or objects to be hidden.

2. Choose Object menu > Hide Selection (Command-U/Ctrl-U) **1**.

**TIP** Individual hidden objects cannot be selectively redisplayed. To redisplay *all* hidden objects, choose Object menu > Show All (Command-Shift-U/Ctrl-Shift-U). You can use the Layers palette to hide or lock all the objects on a layer *(see pages 161–162)*.

**TIP** To hide all *unselected* objects, hold down Option/Alt and choose Object menu > Hide Selection (Command-Option-U/Ctrl-Alt-U).

A locked object cannot be selected or modified. If you close and reopen the file, locked objects will remain locked.

### To lock an object:

1. Select the object or objects to be locked.

2. Choose Object menu > Lock (Command-L/Ctrl-L) **2**.

**TIP** Locked items can't be unlocked individually. To unlock all locked items, choose Object menu > Unlock All (Command-Shift-L/Ctrl-Shift-L). All previously locked objects will be selected and previously selected objects will be deselected.

**TIP** To lock all *unselected* objects, hold down Option/Alt and choose Object menu > Lock (Command-Option-L/Ctrl-Alt-L).

**TIP** To lock a whole layer, use the Layers palette.

### Lock/hide tips

You can't lock or hide part of an object or a path.

To unlock or show only one of several locked or hidden objects, choose Unlock All or Show All from the Object menu, choose the Selection tool, hold down Shift and click on the object you wish to unlock or show, then choose Lock or Hide for the remaining selected objects.

If you chose Lock or Hide for an object within a group, you can unlock or show just that object. Select the group, then hold down Option/Alt and Shift and choose Unlock All or Show All from the Object menu.

**1** *Selection tool.*

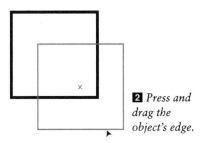

**2** *Press and drag the object's edge.*

## To move an object by dragging:

1. Choose the Selection tool **1**.

2. If your illustration is in Artwork view, press and drag the object's edge **2**.
   *or*
   In Preview view, press and drag the object's edge or the object's fill (if there is one, and the Area Select option is on in Preferences > General). This can also be done with the Direct Selection tool.

**TIP** Press any arrow key to move a selected object the current Cursor Key increment (which is specified in File menu > Preferences > Keyboard Increments). The default is 1 point. Precise methods for moving and aligning objects are discussed in Chapter 21, Precision Tools.

**TIP** If the Snap to Point box is checked in File menu > Preferences > General, the part of the object directly underneath the pointer will snap to the nearest guide or to a point on another object if it comes within two pixels (the pointer will turn white when it's over a guide or the point of another object).

**TIP** Hold down Shift while dragging to constrain the movement to the *x* or *y* axis.

## To drag-copy an object:

1. Choose the Selection tool.

2. Hold down Option/Alt and press and drag the fill or the edge of the object you want to copy (the pointer will turn into a double arrowhead) **3**.

3. Release the mouse, then release Option/Alt. A copy of the object will appear in the new location.

**TIP** To create additional copies of the object, choose Object menu > Transform > Transform Again (Command-D/Ctrl-D) any number of times.

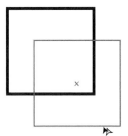

**3** *To copy an object, hold down **Option/Alt** and press and drag the object. Note the double arrowhead pointer.*

*Note:* You can drag-and-drop objects between Illustrator documents or between drag-aware applications. The drag-and-drop method (instructions on the next page) requires fewer steps than does using the Clipboard.

If you select an object or group and then choose the **Cut** or **Copy** command, that object or group is placed onto the **Clipboard,** a temporary storage area in memory. The previous contents of the Clipboard are replaced each time you choose Cut or Copy.

The **Paste** command places the current Clipboard contents in the center of the currently active document window. The same Clipboard contents can be pasted an unlimited number of times.

### To move an object or a group from one document to another:

1. Choose the Selection tool.

2. Click on the object or group.

3. Choose Edit menu > Cut (Command-X/ Ctrl-X) **1**. The object or group will be removed from the current document.
   *or*
   To move a copy of the object or group, choose Edit menu > Copy (Command-C/ Ctrl-C).

4. Click in the destination document window.

5. *Optional:* Select an object to paste in front of or behind.

6. Choose Edit menu > Paste (Command-V/ Ctrl-V) **2**. Or, if you've selected an object in the destination document, choose Edit menu > Paste in Front or Paste in Back.

**TIP** You can place an Illustrator object into a document in another Adobe PostScript application via the Clipboard. *Macintosh users:* If you copy and paste an object from Illustrator into Photoshop 4, a Paste dialog box will open. Click Paste As Pixels (check or uncheck the Anti-Alias box), or click Paste As Paths.

## Moving grouped objects

If you copy an object in a group by dragging (use the Direct Selection tool with Option/Alt held down), the copy will be *part of* that group. If you use the Clipboard to copy and paste an object in a group, the object will paste *outside* the group (the Group command is discussed on page 152).

*Choose **Cut, Copy** **1** or **Paste** from **2** the Edit menu.*

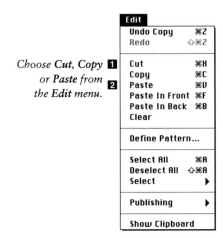

Move an Object to a Different Document

## Drag to the Desktop

If you drag an Illustrator object to the Desktop, a Picture Clipping file will be created in PICT format on Macintosh, a Scrap file in WMF format on Windows. This intermediary file can then be dragged into any drag aware application.

## Drag-and-drop a rasterized object without a mask?

If you drag-and-drop a rasterized object (created without a mask), from Illustrator to Photoshop, the bounding area (background) of the object in Photoshop will become opaque white and will block pixels below it. To make the non-pixel layer areas transparent, use Photoshop's Magic Wand tool to select the white background on that object's layer, then press Delete.

*Note:* To be able to drag-and-drop between Illustrator 7 and Photoshop, you must use Photoshop 4 or later.

## To drag-and-drop a copy of an object (Illustrator-to-Illustrator or between Photoshop and Illustrator):

1. Select the object you want to drag-and-drop in an Illustrator or Photoshop document.

2. Open the Illustrator or Photoshop document to which you want to copy the object.

3. Drag the object into the destination document window, and presto, a copy of the object will appear in the new location. In Photoshop, the object will become pixels on a new layer.

**TIP** Hold down Command/Ctrl when dragging a path object from Illustrator to preserve the object as a path in Photoshop 4.

**TIP** Hold down Shift after you start dragging into Photoshop to position the resulting pixels in the middle of the Photoshop document window.

**TIP** If you drag-and-drop from Photoshop to Illustrator (Move tool), the image will drop as an RGB PICT, 72 ppi. If you're going to print the image, use the following method instead: Convert the file to CMYK Color mode, save the Photoshop file as a TIFF or EPS, and then use the Place or Open command in Illustrator to acquire it.

**TIP** Drag-and-drop does not use the Clipboard, so whatever is currently on the Clipboard is preserved.

Drag-and-drop

The Offset Path command copies a path shape and offsets the copy from the original by a specified distance, and it also reshapes the copy slightly so it fits neatly next to the original path—which doesn't happen if you simply duplicate a path using the Option/Alt drag method or the Scale tool.

We recommend that you use this command on a line or an open path that has a stroke, but no fill. On an object that contains a fill color, you're better off using the Scale tool.

### To offset a copy of a path:

1. Select an object.

2. Choose Object menu > Path > Offset Path.

3. In the Offset field, enter a positive number to place the offset path above the edge of the original path or a negative value to place the copy below the original path 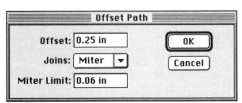. Be sure the Offset value you enter is larger than the stroke weight, if any, so the offset won't overlap the original path.

4. Choose a Joins (bend) style: Round (semicircular), Miter (pointed), or Bevel (square-cornered).

5. *Optional:* Enter a new Miter limit. The Miter limit is the maximum amount the path's line weight (measured from the inside to the outside of the corner point) can be enlarged before the miter join becomes a bevel join. The Miter limit value times the stroke weight value gives the maximum inner-to-outer corner measurement. Increase the Miter limit to have a long, sharp point. Lower the Miter limit to create a bevel join corner.

6. Click OK or press Return/Enter .

**1** *In the* **Offset Path** *dialog box, enter an* **Offset** *amount and choose a* **Joins** *style.*

**2** *The original path—the darkest gray line—with an offset path above it (positive Offset value) and an offset path below it (negative Offset value).*

# RESHAPE PATHS 7

As you learned in Chapter 5, a path is the edge of an object that defines its shape. In this important chapter, you will learn how to change the profile of an object by changing the number, position, or type of anchor points on its path. Using these techniques, you'll be able to draw just about any shape imaginable.

You will learn how to move anchor points or path segments to reshape a path, how to convert a corner anchor point into a curve anchor point (or vice versa) to reshape the segments that it connects, how to add or delete anchor points, how to carve away parts of a path using the Knife tool, how to make cutout shapes using the Slice command, and how to use the Reshape tool to reshape a small or large portion of a path in one simple step.

You will also learn how to split a path, how to align anchor points, how to join endpoints, how to combine paths using the Unite command, and how to trace a placed image automatically or manually.

Also included in this chapter are two practice exercises.

*The angle of a direction line affects the slope of the curve into the anchor point.*

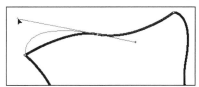

*The length of a direction line affects the height of the curve.*

Béziers

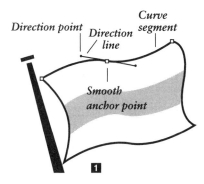

*Direction point  Direction / line  Curve segment*

*Smooth anchor point*

**1**

## What is a Bézier?

In Illustrator, a curve segment is also called a Bézier curve. A Bézier curve consists of two anchor points connected by a curve segment, with at least one direction point and direction line attached to each anchor point **1**. When an anchor point connects a curve and a straight line segment, it has one common direction line. When an anchor point connects two curve segments, it has a pair of direction lines.

If you move an anchor point, the segments connected to it will reshape. If you move a curve segment, the connecting anchor points will remain stationary. If you move a straight line segment, connecting anchor points *will* move.

### To move an anchor point or a segment:

1. Choose the Direct Selection tool ("A" toggles between Direct Selection and Group Selection tools) .

2. Press and drag the anchor point or segment ❷–❸.

**TIP** Hold down Shift to constrain the movement of an anchor point to the nearest 45° angle.

**TIP** If all the anchor points on a path are selected, you will not be able to move an individual point or segment. Deselect the object, then reselect an individual point.

**TIP** To select more than one anchor point at a time, Shift-click them or drag a marquee around them.

In the instructions above, you learned that you can drag a curve segment or an anchor point to reshape a curve. A more precise way to reshape a curve is to lengthen, shorten, or change the angle of its direction lines.

### To reshape a curve segment:

1. Choose the Direct Selection tool.

2. Click on an anchor point ❹.

3. Press and drag a direction point (the end of the direction line) toward or away from the anchor point ❺.

   *or*

   Rotate the direction point around the anchor point ❻ (next page). The anchor point will remain selected when you release the mouse.

❶ *Direct Selection tool.*

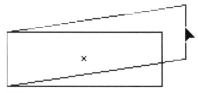
❷ *Moving a segment.*

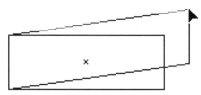
❸ *Moving an anchor point.*

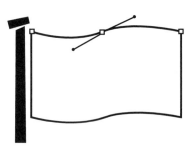
❹ *The original shape with an anchor point selected.*

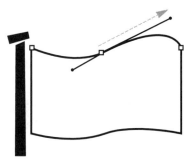
❺ *A direction point is dragged away from its anchor point.*

Move a Point or Segment; Reshape a Curve

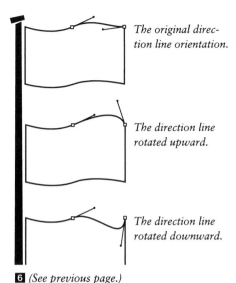

*The original direction line orientation.*

*The direction line rotated upward.*

*The direction line rotated downward.*

**6** *(See previous page.)*

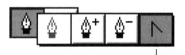

**1** *Convert-direction-point tool. Press "P" to cycle through the pen*

Direction line antennae on a smooth curve move in tandem in a straight line, even if one direction line is moved or the curve segment or anchor point they are connected to is moved.

### To convert a corner anchor point into a curve anchor point:

1. Choose the Direct Selection tool **1**.

2. Click on the edge of the object. The anchor points will be hollow.

3. Choose the Convert-direction-point tool (press "P" to cycle through the pen tools) or hold down Command-Option/Ctrl-Alt with any selection tool active.

4. Press on an anchor point, then drag away from it. Direction lines will be created as you drag. The further you drag, the rounder the curve will become **2**.

5. *Optional:* To further modify the curve, choose the Direct Selection tool, then drag the anchor point or a direction line.

**TIP** If the new curve segment twists around the anchor point as you drag, keep the mouse button down, rotate the direction line back around the anchor point to undo the twist, then continue to drag in the new direction **3**.

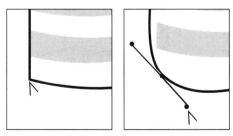

**2** *To convert a corner anchor point into a curve anchor point, click with the **Convert-direction-point** tool on the anchor point, then drag away from it.*

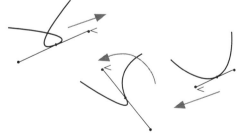

**3** *If the curve twists around the anchor point, rotate the direction line to un-twist it.*

Convert a Corner Point into a Curve Point

## To convert a curve anchor point into a corner anchor point:

1. Choose the Direct Selection tool.

2. Click on the edge of the object to display its anchor points.

3. Choose the Convert-direction-point tool (or hold down Command-Option/ Ctrl-Alt).

4. Click on a curve anchor point—don't drag! Its direction lines will be deleted **1**–**2**.

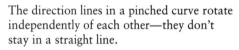

**2** *Click with the Convert-direction-point tool on a curve anchor point to convert it into a corner anchor point.*

The direction lines in a pinched curve rotate independently of each other—they don't stay in a straight line.

## To pinch a curve inward:

1. Choose the Direct Selection tool.

2. Click on the edge of an object to display its anchor points **3**.

3. Choose the Convert-direction-point tool (or hold down Command-Option/ Ctrl-Alt).

4. Press and drag a direction point at the end of one of the direction lines. The curve segment will reshape as you drag **4**.

5. Choose the Direct Selection tool. Click on the anchor point.

6. Drag the other direction line for that anchor point **5**.

**TIP** To revert an independent-rotating direction line pair back to its previous straight-line alignment and produce a smooth, un-pinched curve segment, choose the Convert-direction-point tool, then click on and drag away from the anchor point.

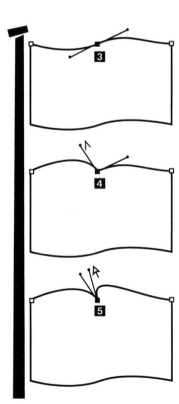

*Direction lines being moved independently to pinch the curve.*

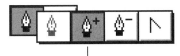

**1** *Add-anchor-point* tool. Press *"P" to cycle through the pen tools.*

**2** *Click on a segment with the **Add-anchor-point** tool to create a new anchor point...*

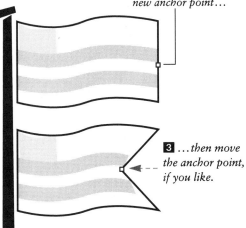

**3** *...then move the anchor point, if you like.*

Another way to reshape an object is to manually add or delete anchor points from its path using the Add-anchor-point or Delete-anchor-point tool. Adding or deleting points from a path will not split or open it. A new anchor point on a curve segment will be a curve anchor point with direction lines. A new anchor point on a straight line segment will be a corner anchor point.

## To add anchor points to a path manually:

1. *Optional:* Select an object to display its anchor points *(see page 66).*

2. Choose the Add-anchor-point tool **1**.

3. Click on the edge of the object. A new, selected anchor point will appear **2**. Repeat, if desired, to add more points.

4. *Optional:* Use the Direct Selection tool to move the new anchor point **3**.

**TIP** If you don't click precisely on a segment of an object, a warning prompt may appear. Click OK, then try again.

**TIP** Hold down Option/Alt to use the Delete-anchor-point tool when the Add-anchor-point tool is selected and is over an anchor point.

*It's difficult to produce a smooth curve if you place anchor points at the top...*

*It's better to place anchor points at the ends of a curve.*

**Add Anchor Points to a Path**

The **Add Anchor Points** command inserts one anchor point midway between every two existing anchor points.

### To add anchor points to a path using the Add Anchor Points command :

1. Select an object or objects.
2. Choose Object menu > Path > Add Anchor Points –**3**.

**1** *The original object.*

**2** *After adding anchor points to the original object and then applying the Punk and Bloat filter (Punk 70%).*

**3** *After adding anchor points and then applying the Punk and Bloat filter (Bloat 70%).*

*Diane Margolin*

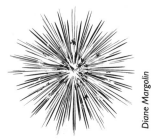

**4** *Delete-anchor-point tool*

### To delete anchor points from a path:

1. Select an object *(see page 66).*
2. Choose the Delete-anchor-point tool **4** ("P" to cycle through the pen tools).
3. Click on an anchor point. The point will be deleted and an adjacent point will become selected **5**. Repeat to delete other anchor points, if desired.

**TIP** If you do not click precisely on an anchor point, a warning prompt may appear. Click OK and try again.

**TIP** Hold down Option/Alt to use the Add-anchor-point tool when the Delete-anchor-point tool is selected and is over a segment.

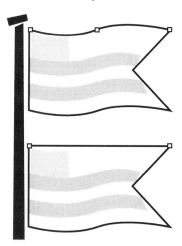

**5** *To delete an anchor point, click on it with the **Delete-anchor-point** tool. The path will reshape.*

**1** *Scissors tool.*

*An open path can be split into two paths and a closed path can be opened using the* **Scissors** *tool. A path can be split at an anchor point or in the middle of a segment.*

## To split a path:

1. Choose any selection tool.

2. Click on an object to display its anchor points.

3. Choose the Scissors tool ("C" to toggle between the Scissors and Knife tools) **1**.

4. Click on the object's path **2**. If you click on a **closed** path, it will turn into a single, open path. If you click on an **open** path, it will split into two paths.

 If you click on a **segment**, two new endpoints will appear, one on top of the other. If you click on an **anchor** point, a new anchor point will appear on top of the existing one. The new endpoints will be selected and they will overlap each other.

*To move the new endpoints apart:*

5. Choose the Direct Selection tool.

6. Click away from the object to deselect it **3**.

7. Click on the object's path.

8. Click on the new endpoint **4**, then drag it away to reveal the endpoint underneath **5**.

**TIP** You can apply a fill color to an open path. If you apply a stroke color, you will be able to see where the missing segment is **6**.

**TIP** You cannot split an open path if it has text on it or inside it.

**2** *Click with the Scissors tool on a path.*

**3** *Click with the* **Direct Selection** *tool away from the path.*

**4** *Click with the* **Direct Selection** *tool on the new endpoint.*

**5** *Move the new endpoint.*

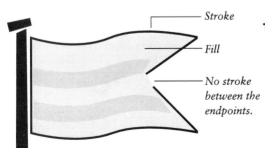

— Stroke

— Fill

— No stroke between the endpoints.

**6** *An open path can have a fill and a stroke.*

**Split a Path**

81

The **Average** command reshapes one or more paths by precisely realigning their endpoints or anchor points along the horizontal and/or vertical axis.

## To average anchor points:

1. Choose the Direct Selection tool.

2. Shift-click on two or more anchor points. You might want to zoom in on the objects so you can clearly see the selected points.

3. Choose Object menu > Path > Average (Command-Option-J/Ctrl-Alt-J) 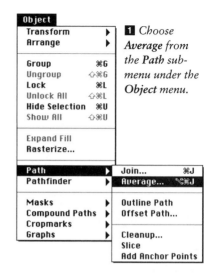.

4. Click **Horizontal** to align the points along the horizontal (x) axis.
   *or*
   Click **Vertical** to align the points along the vertical (y) axis 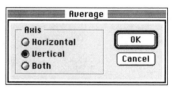.
   *or*
   Click **Both** to overlap the points along both the horizontal and vertical axes. Choose this option if you want to join them later into one point *(instructions on the following page)*.

5. Click OK or press Return/Enter **3**.

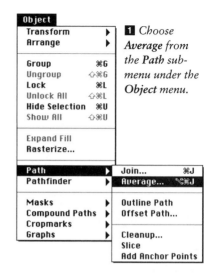
**1** *Choose Average from the Path submenu under the Object menu.*

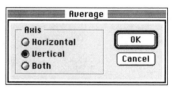
**2** *Click an Axis button in the Average dialog box.*

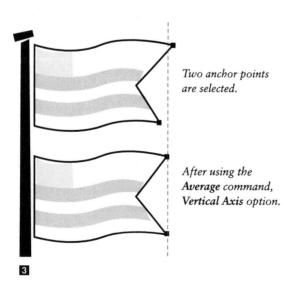
*Two anchor points are selected.*

*After using the Average command, Vertical Axis option.*

**3**

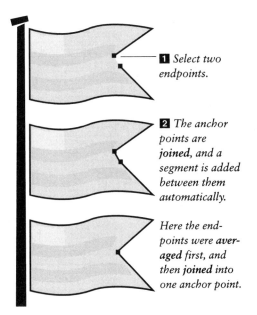

**1** *Select two endpoints.*

**2** *The anchor points are joined, and a segment is added between them automatically.*

*Here the end-points were aver-aged first, and then joined into one anchor point.*

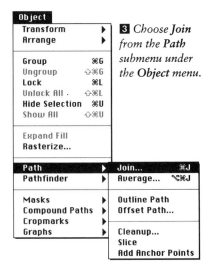

**3** *Choose Join from the Path submenu under the Object menu.*

**4** *Click Points: Corner or Smooth in the Join dialog box.*

If you align two endpoints on top of each other that are both selected and then execute the **Join** command, they will combine into one anchor point. If the endpoints are not on top of each other, a new straight line segment will be created between them. The Join command will not add direction lines to the new anchor point. The endpoints can be on separate open paths or one open path.

## To join two endpoints:

1. Choose the Direct Selection tool.

2. *Optional:* If you want to combine two endpoints into one, move one endpoint on top of the other manually and marquee them to select them both, or use the Average command (Axis: Both) to align them *(instructions are on the previous page).*

3. Shift-click on two endpoints, or marquee them **1**.

4. Choose Object menu > Path > Join (Command-J/Ctrl-J). If the endpoints are not on top of each other, the Join command will connect them with a straight line segment **2**. If the endpoints are aligned on top of each other and both are selected (marquee them, if necessary), the Join dialog box will open **4**. In the Join dialog box:

   Click **Corner** to join corner points into one corner point with no direction lines or to connect two curve points (or a corner point and a curve point) into one curve point with independent-moving direction lines. This is the default setting.
   *or*
   Click **Smooth** to connect two curve points into a curve point with direction lines that move in tandem.

5. Click OK or press Return/Enter.

**TIP** To average and join two selected endpoints using one keystroke: Command-Option-Shift-J/Ctrl-Alt-Shift-J.

**Join Endpoints**

The Pathfinder commands combine multiple objects into one new object. Most of the Pathfinders are covered on pages 97–100, but here's an introduction to one of the most useful: The Unite command.

### To combine two or more objects into one using the Unite command:

1. Position two or more objects so they overlap **1**.

2. Choose any Selection tool.

3. Marquee at least some portion of all the objects.

4. Choose Object menu > Pathfinder > Unite. The individual objects will combine into one closed object **2**–**5**, and will be colored with the topmost object's paint attributes.

**TIP** If you apply a stroke color to the new object, you will see that its previously overlapping segments were removed.

**TIP** You can use the new closed object as a masking object. (You could not have created a mask with the original objects before they were united.)

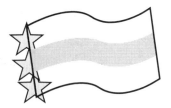

**1** *Overlap two or more objects, then select them all.*

**2** *The individual shapes are combined into a single shape.*

**3** *These numbers were converted to outlines before applying the Unite command.*

**4** *The outer shape of this tag was created by placing a rectangle over a circle and then applying the Unite command.*

PETER FAHRNI

**5** *Before applying the Unite command.* *After applying the Unite command.*

Unite Objects

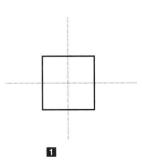

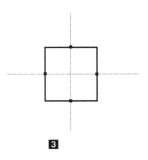

**2** *Add-anchor-point* tool.

**Convert-direction-point** *tool*

**Delete-anchor-point** *tool*

*Press "P" to cycle through the pen tools.*

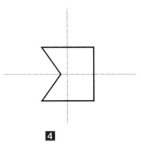

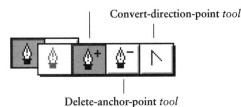

## Exercise

### Change a square into a star (or a clover):

1. If the rulers are not displayed, choose View menu > Show Rulers (Command-R/Ctrl-R).

2. Choose the Rectangle tool (M).

3. Click on the Artboard.

4. In the Rectangle dialog box, enter 3" in the Width and Height fields, then click OK.

5. Choose the Selection tool.

6. Press and drag a guide from the horizontal ruler. Release the mouse when the guide is over the rectangle's center point.

7. Press and drag a guide from the vertical ruler. Release the mouse when the guide is over the rectangle's center point **1**.

8. Choose the Add-anchor-point tool **2**.

9. Position the pointer over the intersection of a ruler guide and the edge of the rectangle, then click to add a point in the middle of the segment **3**, then add points to the other segment midpoints.
   *or*
   Choose Object > Path > Add Anchor Points.

10. Choose the Direct Selection tool.

11. Drag each of the midpoints inward toward the center point **4**.

*(Continued on the following page)*

**Exercise: Square to Star**

12. You should now have a star with four narrow spokes **1**. Choose the Convert-direction-point tool **2**.

13. Drag from each of the outer anchor points to convert the corners into smooth curves **3**.

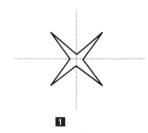

**1**

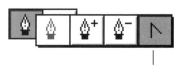

**2** *Convert-direction-point tool.*

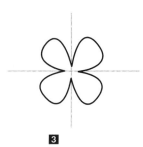

**3**

### Change the star (or clover) back into a square:

1. If the star is not selected, select it with a selection tool.

2. Choose the Convert-direction-point tool.

3. Click (but don't drag) on the curve points to convert them back into corner points.

4. Choose the Delete-anchor-point tool.

5. Click on each of the inner anchor points. The outer points will be reconnected by single segments, and the object will be square again.

## Exercise

### Create a flag:

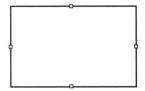

**1.** *Draw a rectangle. Apply a white fill and a black stroke. Add points to the middle of the segments using the Add-anchor-point tool.*

**2.** *Drag with the Convert-direction-point tool from the top and bottom midpoints.*

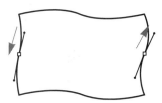

**3.** *Drag with the Convert-direction-point tool from the side midpoints.*

**4.** *Using the Direct Selection tool, move the left midpoint inward, then rotate the direction lines. Drag the right midpoint direction lines away from their anchor point.*

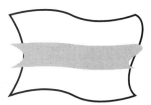

**5.** *Select the whole object, then double-click the Scale tool. Enter Non-uniform: Horizontal 120%, Vertical 30%, then click Copy. Apply a gray fill and a stroke of None.*

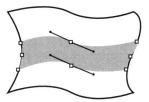

**6.** *Using the Direct Selection tool, rotate the top and bottom midpoints' direction lines to match the flag's curves. Select the large flag. Choose Edit menu > Copy. Select the gray shape. Choose Edit menu > Paste in Front. Shift-select the gray shape again. Choose Object menu > Pathfinder > Crop. The gray shape now conforms to the flag.*

**7.** *To cover the edges of the selected gray shape with a copy of the flag, choose Edit menu > Paste in Front. With this newly pasted shape now selected, apply a fill of None and a Black stroke in a slightly thicker weight. Marquee all the shapes with the Selection tool, then choose Object menu > Group.*

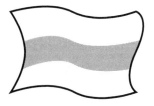

Using the Reshape tool, you can quickly reshape part of a path simply by dragging the path's edge. That portion will reshape smoothly—that's the beauty of this tool. Use it to stretch or add a twist or bend to any part of an existing path.

### To use the Reshape tool:

1. Click on the edge of a path using the Direct Selection tool. Only one point or segment should be selected.

2. Choose the Reshape tool (press "S" to toggle between the Scale and Reshape tools) **1**.

3. Drag any visible point. A square border will display around the point when you release the mouse.
   *or*
   Drag any segment of the path. A new square border point will be created.
   *or*
   Shift-click multiple points on the path or drag a marquee around them (squares will display around these points), then drag. For smooth reshaping, leave at least one point on the path unselected (with no square around it) to act as an anchor for the shape **2**–**3**.

4. *Optional:* Select other points (marquee or Shift-click with the Reshape tool) and/or drag again with the Reshape tool to further reshape.

**TIP** Choose Edit menu > Undo to undo the last Reshape. Undo will also automatically select the whole shape. Before continuing to work with the Reshape tool, you must deselect the shape, and then click again on the edge of the shape with the Direct Selection tool.

**TIP** The Reshape tool works well for stretching or bending an open path or paths. Marquee the endpoints on one end of the paths with the Direct Selection tool, marquee all the points except the endpoints on the other side with the Reshape tool, then stretch and bend the paths.

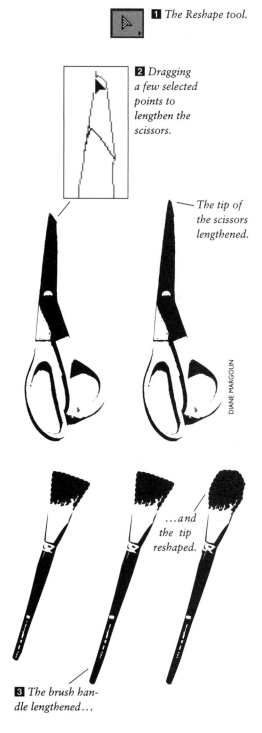

**1** *The Reshape tool.*

**2** *Dragging a few selected points to lengthen the scissors.*

*The tip of the scissors lengthened.*

DIANE MARGOLIN

*...and the tip reshaped.*

**3** *The brush handle lengthened...*

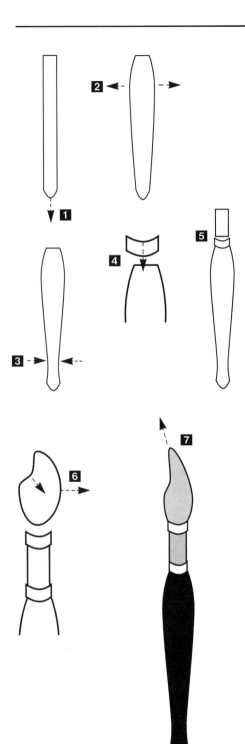

## Exercise

### Draw a paintbrush using the Reshape tool:

1. Draw a narrow vertical rectangle, white fill, black stroke.

2. Deselect the shape. Click on the path edge with the Direct Selection tool (A).

3. Choose the Reshape tool (S) and drag down from the middle of the bottom segment **1**.

4. Drag the upper middle of the right vertical segment slightly outward **2**. And drag the upper middle of the left vertical segment outward the same distance.

5. Drag each side of the bottom vertical segments inward to pinch the stem **3**.

6. Draw a small horizontal rectangle. Deselect it. Click on the path's edge with the Direct Selection tool.

7. Choose the Reshape tool, click the middle of the top segment, Shift-click the middle of the bottom segment, then drag downward **4**.

8. Place the rectangle over the top of the brush stem, and scale it to fit.

9. Draw a vertical rectangle above the horizontal rectangle with a slightly narrower width. Choose Object menu > Arrange > Send to Back **5**.

10. Option-Shift/Alt-Shift drag the horizontal rectangle upward to create a copy placed at top of vertical rectangle.

11. Drag an oval for brush tip. Deselect, then click on path edge with Direct Selection tool.

12. Choose the Reshape tool, drag the right middle point outward, drag the upper left segment inward **6**, then drag the top point upward to lengthen brush tip **7**.

13. Position the brush tip shape over the brush stem, then choose Object menu > Arrange > Send to Back.

Exercise: Paintbrush (Reshape Tool)

The **Auto Trace** tool automatically traces a path over a PICT, TIFF or EPS image that's opened via the File menu > Place command. A flaw of this tool is that it can create extraneous anchor points or place points in inappropriate locations, so autotraced shapes usually need to be cleaned up—points removed, etc. The Auto Trace tool works best on high contrast artwork, or if you're looking for a rough, hand-drawn look. Photographs, on the other hand, are best traced manually using the Pen or Pencil tool.

The exactness with which the Autotrace tool traces a path is determined by the Auto Trace Gap and Curve Fitting Tolerance settings in File menu > Preferences > General. The Auto Trace Gap (0–2) is the minimum width in pixels a gap in linework must be in order to be traced. A high Auto Trace Gap setting may result in the creation of a lot of extraneous points. The higher the Curve Fitting Tolerance, the less precisely an object will be traced, and the fewer anchor points will be created.

*Note:* Adobe's Streamline program traces more accurately and offers more options than Illustrator's Auto Trace tool. You can also color adjust a bitmap image in Streamline before using the program to trace it.

### To use the Auto Trace tool:

1. Open a file, then choose File menu > Place.

2. Locate and highlight a bitmap file (PICT, TIFF or EPS), then click Place **1**.

3. *Optional:* Set up a fill of None and a black stroke.

4. Create a new layer for the tracing shapes so you can view and select them separately from other elements in the artwork.

5. Choose the Auto Trace tool (press "B" to toggle between Blend and Auto Trace) **2**.

6. Click on areas or edges of the placed shape or press and drag to define an area to be traced. The shape will be traced automatically **3**–**4**. Experiment!

7. Fill the traced shapes, as desired **5**.

**1** *The placed artwork in the document window. When placing an EPS for tracing, do not link the file, as this will produce a poorer screen image.*

**2** *Auto Trace tool.*

**3** *The outer path traced. Apply a fill of None to prevent the new tracing shapes from blocking out the placed image.*

**4** *The outer and inner paths traced.*

**5** *The final objects after applying black and white fills.*

**1** *A closeup of an Auto Trace of the letters. Note the non-systematic distribution of anchor points and direction lines.*

**2** *A closeup of the placed artwork.*

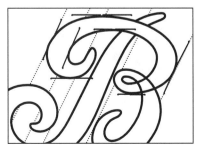

**3** *The letters drawn manually (the artwork is hidden). Direction lines are horizontal or on the same diagonal.*

## To trace letters manually:

The Auto Trace tool traces quickly and is useful if the feel of the relatively coarse rendering it produces is appropriate for your particular project. If you need to create smoother shapes, you can refine the Auto Trace tool paths or trace the template manually **1**. What follows is a description of how designer Peter Fahrni uses Illustrator to produce his own letterforms.

### 1. Scan the artwork

To make sure the baseline of your letterwork squares with the horizontal guidelines in Illustrator, trim the edge of your drawing parallel to the baseline, then slide it against the glass frame of the scanner. Scan your artwork at a resolution between 72 and 150 ppi. Save it as a PICT, TIFF or EPS. Even at 300% view, you will see only a minor difference in crispness between a placed 72 ppi PICT image and a placed, non-linked, 250 ppi EPS.

### 2. Trace manually

Use the File menu > Place command to locate and place an image **2**. If you wish, put the placed image on its own layer, and dim and/or lock this layer using Layer Options to make tracing easier (see page 160). Using the Pen tool, most round shapes can be created with as few as four anchor points.

To trace the upright letters in the illustration at left, anchor points were placed on the topmost, bottommost, leftmost, and rightmost parts of the curve. Shift was held down to draw out the direction lines horizontally or vertically.

To create the inclined letter shown in **3**, a line was drawn following the inclination of a stem, (in this case the lower case "t"), and then it was copied and converted into a guide for positioning the direction lines (choose View menu > Make Guides). The direction lines of the leftmost and rightmost

*(Continued on the following page)*

**Manual Trace**

points were extended to align with the guides.

### 3. *Fine tune the flow of curves*

Select an anchor point, then move it by pressing the arrow keys. The length and the angle of the direction lines won't change. Select a curve segment, and press the arrow keys to adjust its shape. The length, but not the angle, of the direction lines will change.

The manually traced "B" consisted of two closed, crisscrossing paths **1**. The Unite command was applied to combine the two paths into one **2**.

**1** *The hand-drawn "B."*

**2** *The final "B" after applying the Unite command.*

**A comparison between an Auto Traced character and an Adobe font character**

*Placed artwork in Illustrator.*

*The character Auto Traced.*

*A character in the Goudy 100 Adobe PostScript font, created as type in Illustrator.*

**Manual Trace**

**1** *A placed PICT image.*

**2** *After tracing the PICT using the Pen tool, filling and stroking the paths with various shades of black, and applying the Roughen filter with low Size and Detail settings to give the path strokes a more handmade appearance.*

Using the Pen or Pencil tool, you can manually trace over any placed PICT, TIFF, or EPS image. When you manually trace an image, you can organize and simplify path shapes as well as control their stacking order. If you like, you can even place different path shapes on different layers as you trace.

### To manually trace over a placed image:

1.  Place a TIFF, PICT, or non-linked EPS image using the File menu > Place command *(see page 41)* **1**.

2.  On the Layers palette, click on the name of the layer that contains the placed image, then click the lock icon (second box from the left) so the image can't be selected while you trace over it.

3.  *Optional:* Double-click the layer name, check the Dim Images box to dim the placed image so your pen paths will stand out more distinctly, then click OK.

4.  On the Layers palette, create a new layer for the tracing shapes so you can view and select them separately from other artwork.

5.  Choose the Pen (P) or Pencil (Y) tool.

6.  Trace the placed image **2**.

**TIP** You can move the placed image anywhere on your Artboard, provided the layer is not locked. You can also transform a placed image before you trace it.

Manually Trace a Placed Image

The Knife tool reshapes paths like a carving knife, and is a wonderful tool for artists who have a freehand drawing style.

**1** *Knife tool.*

### To cut an object into separate shapes:

1. Choose the Knife tool (Press "C" to toggle between the Scissors and Knife tools) **1**.

2. Starting from outside the object's edge, drag the Knife tool completely across an object to divide it, or end up outside the object again to reshape it **2**–**4**. Hold down Shift while dragging to cut in a straight line.

**TIP** Choose Object menu > Group to group separate shapes into one object, and then use the Direct Selection tool if you need to select separate shapes within the group.

**TIP** If you drag the Knife tool completely inside the object (and not outside-to-inside the object), the resulting shape will be a compound. If you choose Artwork view, you'll see a cutout shape and a copy of the cutout shape directly behind the object.

If you draw a line completely inside an object with the Knife tool, you will create a tear in the object. To open the tear, select the inner line shape of what is now a compound path and pull the direction lines.

**TIP** The Knife tool won't cut a line or an open path. If a Stroked line is among the stack of objects cut by the Knife tool, the line will be sent to the back of the stack.

**TIP** If the Knife tool cuts through a mask, any objects within the mask that the Knife tool passes over, and any shapes stacked above it, will be released from the mask and will be cut by the Knife. The mask and any uncut masked objects won't be affected.

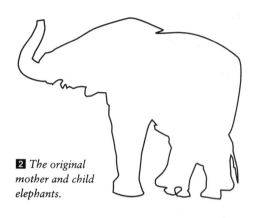

**2** *The original mother and child elephants.*

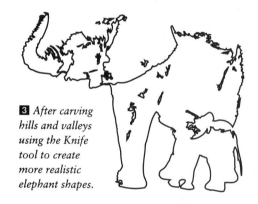

**3** *After carving hills and valleys using the Knife tool to create more realistic elephant shapes.*

**4** *The final image, after applying a black Fill.*

Diane Margolin

Knife Tool

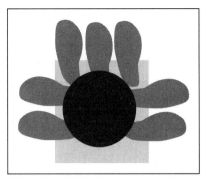

**1** *The black circle is the cutting object.*

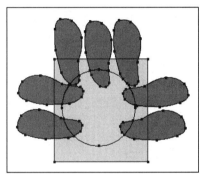

**2** *After applying the **Slice** command.*

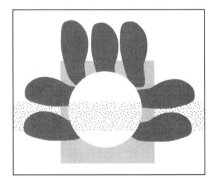

**3** *After deleting the cutting object and the inner part of each petal. The pattern behind all the objects shows that the slicing circle produced a cutout.*

The Slice command uses the topmost object to cut the underlying objects beneath it.

## To cut objects using the Slice command:

1. Create or select an object to be used as the cutting shape. The Slice command will cause this object to be deleted, so make a copy of it if you want to preserve it.

2. Place the cutting object on top of the objects you want to cut **1**.

3. Make sure no other objects are selected except the cutting object.

4. Choose Object menu > Path > Slice. The topmost shape will be deleted and the underlying objects will be cut where they meet the edge of the cutting object **2**–**4**.

**TIP** Using the Slice command on top of objects within a mask will release those objects from the mask.

**TIP** The Slice command gathers objects from different layers onto the layer of the cutting object. To prevent any object from being affected, hide it or lock its layer.

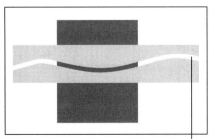

**4** *To create this cutout shape, a stroke was drawn with the Paintbrush tool and the Slice command was applied to it. Then the resulting cut shape was selected using the Direct Selection tool and deleted.*

**Slice**

Some of the Illustrator filters can be used to expand a simple shape into a more complex one. The Zig Zag filter adds anchor points to a path or line and then moves those points to produce zigzags or waves. Other filters are discussed in Chapter 19.

### To create a zigzag or wavy line:

1. Select a path.

2. Choose Filter menu > Distort > Zig Zag.

3. Check the Preview box **1**.

4. Click Points: Smooth to create a wavy line or click Corner to create a zigzag line.

5. Choose an Amount for the distance added anchor points will move.

6. Choose a number of Ridges for the number of anchor points to be added between existing points. If you enter a number, press Tab or uncheck and then check the Preview box to preview.

7. Click OK or press Return/Enter.

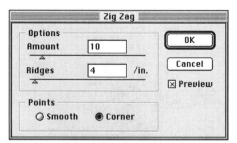

**1** In the **Zig Zag** dialog box, click the **Preview** box, click **Smooth** or **Corner**, and choose an **Amount** and number of **Ridges**.

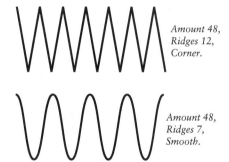

The original line.

Amount 48, Ridges 12, Corner.

Amount 48, Ridges 7, Smooth.

The original star.

Amount 45, Ridges 4, Smooth.

The original spiral.

Amount 0, Ridges 0, Corner.

The original star.

Amount 17, Ridges 20, Smooth.

Zigzag or Wavy Lines

**1** *The original objects.*

**2** *Unite command.*

**3** *The original objects.*

**4** *Intersect command.*

**5** *The original objects.*

**6** *Exclude command.*

**7** *The original objects. The white circle is placed over the black circle.*

**8** *Exclude command. One new object is formed. The "white" area is transparent.*

**9** *The original objects.*

**10** *The Exclude command.*

## The Pathfinders

The Pathfinder commands are among Illustrator's most powerful and useful features. They create a new, closed object or objects or a compound path (a group of two or more closed shapes) from two or more selected and overlapping objects by joining, splitting, or cropping them. The Pathfinder commands fall into four general categories: Combining, dividing, color mixing and trapping.

*Notes:* If a Pathfinder command is applied to an open path, Illustrator closes the path before performing the command. If you want to control how a path is closed, apply Object menu > Path > Outline Path before applying a Pathfinder command.

To access certain Object menu commands (Path > Offset Path, or Outline Path and all the Pathfinder commands) on a Quadra, a math coprocessor must be installed.

**TIP** Use this shortcut to repeat the last-used Pathfinder command: Command-4/Ctrl-4.

### Combining commands

**Unite:** Joins selected objects into one compound path object. Interior objects are deleted. The paint attributes of the front-most object, including any stroke, are applied to the new object **1**–**2** *(see also page 84)*.

**Intersect:** Deletes any non-overlapping areas from overlapping, selected objects. The paint attributes of the frontmost object are applied to the new object **3**–**4**. The selected objects must partially—not completely—overlap to apply this command.

**Exclude:** Makes areas where selected objects overlap transparent. The paint attributes of the frontmost object, including any stroke, are applied to the new object **5**–**10**.

**Minus Front:** The backmost selected object is "cut away" where selected objects overlap it, and objects overlapping the backmost object are deleted. The paint attributes of the backmost object, including any stroke, are preserved. This command works like the Make Compound Paths command if the original frontmost objects do not extend beyond the edge of the backmost object **1**–**4**. *(see also page 219)*

**Minus Back:** The frontmost selected object is "cut away" where selected objects overlap it. Objects overlapping the frontmost object are deleted; the paint attributes of the frontmost object, including any stroke, are preserved **5**–**6**. The selected objects must partially—not completely—overlap to apply this command.

**1** *The original objects.*

**2** *Minus Front command.*

**3** *The original objects.*

**4** *Minus Front command.*

**5** *The original objects.*

**6** *Minus Back command.*

## Dividing commands

These commands divide overlapping areas of selected objects into separate, non-overlapping closed objects (fills) or lines (strokes).

**Divide:** The new objects retain their previous fill and gradient colors. Stroke colors are retained **7**–**10**. *(see also page 220)*

**7** *The original objects.*

**8** *Divide command (pulled apart for emphasis).*

**9** *The original objects.*

**10** *Divide command (pulled apart for emphasis).*

**1** *The original objects.*

**2** *Outline command (pulled apart for emphasis).*

**3** *The original objects.*

**4** *Trim command (pulled apart for emphasis).*

**5** *The original objects.*

**6** *Merge command (pulled apart for emphasis).*

**7** *The original objects.*

**8** *Crop command.*

**9** *The original objects.*

**10** *Crop command.*

**Outline:** Objects turn into stroked lines. The fill colors of the original objects become the stroke colors, and fill colors are removed **1**–**2**. Use this command to create partial strokes on objects that had no stroke originally.

**Trim:** The frontmost object shape is preserved; parts of objects that are behind it and overlap it are deleted. Adjacent or overlapping objects of the same color or shade remain separate (unlike the Merge command). Objects retain their original solid or gradient fill colors; stroke colors are deleted **3**–**4**.

**Merge:** The frontmost object shape is preserved; adjacent or overlapping objects of the same color or shade are combined. Objects retain their original solid or gradient fill colors; stroke colors are deleted **5**–**6**.

**Crop:** The frontmost object "trims" away areas of selected objects that extend beyond its borders. The remaining non-overlapping objects retain only their fill colors; stroke colors are removed. The frontmost object is also removed **7**–**10**. Unlike a mask, the original objects can't be restored.

**Outline; Trim; Merge; Crop**

## Color mixing commands

The color mixing commands convert areas where objects overlap into separate objects. The new fill colors are a mixture of the overlapping colors, and stroke colors are removed.

**Hard:** Simulates overprinting. The highest CMYK values from each object are mixed in areas where they overlap. The resulting effect is most noticeable where colors originally differed most **1**–**2**.

**Soft:** Creates an illusion of transparency. The higher the Mixing rate you enter in the Pathfinder Soft dialog box, the more transparent the frontmost object will appear **3**–**6**. To create a painterly effect, layer three color objects, then apply the Soft command at about 75%. Or, to lighten the underlying colors, place an object with a white fill across other filled objects and enter a Mixing rate between 75% and 100%.

**1** *The original objects.*

**2** *Hard command.*

**3** *The original objects.*

**4** *Soft command (90%).*

**5** *The original objects.*

**6** *Soft command (40%).*

Hard; Soft

**1** *Select an object with a stroked path. To produce the button shown below, a gradient fill and a stroke were applied to the object before applying the* **Outline Path** *command.*

If you want to apply a Pathfinder command to an open path, the path is closed automatically. You may want to apply the Outline Path command first (instructions on this page) to close the path yourself. Another reason to apply Outline Path is to convert a line or a stroke into a closed path so you can apply a gradient or pattern to it.

*Note:* This command produces the most predictable results when it's applied to an object with wide curves. It may produce odd corner shapes if it's applied to an object that has sharp corners. Use Object menu > Pathfinder > Unite to eliminate odd corner shapes.

### To turn a stroke or an open path into a closed, filled object:

1. Select an object that has a Stroke color **1**.

2. Choose Object menu > Path > Outline Path. The width of the new filled object will be the same thickness that the original Stroke was **2**.

**TIP** If you apply the Outline Path command to a closed path to which fill and stroke colors have been applied, you'll end up with two separate objects: a fill object and a compound stroke object.

**2** *The* **Outline Path** *command converted the stroke into a compound path. To produce this button, the compound path was selected with the Selection tool and a gradient fill was applied to it. Then the Gradient tool was dragged across it to make it contrast with the gradient fill in the inner circle.*

*The thread was created using the Pencil tool. The* **Outline Path** *command was applied to it, and then it was also filled with a gradient.*

**Outline Path**

### Exercise
### Create a light bulb.

**1.** *Draw a* **circle** *and a* **rectangle**. *Apply a fill of None and a 4-point gray stroke to both objects.*

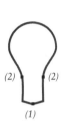

**2.** *Select the bottom point of the circle with the* **Direct Selection** *tool. Drag the point downward. Select* **both** *objects.*

**3.** *Apply the* **Unite** *command (Object menu > Pathfinder). Use the* **Add-anchor-point** *tool to add a point on the bottom segment (1), then use the* **Direct Selection** *tool to drag it downward.*

*Rotate the direction lines upward for the points where the curve meets the straight line segment (2).*

**4.** *Apply the* **Outline Path** *command (Object menu > Path).*

**5.** *Create a rounded rectangle or an oval that's wider than the base of the bulb. Rotate it using the* **Rotation** *tool. Option-Shift/Alt–Shift drag two copies downward.*

**6.** *Fill the ovals, and position them on the bottom of the bulb.*

**7.** *Use the* **Star** *tool to create a 20-point star (1st radius: .4", 2nd radius: .69"). Apply a gray fill that is lighter than the fill on the bulb, and a stroke of None. Scale the Star so it's much larger than the bulb.*

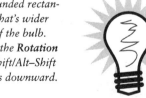

**8.** *Position the star over the bulb. Select the Star, then choose* **Send to Back** *(Object menu > Arrange).*

**9.** *Shift-select the bulb, then apply the* **Divide** *command to the star and bulb to divide the star. Select and delete the part of the star inside the bulb (use the Direct Selection tool).*

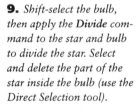

**10.** *Use the* **Pencil** *tool to draw a filament line inside the bulb. Apply a fill of None and a black stroke to the filament.*

**11.** *Bulb variation: Before applying the* **Divide** *command (step 9), apply the* **Roughen** *filter (Distort submenu) to the star (Size: 2, Detail: 3–6).*

# PEN TOOL 8

The Pen tool creates precise curved and straight line segments connected by anchor points. If you click with the Pen tool, you will create corner points and straight line segments with no direction lines. If you drag with the Pen tool, you will create smooth curve points and curve segments with direction lines. The distance and the direction in which you drag the mouse determines the shape of the curve segment.

Mastering the Pen tool—Illustrator's most difficult tool—requires patience and practice. Once you become comfortable creating Pen tool paths, read Chapter 7 to learn how to reshape them. If you find the Pen tool to be too difficult to use, remember that you can transform a simple shape (Chapter 5) into a complex shape using the point and path editing tools (Chapter 7).

*The true story behind Systems Crash: Along with the pictures of beautiful women that Spollen downloaded from Holland on his foreign server came a little monster virus that destroyed everything on his hard drive.*

Chris Spollen, **Systems Crash**

Click with the Pen tool to create an open or closed straight-sided polygon.

**1** *Pen tool.*

### To create a straight-sided object using the Pen tool:

1. Choose the Pen tool (Press "P" to cycle through the pen tools) **1**.

2. Click to create an anchor point.

3. Click to create a second anchor point. A straight line segment will connect the two points.

4. Click to create additional anchor points. They will be also connected by straight line segments.

5. To complete the shape as an **open** path:

   Click the Pen tool or any other tool on the Toolbox.
   *or*
   Hold down Command/Ctrl and click outside the new shape to deselect it.
   *or*
   Choose Edit menu > Deselect All.

   To complete the shape as a **closed** path, position the Pen pointer over the starting point (a small circle will appear next to the pointer), and click on it **2**.

**TIP** If you use the Pen tool when your illustration is in Preview view and a color is selected for the Fill box on the Toolbox, the Pen path will be filled as soon as three points are created. To create segments that appear as lines only, choose a stroke color and a fill of None before, during, or after drawing the path *(see page 115)*.

**TIP** Hold down Shift while clicking with the Pen tool to constrain a segment to the nearest 45° angle.

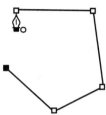

**2** *The Pen tool pointer positioned over the starting point. Note the small circle next to the pointer.*

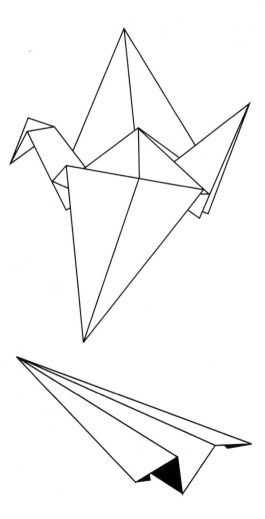

**1** *Press and drag to create the first anchor point.*

Follow these instructions to create continuous curves, which are smooth anchor points connected by smooth curve segments, each with a pair of direction lines that move in tandem. The longer the direction lines, the larger the curve. You can practice drawing curves by tracing over a placed image that contains curve shapes or by converting curved objects into guides and then tracing over the guide lines.

### To create continuous curves using the Pen tool:

1. Choose the Pen tool.

2. Press and drag to create the first anchor point **1**. The angle of the pair of direction lines that you create will be determined by the direction you drag.

3. **Release** the mouse, **move** it away from the last anchor point, then press and drag in the direction in which you want the curve to follow to create a second anchor point **2**. A curve segment will connect the first and second anchor points, and a second pair of direction lines will be created. The shape of the curve segment will be defined by the length and direction you drag the mouse. Remember, you can always reshape the curves later (see Chapter 7).

4. Drag to create additional anchor points and direction lines **3**–**4**. The anchor points will be connected by curve segments.

*(Continued on the following page)*

**2** *Release and reposition the mouse, then drag in the direction you wish the curve to follow.*

**3** *Continue to reposition and press-and-drag the mouse.*

**4** *Continue to reposition and press-and-drag. To complete the object as an open path, click the **Pen** tool on the toolbox.*

Create Continuous Curves

**5.** To complete the object as an **open** path:

Click the Pen tool on the Toolbox.
*or*
Click a selection tool (or hold down Command/Ctrl), then click away from the new object to deselect it.
*or*
Choose Edit menu > Deselect All.

To complete the object as a **closed** path, position the Pen pointer over the starting point (a small circle will appear next to the pointer) **1**, drag, then release the mouse.

**TIP** The fewer the anchor points, the smoother the shape. Too many anchor points will produce bumpy curves.

**TIP** Hold down Command/Ctrl to use the Selection tool or Direct Selection tool (whichever was last highlighted) while the Pen tool is selected.

**TIP** If the last created anchor point was a curve point and you want to convert it into a corner point, click on it with the Pen tool, and continue to draw. One direction line will disappear.

If the last created anchor point was a corner point and you want to convert it into a curve point, position the Pen tool pointer over it, then press and drag. A new direction line will appear.

*Drawing a path...*

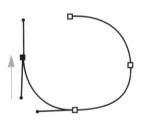

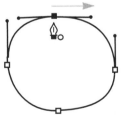

**1** *...and completing it by dragging over the starting point.*

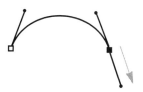

**1** *Press and drag to create the first anchor point.*

**2** *Release the mouse, reposition it, then press and drag to create a second anchor point.*

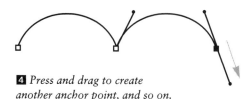

**3** *Hold down Option/Alt and press and drag from the last anchor point in the direction you want the new curve to follow. The direction lines are on the same side of the curve segment.*

**4** *Press and drag to create another anchor point, and so on.*

You can use the Pen tool to create non-continuous curves, which are segments that curve on only one side of an anchor point, like a series of archways. (In a continuous curve, segments curve on both sides of an anchor point.) The anchor point that connects non-continuous curves is called a corner point. If you move one direction line from a corner point, only the curve on the same side of the point will reshape. Continuous and non-continuous curves can be combined in the same path.

Two methods for producing non-continuous curves follow. In the first set of instructions, you will press and drag to create an anchor point first, then hold down Option/Alt to redraw the direction line for that anchor point.

### To create non-continuous curves (Pen tool method):

1. Choose the Pen tool.
2. Press and drag to create the first anchor point **1**.
3. **Release** the mouse, **move** it away from the last anchor point, then press and drag to create a second anchor point **2**. A curve segment will connect the first and second anchor points, and a second pair of direction lines will be created. The shape of the curve segment will be determined by the length and direction you drag.
4. Hold down Option/Alt and press and drag from the last anchor point in the direction you wish the new curve to follow **3**. A new direction line will be created.
5. Repeat steps 3 and 4 to create a series of anchor points and curves **4**.

**Create Non-Continuous Curves**

## To create non-continuous curves (Convert-direction-point tool method):

1. Follow the steps on page 105 to create an open path with smooth curves.

2. Choose the Direct Selection tool **1**.

3. Click on the path **2**.

4. Click on the anchor point to be modified **3**.

5. Hold down Command-Option/Ctrl-Alt to temporarily use the Convert-direction-point tool, and rotate the direction line so it forms a "V" shape with the other direction line **4**. The curve segment will be on the same side of the anchor point as the previous curve segment.

6. Release Command-Option/Ctrl-Alt and the mouse.

7. Repeat steps 4–6 to convert other anchor points **5**.

**TIP** Hold down Option/Alt to use the Convert-direction-point tool to move a direction line when the Pen tool is selected.

**TIP** To convert a pair of direction lines back into a smooth curve, choose the Direct Selection tool, click on the anchor point, choose the Convert-direction-point tool (or hold down Command-Option/Ctrl-Alt), then drag out new direction lines from the anchor point.

**1** *Direct Selection tool.*

**2** *Click on the path.*

**3** *Click with the Direct Selection tool on the anchor point you want to modify.*

**4** *Hold down **Command-Option/Ctrl-Alt** and rotate the direction line, then release those keys.*

**5** *Repeat steps 4–6 for other anchor points you want to convert.*

**Create Non-Continuous Curves**

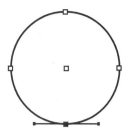

**1** *Click on the bottom edge of the circle.*

**2** *Move the bottom anchor point downward.*

## Exercise

### Convert a circle into a heart:

1. Draw a perfect circle with the Oval tool (hold down Shift while dragging).

2. Choose the Direct Selection tool.

3. Click away from the object to deselect it.

4. Click on the bottom edge of the circle **1**.

5. Select the bottom anchor point, start dragging it downward, hold down Shift, then continue to drag **2**.

6. Hold down Command-Option/Ctrl-Alt to temporarily use the Convert-direction-point tool and press and drag one of the direction lines for that anchor point upward to form a non-continuous curve **3**.

7. Release Command-Option/Ctrl-Alt.

8. Click on the bottom anchor point to reselect it, then drag the second direction line upward. The bottom of the circle will become a corner point with handles **4**. Deselect.

9. Hold down Shift and drag the anchor point from the top of the circle downward **5**.

*(Continued on the following page)*

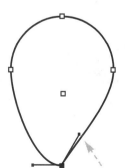

**3** *Hold down **Command-Option/Ctrl-Alt** and move one of the direction lines upward.*

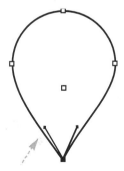

**4** *Reselect the bottom anchor point, then drag the second direction line upward.*

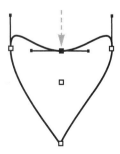

**5** *Move the top anchor point downward.*

10. Hold down Command-Option/ Ctrl-Alt to temporarily use the Convert-direction-point tool, and drag a direction line connected to the top anchor point upward to form a non-continuous curve **1**.

11. Release Command-Option/Ctrl-Alt.

12. Click on the top anchor point to reselect it, then drag the second direction line upward. The top of the circle will become a corner point with handles **2**–**3**.

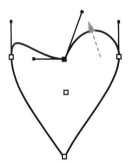

**1** Hold down **Command-Option/Ctrl-Alt**, drag one of the top direction lines upward, then release the keys.

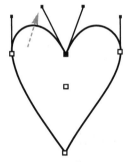

**2** Click on the top anchor point, then drag the second direction line upward.

**3** The completed heart.

# COLORING 9

*In this chapter you will learn to fill the inside or stroke the edge of an object with a color or shade, and choose stroke attributes like dashes and joins. You'll learn how to mix a process color, save a color as a swatch, copy swatches from another library or document, and edit, replace, delete, move, and duplicate swatches. You'll learn to sample colors from any window using the Eyedropper tool and apply fill and stroke colors simultaneously using the Paint Bucket tool. Finally, you'll learn to adjust colors, colorize a TIFF, saturate/desaturate, invert, blend, and globally replace colors. Gradients and patterns are covered in the following two chapters, respectively.*

The color applied to the inside of a closed or open shape is called the fill. A fill can be a flat color, a pattern, or a gradient. The flat color that's applied to a line or the outer edge of a shape is called the stroke. A stroke can be solid or dashed. You can choose a pre-mixed swatch, mix your own gray percentage, mix a process color using Cyan, Magenta, Yellow and Black or Red, Green, and Blue percentages, or choose a swatch from a matching system, like Pantone or Trumatch.

Colors are applied using the Color, Stroke, Swatches, and Tools palettes. The Stroke palette is also used to apply characteristics such as a stroke's thickness (weight) and style (dashed or solid). You can store any color, pattern, or gradient on the Swatches palette for later use. The color attributes of a selected object are displayed on the Tools, Color, and Stroke palettes. The current fill and stroke colors are automatically applied to any new object you create.

For the instructions in this chapter, open the Color, Stroke, and Swatches palettes. And work with your illustration in Preview view so you can see colors on screen as you apply them.

CHRIS SPOLLEN

This is the quick-and-dirty method for applying color, just to get you started. The beauty of this method is that you don't need to choose a specific tool or select anything in your document. Keep on reading to learn how to mix and save process and spot colors, and how to use the Swatches palette.

### QuickStart drag-color:

Drag from the Fill **1** or Stroke **2** box on the Toolbox, from the Color box from the Color or Gradient palette **4**, or from the Swatches palette right over the object's fill or stroke, whichever you want to recolor. The attribute that is currently active—fill or stroke—is the one that will be applied.

### To apply a fill or stroke of black or white:

1. Select an object.

2. Click the Fill or Stroke box on the Toolbox **1**–**2**.

3. To apply a white fill *and* a black stroke, click the Default Colors icon (D) on the Toolbox **3**.
   *or*
   Click the small white square at the right end of the spectrum bar on the Color palette to make the current color white, or click the black square to make the current color black **5**.
   *or*
   Click the white or black swatch on the Swatches palette **6**.

### Fill and Stroke boxes on the Toolbox

The Fill and Stroke boxes on the Toolbox reflect those attributes of the currently or last selected object. If the Fill box is currently active, any changes you make on the Color or Swatch palette will change that fill color. If the Stroke box is active, the stroke color will change.

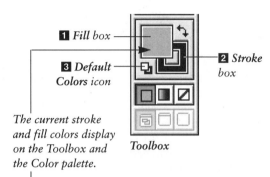

**1** *Fill box*

**3** *Default Colors icon*

**2** *Stroke box*

*The current stroke and fill colors display on the Toolbox and the Color palette.*

*Toolbox*

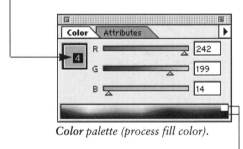

*Color palette (process fill color).*

**5** *Black and white squares*

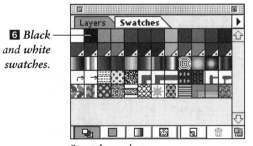

**6** *Black and white swatches.*

*Swatches palette.*

## Remember these basic coloring steps

You'll be working with four palettes:
Toolbox, Color, Swatches, and Stroke.

■ Select (or draw) the objects whose color attributes you want to change.

■ Make sure the box for the attribute that you want to change is active on the Toolbox—Fill or Stroke. Press "X" to toggle between the two. (To change the color of the non-active box, Option/Alt drag on the spectrum bar on the Color palette.)

■ Use the Color palette to create or modify a color. To choose a solid color, first click the Color button on the Toolbox (or press "," on the keyboard) to make the Color palette come to the forefront of its group. (The color box on the Color palette will display the current Fill or Stroke box color, whichever box is currently active on the Toolbox.)
*or*
Click a swatch on the Swatches palette to assign an existing color to a selected object. You can also drag a swatch over an unselected object.

■ Adjust the line weight and other stroke attributes using the Stroke palette.

■ To save the current color, drag the color box from the Color palette or the Toolbox onto the Swatches palette.

*An object with a **stroke** color and a fill of **None**.*

*An object with a **fill** color and a stroke of **None**.*

*An object with a **fill** color and a stroke color.*

*Type with a **fill color** and a **stroke** of **None**.*

Apple & pear

## What's the difference between a spot and a process color?

A spot color appears on its own plate after color separation. It can be a color that you mix yourself or a pre-mixed color from a matching system, like PANTONE. If you mix your own spot color, to ensure that it separates onto its own plate, double-click the swatch for the color on the Swatches palette, choose Color Mode: Spot Color, then click OK. You can use spot colors exclusively if your illustration doesn't contain continuous tone images—just type and flat-color illustrations to which a handful of colors have been applied.

**TIP** You can achieve a pleasing range of tints using a black plate and a single spot color plate by varying the tint percentages of that spot color throughout the illustration.

A process color, on the other hand, is printed via four plates, one each for Cyan (C), Magenta (M), Yellow (Y), and Black (K). You can enter process color percentages yourself, or you can choose a pre-mixed process color from a matching system, like TRUMATCH, FOCOLTONE, or PANTONE Process ProSim. Process printing *must* be used for any document that contains continuous tone images. Spot color plates can be added to a four-color process job—budgetary constraints will be the only limiting factor.

**TIP** For on-screen output, use the RGB color model when mixing colors.

*Note:* Normally, Illustrator converts all spot colors into process colors when they are color separated. To make your spot colors separate to their own plates—which is what they should do—uncheck the Convert to Process option in the Separation Setup dialog box.

## Don't let your monitor fool you

Illustrator's Color Settings command works with the system's color management software to provide more accurate color matching between the on-screen display of CMYK and RGB colors and the same colors when printed using a specific printer. This command utilizes monitor and printer device profiles and output intents, all chosen by the user, to better translate color between devices. Beware, though, the profiles are not completely capable of producing exact on-screen proofs.

For a print job, you shouldn't mix process colors or choose spot (Pantone) colors based on how they look on the screen. Screen colors—which are seductively bright and luminous—don't accurately simulate printed colors. To avoid an embarassing and costly post-press surprise, use matching books to choose spot colors or mix process colors, and run color proofs of your job. Color output methods are discussed on page 270.

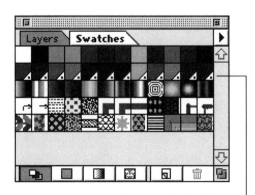

*Spot color swatches display a dot in the lower right corner.*

**1** *Fill box*

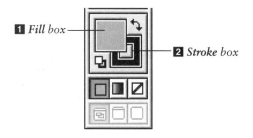

**2** *Stroke box*

*Tint slider*

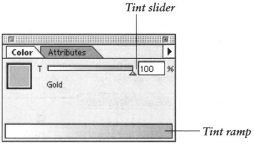

*Tint ramp*

**3** *The Color palette for a spot color.*

## Swatches palette

The Swatches palette contains swatches for process (RGB, HSB, or CMYK) colors, spot colors, patterns, and gradients. A default set of process color, spot color, pattern, and gradient swatches is supplied with Illustrator. You can also save user-defined solid color, pattern, or gradient swatches for each document. If you click a swatch, that color will display on the Color palette and in the current Fill or Stroke box (whichever is currently active) on the Toolbox, and it will apply to any currently selected object or objects.

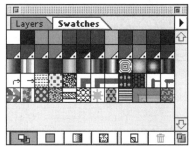

**4** *Swatches palette.*

## To color an object while or after you draw it:

1. Select an existing object (not all the anchor points need to be solid).
   *or*
   Choose the tool with which you want to draw a new object.

2. Click the Fill **1** or Stroke **2** box on the Toolbox. To toggle between these two boxes, press "X".

3. Click a swatch on the Swatches palette. If you chose a spot color swatch, you can move the Tint slider on the Color palette or click or drag inside the Tint ramp bar to adjust the percentage of that color **3**.
   *or*
   Choose a color model from the Color palette pop-up menu and choose color percentages (instructions on the next page).

4. If you're applying a stroke color, define stroke attributes using the Stroke palette (see page 125).

5. If you don't have an existing object, draw it now. It will reflect the current Color and Stroke palette settings.

**TIP** A gradient can't be applied as a stroke. For a workaround, see page 101.

**TIP** To display the process color breakdown of a spot swatch, click the spot swatch, then choose the RGB or CMYK color model from the Color palette pop-up menu.

**TIP** To define a color as process or spot, double-click the swatch on the Swatches palette **4**, choose Color Mode: Spot Color or Process Color, then click OK.

**Color an Object**

Follow these instructions to mix your own process color. *Note:* To apply a color from a color matching system, like TRUMATCH or FOCOLTONE, see page 118).

### To mix a process color:

1. *Optional:* If you want to recolor an existing object or objects, select them now, and click the Fill or Stroke box on the Toolbox (X). Otherwise, make sure no objects are selected.

2. Choose a color model from the Color palette pop-up menu :

   Choose Grayscale to remove color from any selected objects and/or to choose gray shades.

   Choose RGB to mix colors for output on a monitor—video or Web graphics.

   Choose HSB to individually adjust a color's hue, saturation, or brightness.

   Choose CMYK to create process colors for output on a four-color press.

3. Click a color on the spectrum bar at the bottom of the Color palette **2**.
   *and/or*
   Move the sliders to adjust the individual color percentages.

   *Note:* If an exclamation point appears below the Color box on the Color palette **3**, you have mixed an RGB or HSB color that has no CMYK equivalent, which means it isn't printable on a four-color press. If you click the exclamation point, Illustrator will substitute the closest CMYK equivalent.

4. *Optional:* To save the newly mixed color as a swatch, see the next page.

**TIP** Premixed swatches and colors applied to objects remain associated with their color model. If you click on a swatch or on an object to which a color is applied, the Color palette will reset to reflect that color's model.

**TIP** Hold down Option/Alt and drag on the spectrum bar to modify the stroke while the Fill box is active, or vice versa.

### Color palette

The Color palette is used to adjust process and spot color percentages. The color box on the Color palette displays the current fill or stroke color of the currently selected or last selected object, depending on whether the Fill or Stroke box is currently active on the Toolbox.

*The **Fill** color box.*

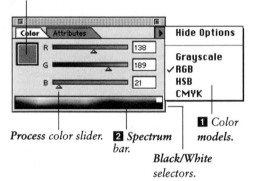

*Process color slider.* **2** *Spectrum bar.*  **1** *Color models.*

*Black/White selectors.*

*The **Stroke** color box.*

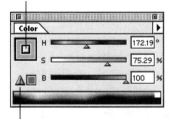

**3** *An **exclamation point** will appear if you mix a color that's out of the printable CMYK gamut.*

*If the fill or stroke colors differ among the selected objects, a **question mark** will appear in the corresponding Fill or Stroke box on the Toolbox, but you can go ahead and apply a new fill and/or stroke color to all the selected objects.*

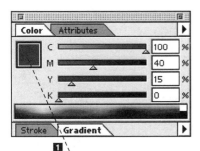

**1**

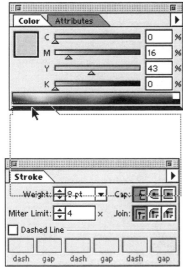

**2** *New Swatch icon*

Swatches that are stored on the Swatches palette are saved only with the current document, not with the application as a whole.

## To save the current fill or stroke color as a new swatch:

Drag the color box from the Color palette or drag the Fill or Stroke box from the Toolbox to an empty area of the Swatches palette to make it appear as the last swatch **1**. Or release the mouse between two colors to insert the new color between them.

*or*

Click the New Swatch icon at the bottom of the Swatches palette **2**.

*or*

Choose New Swatch from the Swatches palette pop-up menu, enter a name for the swatch, choose Color Mode: Spot Color or Process Color, then click OK.

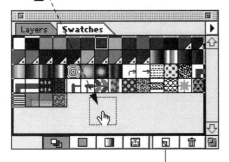

**3** *To dock a palette, drag it its folder tab to the bottom of another palette or palette group. Release the mouse when a black line appears at the **bottom** of the palette you're docking to.*

### Dock 'em

By default, the Stroke and Gradient palettes are docked to the bottom of the Color and Attributes palette group. These four palettes can be moved around the screen together as one super-group. You could also dock the Swatches palette to the bottom of the Stroke/Gradient palette group to create an even larger super-group. An illustration of docking is at left **3**.

Click the zoom box of the topmost palette to reduce the super-group to just the folder tab names. Click the zoom box again to restore the last used palette configuration.

*Save a Color as a Swatch*

In order to apply a color from a matching system, like the PANTONE, FOCOLTONE, TRUMATCH, or TOYO or from the Web palette you must open the swatch library that contains those swatches, then drag a swatch onto the main Swatches palette. The name of the newly opened library will appear as a new tab on a secondary palette.

### To copy swatches from another library:

1. Display the Swatches palette.

2. Choose a matching color system name from the Swatch Libraries submenu under the Window menu.

3. Click the tab for the desired color system, if it isn't already displayed.

4. Locate the desired color on the newly opened swatch palette, and drag it into the document's Swatches palette **1**. To add multiple swatches at a time, Command/Ctrl click them individually or click, then Shift-click a contiguous series of them before dragging.
   *or*
   Choose Add to Swatches from the secondary swatch palette's option menu. The new color will be added to the document's Swatches palette.

**TIP** You *can* directly apply a color to a shape using the secondary swatch palette, but you must add the color to the current document's Swatches palette in order to save it as a swatch.

**TIP** You cannot modify swatches on a secondary palette (note the non-edit icon in lower left corner of palette)—the Swatch Options dialog box isn't available. You can, of course, edit a swatch once it's saved on the document Swatches palette.

**TIP** If you open more than one swatch library to the secondary palette and then you want to close one of them, drag its tab out of the secondary palette window and then close it.

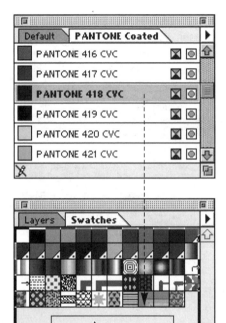

**1** *Dragging a spot color from the swatch library to the current document.*

### Oops

Did you apply a swatch to a shape and forget to copy it to the Swatches palette before closing the secondary swatch library that it originated from? Don't dismay. Select the shape, then drag the Fill, Color, or Gradient box from the Toolbox to the Swatches palette.

Copy Swatches from another Library

## Combine your spots

Normally, Illustrator treats each spot color that's applied in a document as a separate color, even if it has the same name and same color breakdown as another spot color. This means that each instance of a spot color will have it's own printing plate when the illustration is color separated. To combine all the spot colors in the same document that have the same name and the same color breakdown into one spot color, choose Filter menu > Color > Merge Spot Colors. You don't have to select any objects or swatches to apply this filter.

**1** *Using the **Swatch Options** dialog box, you can **convert** a process color into a spot color, or vice versa, or **rename** a color.*

**TIP** If you turn on the Persistent command on the secondary swatch palette pop-up menu, the secondary swatch palette with the currently selected tab library will reopen automatically when you re-launch Illustrator.

## To convert a process color into a spot color or vice versa:

1. Mix a color on the Color palette.
   *or*
   Select an object that contains the color you want to convert.

2. If the color isn't already on the Swatches palette, drag the Fill or Stroke box from the Color palette or the Toolbox onto the Swatches palette.

3. Double-click the swatch to open the Swatch Options dialog box **1**.

4. Choose Color Mode: Spot Color or Process Color, rename the color, if you like, then click OK.

**TIP** A spot color, by default, is converted to a process color during color separation. For any spot color that you don't want converted, choose File menu > Separation Setup, then uncheck the Convert to Process box.

A 1-bit TIFF image opened or placed in Illustrator can be colorized via the Color palette. Black areas in the TIFF will recolor; white areas will remain transparent.

*Note:* A 1-bit-TIFF copied using the drag-and-drop method can't be colorized.

## To colorize a 1-bit TIFF image:

1. Use File menu > Open or Place to open a 1-bit TIFF image in Illustrator.

2. Select the TIFF image.

3. Apply a fill color.

**TIP** To make transparent areas in a 1-bit TIFF look as if they're colorized, create an object with the desired "background" color and send it behind the TIFF.

Convert Process Color to Spot Color

## Color editing shortcuts

■ Shift-click the color box or the spectrum bar on the Color palette to cycle through the different color **models.** You can also convert the current color by choosing a different color model from the palette pop-up menu or by choosing Filter menu > Colors > Convert to CMYK, Convert to Grayscale, or Convert to RGB. If the color has been saved as a swatch, the swatch itself won't change.

■ Press "X" to toggle between the Fill and Stroke boxes on the Toolbox and Color palette.

■ Command/Ctrl click the color box on the Color palette to convert the current color into its **complementary** color. This shortcut won't change the color model.

■ To make the fill color the **same** as the stroke color, or vice versa, drag one box over the other on the Toolbox.

■ Shift-drag any RGB, HSB or CMYK slider on the Color palette to change that color's strength—the other sliders will readjust automatically.

■ To select multiple objects with the same paint attributes, see page 132.

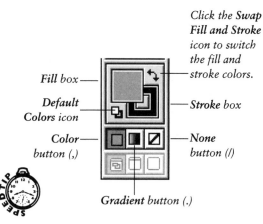

*Click the Swap Fill and Stroke icon to switch the fill and stroke colors.*

*Fill box*

*Default Colors icon*

*Stroke box*

*Color button (,)*

*None button (/)*

*Gradient button (.)*

## The Color, Gradient, and None buttons

Click the **Color, Gradient,** or **None** button on the Toolbox to change the currently selected fill to a solid Color, a Gradient, or a fill of None, respectively, or the current stroke to a solid Color or None. The Color button displays the last chosen solid color; the Gradient buttons displays the last chosen gradient. If an object is selected, it will be recolored (or its color removed) when you choose a different button. When you click the Color button on the Toolbox (or use the Command-I/Ctrl-I shortcut), the Color palette and any other palettes that are grouped with or docked to the Color palette will display.

### Apply color the speed-demon way

These are the shortcuts for activating the Color, Gradient, and None buttons:

Color , (comma)

Gradient . (period)

None / (backslash)

The comma, period, and backslash keys appear next to each other on the keyboard, which makes them easy to remember. Let's say the Fill box on the Toolbox happens to be selected and you want to remove a stroke from a selected object. Press "X", then "/", then "X" again. No mousing around.

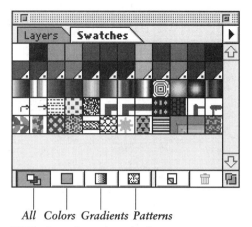

All  Colors  Gradients  Patterns

**1** *The Swatches palette display options.*

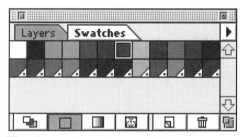

**2** *Color swatches only displayed.*

*This swatch is*
*a process color.*

*This icon*
*indicates this*
*swatch is a*
*spot color.*

*The color model.*

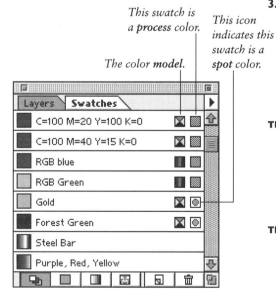

**3** *The swatches displayed by name.*

You can control whether the Swatches palette displays all types of swatches or only certain categories of swatches, and whether the swatches are large or small. A dot in the corner signifies the swatch is a spot color.

Swatches—even process colors—can be displayed with names. The RGB, HSB, or CMYK breakdown will be displayed for any process color that doesn't have a name. In Name view, the palette also displays an icon for the color's color model, so a CMYK color will have a four-part square and an RGB or HSB color will have vertical bars inside a square.

## To choose swatch display options:

1. Click a display icon at the bottom of the Swatches palette to control which category of swatches is displayed **1**: All, for all types (colors, gradients, and patterns); Colors, for solid process and spot colors only **2**; Gradients, for gradients only; or Patterns, for patterns only.

2. Choose a swatch display mode from the palette pop-up menu: Name **3**, Small Swatch, or Large Swatch (good for patterns).

3. Choose Sort by Name from the palette pop-up menu to sort the swatches alphabetically by name.
   *or*
   Choose Sort by Kind to sort swatches into color, gradient, and pattern groups (use when all categories of swatches are displayed).

**TIP** You can choose a swatch by typing in the color name (use when swatches are viewed By Name). Command-Option/Ctrl-Alt click in the palette, then start typing. Click the swatch name or press Return/Enter to apply the swatch and restore the focus to your illustration.

**TIP** Hold down Option/Alt when choosing a display mode from the palette pop-up menu to force all the display icons to show in that mode when clicked on (i.e. Option/Alt choose Name to see all the display options by Name).

**Swatch Display Options**

If you replace a spot color swatch with a different swatch, that color will automatically change in *all* the objects to which it has already been applied, whether or not those objects are selected. Any object to which the original color, or any tint of the original color, was previously applied will be recolored with the new one. The object's previous tint value will be preserved.

If you replace a process color swatch, only the currently *selected* shape or shapes (if any) containing that color will be recolored.

### To globally replace a spot color:

1. Click the swatch you want to edit or replace.

2. On the Color palette, adjust the sliders for a process color, or adjust the tint slider for a different spot color.
   *or*
   Use the Gradient palette to edit a gradient (see page 137).

3. Option/Alt drag from the Fill or Stroke box on the Color palette or the Toolbox over the swatch you want to replace.

**TIP** You can also replace a swatch by Option/Alt dragging another swatch over it.

**TIP** If you change your mind and you want to add the newly adjusted color to the Swatches palette without changing the originally selected swatch, drag without holding down Option/Alt (step 3, above).

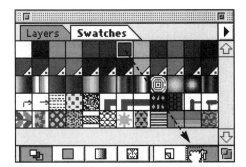

## To delete a swatch or swatches:

Select a swatch (then, if desired, Shift-click the last swatch in a series of contiguous swatches, or Command/Ctrl click to select additional swatches), then click the trash icon on the Swatches palette or choose Delete Swatch from the palette pop-up menu.
*or*
Drag the swatch you want to delete over the trash icon.

**TIP** Choose Undo to restore the deleted swatch.

**TIP** To select only swatches that are *not* currently applied to objects in your document, choose Select All Unused from the palette pop-up menu.

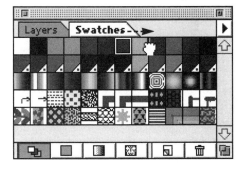

## To move a swatch or swatches:

Drag a swatch to a new location on the palette. A thin white vertical line will show the swatch location as you drag it. (To select multiple swatches, click a swatch, then Shift-click the last swatch in a series of contiguous swatches, or Command/Ctrl click to select individual swatches.)

**TIP** Option/Alt drag a swatch over another swatch to replace that swatch with the one you are dragging.

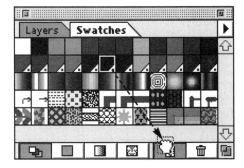

## To duplicate a swatch:

Select the swatch you want to duplicate, then choose Duplicate Swatch from the palette pop-up menu, or click the New Swatch icon.
*or*
Drag the swatch over the New Swatch icon. The duplicate swatch will be placed at the bottom of the palette.

**TIP** If no swatch is selected and you click the New Swatch icon, a new swatch will be created for the current fill or stroke color.

Delete Swatch; Move Swatch; Duplicate Swatch

### To load swatches from another Illustrator document:

1. Choose Window > Swatch Libraries > Other Library.

2. Locate the Illustrator file from which you want to copy the swatches, then click Select.

3. Drag an individual swatch from the newly opened Swatches palette into the current document's Swatches palette **1**. To add multiple swatches at a time, first Command/Ctrl click them individually or click, then Shift-click a contiguous series of them.
*or*
Choose Add to Swatches from the secondary Swatches palette's option menu. The new color will be added to the current document's Swatches palette.

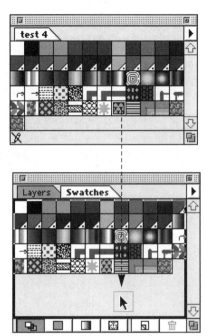

**1** *Moving a swatch from one document to another.*

If you drag individual process (not spot) color swatches from the Default palette to your current document, you may inadvertently add a default swatch that you already have. There's no easy way to detect this duplication. You have two choices: Either carefully copy swatches individually or delete your entire Swatches palette and replace it with the Default palette. Any non-default swatches will be removed if you use the latter method.

### To restore the default swatch palette:

1. Choose Window menu > Swatch Libraries > Default.

2. *Optional:* Delete any or all of the swatches in your current document.

3. On the Default Swatches palette, select the swatches you want to restore to your document (Shift-click or Command/Ctrl click to select multiple swatches).

4. Drag those swatches to the current document's Swatches palette.
*or*
Choose Add to Swatches from the secondary Swatch palette's option menu.

### Custom Swatches palette upon launching

If you want to control which colors appear on the Swatches palette upon launching the application, create a custom startup file that contains those colors (see page 263).

*Load Swatches from Another Doc; Default Palette*

**1** *Enter a value in the stroke **Weight** field, click the up or down arrow, or choose from the drop-down menu.*

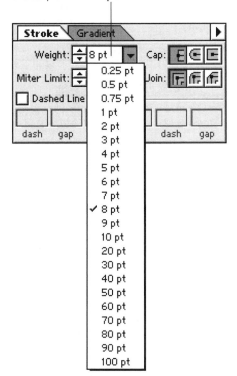

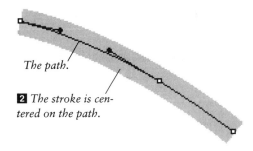

*The path.*

**2** *The stroke is centered on the path.*

You can change a stroke's color, weight (thickness), and style (dashed or solid, rounded or sharp corners, flat or rounded ends).

### To change a stroke's thickness:

1. Select an object.

2. On the Stroke palette:

   Enter a width in points in the Weight field (0 to 1000 pts) **1**.
   *or*
   Choose a preset weight from the Weight drop-down menu.
   *or*
   Click the up or down arrow to increase/decrease, respectively, the current stroke weight one unit at a time.

   Half a stroke's width is applied on one side of the path, the other half is applied on the other side of the path **2**.

   **TIP** A line weight of 0, output on a high resolution printer, will be a one-pixel wide hairline.

   **TIP** Don't apply a large stroke weight to small type—it will distort the letterforms.

   **TIP** If the object had a stroke of None and then you chose a stroke Weight other than zero via the Stroke palette, the currently chosen stroke color (or fill color, if the stroke color is None) will be applied. You don't have to active the Stroke box on the Toolbox.

   **TIP** You can also enter a number in inches (in), millimeters (mm), centimeters (cm), or picas (p) in the stroke Weight field.

**Stroke Thickness**

### To create a dashed stroke:

1. Select an object, and make sure it has a stroke color and weight.

2. If the Stroke palette options aren't fully displayed, choose Show Options from the palette pop-up menu.

3. Click a Cap icon (the dash shape) 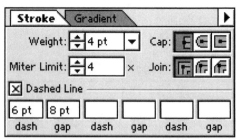.

4. Click the Dashed Line box.

5. Enter a number in the first dash field (the length of the first dash, in points), then press Tab or Return/Enter to apply.

6. *Optional:* To create dashes of varying lengths, enter other amounts in the other dash fields. If you enter an amount only in the first dash field, that amount will be repeated for all the dashes.

7. Enter an amount in the gap field (the length of the first gap after the first dash), then press Tab or Return/Enter to apply.

8. *Optional:* Enter other amounts in the other gap fields to create gaps of varying lengths. If you enter an amount only in the first gap field, that amount will apply to all the gaps.

**TIP** To create a dotted line, click the second Cap icon, enter 0 for the Dash value, and enter a Gap value that is greater than or equal to the stroke Weight. You can enter a value in inches (in), millimeters (mm), centimeters (cm), or picas (p) in the dash or gap fields. That number will be translated automatically into points.

**TIP** The default first dash unit is 12 pt. Any user-defined values will remain in effect until you change them or quit/exit Illustrator.

**1** *Stroke palette settings for a dashed line with a 6-pt. dash length and an 8-pt. gap between dashes.*

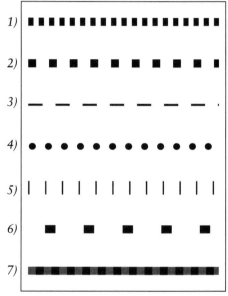

*A variety of dashed lines (the first Caps icon was selected for all except #4):*

1) *stroke 6, dash 4, gap 4.*

2) *stroke 6, dash 6, gap 10.*

3) *stroke 1.5, dash 11, gap 10.*

4) *stroke 5, dash 0, gap 12 (round caps).*

5) *stroke 10, dash 1, gap 12.*

6) *stroke 6, dash 0, gap 10, dash 8, gap 10.*

7) *stroke 6, dash 6, gap 6 (pasted in front of a 6-point gray stroked line).*

**Dashed Stroke**

*Nancy Stahl, **Flying Hats***

*Nancy Stahl, **Cable Man***

# IMAGES

*Michael Bartalos, for Mohawk Paper Mills, Inc.*

*Michael Bartalos, **Tropical Beat**, CD gift box design for Koolwraps*

*Michael Bartalos, **Jazzmatazz**, CD gift box design for Koolwraps*

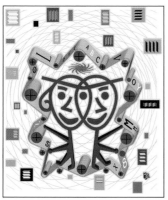

John Hersey, **Cross Swatchbook Cover**

John Hersey, **Dazed**,
T-shirt for Fisher Bicycles

Chris Spollen, **Internet Theft**

John Hersey, illustration for Walldata Corporation

*Chris Spollen,* **Message from Cyberspace**

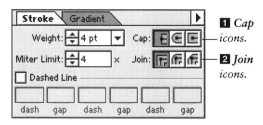

**1** *Cap icons.*

**2** *Join icons.*

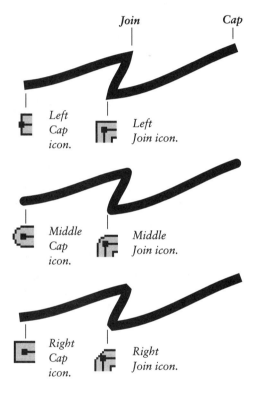

*Left Cap icon.*

*Left Join icon.*

*Middle Cap icon.*

*Middle Join icon.*

*Right Cap icon.*

*Right Join icon.*

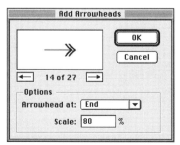

**3** *Choose a style, location (Start, End, or Both Ends) and Scale in the Add Arrowheads dialog box.*

## To modify stroke caps and/or joins:

1. Select an object, and make sure it has a stroke color and weight.

2. If the Stroke palette options aren't fully displayed, choose Show Options from the palette pop-up menu.

3. To modify the endpoints of a solid line or all the dashes in a dashed line:

   Click the left **Cap** icon **1** to create square-cornered ends in which the Stroke stops at the endpoints or to create square-cornered dashes. Use this option to align paths very precisely.

   Click the middle **Cap** icon to create round ends or round-ended dashes.

   Click the right **Cap** icon to create square-cornered ends in which the stroke extends beyond the endpoints or to create rectangular dashes.

4. To modify the line bends:

   Click the left **Join** icon to produce pointed bends (miter joins) **2**.

   Click the middle **Join** icon to produce semicircular bends (round joins).

   The right **Join** icon to produce square-cornered bends (bevel joins).
   The miter limit is discussed on page 74.

## To create arrowheads:

1. Select an open path.

2. Choose Filter menu > Stylize > Add Arrowheads.

3. Click the left or right arrow to choose from the various head and tail designs **3**.

4. Choose a location for the arrowhead (Start, End, or Both Ends) from the Arrowhead at drop-down menu.

5. *Optional:* Resize the arrowhead by entering a different Scale percentage.

6. Click OK or press Return/Enter. The arrowhead can be reshaped like any other path.

**Stroke Caps and Joins; Arrowheads**

If you click with the Paint Bucket tool on an object, that object will be filled *and* stroked using the current Color and Stroke palettes settings. Neither palette needs to be displayed for you to use the Paint Bucket tool.

 **1** *Paint Bucket tool.*

### To use the Paint Bucket tool:

1. With no objects selected, choose the Paint Bucket tool (K) **1**.

2. Choose fill and stroke colors from the Color or Swatches palette.
   *or*
   Option/Alt click on a color anywhere in any open Illustrator window (this is a temporary Eyedropper).

3. Enter a stroke weight. Choose other stroke options, if desired.

4. Click on an object (the object does not have to be selected). The object will become selected and colored with the current Color and Stroke palette attributes **2**–**3**. For an object without a fill color, or if you're working Artwork view, position the black spill of the Paint Bucket cursor on the path outline before clicking.

**2** *The original illustration.*

**3** *After using the Paint Bucket to apply a white fill and a dashed stroke to the leaves on the left side.*

Diane Margolin

Use the Paintbucket/Eyedropper dialog box to change the default attributes for either or both tools.

### To choose paint attributes the Paint Bucket applies or the Eyedropper picks up:

1. Double-click the Paint Bucket or Eyedropper tool.

2. Click check box options on or off **4**.

**4** *Click check boxes on or off in the Paintbucket/ Eyedropper dialog box.*

Paint Bucket

### Grab a color from another application

Open the application that you want to sample colors from. If the application has a color palette that stays open even if the application isn't currently active (like Director), open that as well. Move the windows and/or palettes that you want to sample from over to one side of the screen.

Move the Illustrator document window so that you can see the other application windows behind it. Choose the Eyedropper tool, drag from the Illustrator document window over a color in another application window (the color will appear on Illustrator's Toolbox and Color palette), then save the color as a swatch. Repeat for other colors.

**1** *Eyedropper tool.*

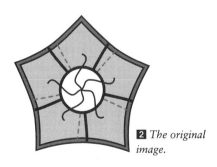

**2** *The original image.*

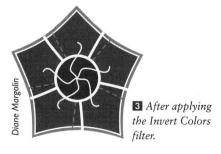

**3** *After applying the Invert Colors filter.*

Diane Margolin

If you click on an object or a placed image with the Eyedropper tool, it will pick up the object's paint attributes, display them on the Tools, Color, and Stroke palettes, and apply them to any currently selected objects.

### To use the Eyedropper tool:

1. *Optional:* Select an object or objects if you want to recolor them immediately with the attributes you pick up with the Eyedropper.

2. Chose the Eyedropper tool (I) **1**.

3. Click on an object in any open Illustrator window that contains the color you want to sample. The object doesn't have to be selected. You can also drag from Illustrator into any location on your screen—in another application or on the Desktop.

   If you selected any objects (step 1), they will take on the paint attributes of the object you click on.

**TIP** Hold down Option/Alt to use the Paint Bucket tool while the Eyedropper is selected, or vice versa.

**TIP** To preserve the sampled color to use again, drag the Fill or Stroke box from the Toolbox or the Color palette onto the Swatches palette.

**TIP** Shift-click a color on an unselected object to copy that color to only the fill or stroke (whichever box is currently active on the Toolbox) of any selected objects.

The Invert Colors filter converts process colors into their process color opposites (like a photo negative). Spot colors, gradients, and patterns cannot be inverted.

### To invert colors:

1. Select the object or objects whose colors you want to invert.

2. Choose Filter menu > Colors > Invert Colors **2**–**3**.

Eyedropper; Invert Colors

Use the Adjust Colors filter to adjust colors in one or more selected objects, including text objects (but not gradients or patterns).

### To adjust colors:

1. Select the object or objects whose colors you want to adjust.

2. Choose Filter menu > Colors > Adjust Colors.

3. Check the Preview box to preview color adjustments in your illustration while the dialog box is open 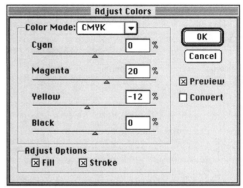.

4. Check the Adjust Options: Fill and/or Stroke box to adjust one or both of those attributes.

5. At first the sliders will reflect the color mode of the currently selected object or objects, and only colors in that mode will be adjusted when you move the sliders. Move the sliders or enter percentages in the fields (the amount you want to increase or decrease that particular color).

   *Note:* If selected objects' colors are in more than one color mode, the sliders will display first in CMYK mode, if any colors are in that mode. If no CMYK colors are present, the sliders will display in RGB mode, then in grayscale mode. After you adjust colors in one mode, you can choose another mode, and adjust again.

   If you want to convert all the currently selected objects to one color mode, check the Convert box, choose from the Color Mode pop-up menu, then move the sliders.

6. Click OK or press Return/Enter.

**1** *In the* **Adjust Colors** *dialog box, enter Process color or Custom color tint percentages or move the sliders.*

**Adjust Colors**

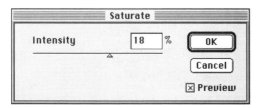

**1** *In the **Saturate** dialog box, choose a positive percentage to saturate or a negative percentage to desaturate.*

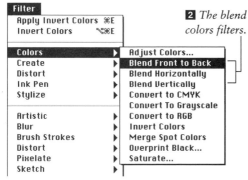

**2** *The blend colors filters.*

**3** *The original image.*

**4** *After applying the Blend Horizontally filter.*

The Saturate filter deepens or fades colors in selected objects by a specified percentage.

### To saturate or desaturate colors:

1. Select the object(s) whose colors you want to saturate or desaturate.

2. Choose Filter menu > Colors > Saturate.

3. Check the Preview box to preview color changes in your illustration **1**.

4. Move the Intensity slider or enter a percentage between 100% and –100% for the amount you want to intensify or fade the color or colors.

5. Click OK or press Return/Enter.

### To blend fill colors between objects:

1. Select three or more objects.

   *Note:* The two objects that are farthest apart (or frontmost and backmost) cannot contain gradients, patterns, or different spot colors. The frontmost and backmost objects can contain different tints of the same spot color. Objects with a fill of None won't be recolored.

2. From the Colors submenu under the Filter menu **2**, choose:

   **Blend Front to Back** to create a blend using the fill colors of the frontmost and backmost objects as the starting and ending colors. Objects will stay on their respective layers.

   **Blend Horizontally** to create a color blend using the fill colors of the leftmost and rightmost objects as the starting and ending colors **3**–**4**.

   **Blend Vertically** to create a color blend using the fill colors of the topmost and bottommost objects as the starting and ending colors.

   Any selected objects that are stacked between the frontmost and backmost objects (or positioned between the leftmost and rightmost or topmost and bottommost objects) will be assigned intermediate blend colors.

*Saturate/Desaturate; Blend Colors*

### To select objects with the same paint attributes for recoloring:

1. Select an object whose paint attributes (fill color, stroke color, stroke weight, etc.) you want to replace.
*or*
Choose the attributes that you want to search for from the Color and/or Stroke palettes and leave the Color palette Color box selected, or click a swatch on the Swatches palette.

2. Choose Edit menu > Select > Same Paint Style, or Same Fill Color, or Same Stroke Color to select objects with the same paint attributes as you chose in the previous step **1**. All occurrences of those paint attributes will now be selected.

3. With the shapes still selected, mix a new color using the Color palette.
*or*
Click a new swatch on the Swatches palette.
*or*
Choose a new Weight or other attributes on the Stroke palette.

**TIP** The Select > Same Fill Color command selects all objects containing the same spot color, regardless of any differences in tint strength among those objects.

**TIP** You can also globally change a spot color by replacing its swatch (see page 122).

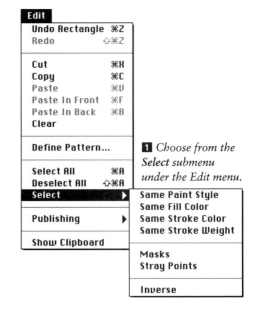

**1** *Choose from the Select submenu under the Edit menu.*

# GRADIENTS 10

*A gradient fill is a gradual blend between two or more colors. In this chapter you will learn how to create two-color and multi-color gradients and how to change the angle or order of gradient colors using the Gradient palette.*

The simplest gradient fill consists of a starting color and an ending color, with the point where the colors are equally mixed together midway between them. A gradient can be linear (side-to-side) or radial (out-from-center). You can apply a gradient fill to one object or across several objects. A set of predefined gradients is supplied with Illustrator, but you can also create your own gradients using the Gradient palette.

Once an object is filled with a gradient, you can use the Gradient tool to modify how the fill is distributed within the object. You can change the direction of the gradient, how quickly one color blends into another, or the placement of the center of a radial gradient fill.

Chris Spollen, **New York Retro**

Follow these instructions to apply an existing gradient, which can be a gradient that's supplied with Illustrator or a gradient that you have already created. To create your own gradient, follow the next set of instructions.

*Note:* Open the Color, Gradient, and Swatches palettes for the instructions in this chapter.

### To fill an object with a gradient:

1. Select an object.

2. On the Swatches palette, click a Gradient swatch .
   *or*
   To apply the last selected gradient, click the Gradient Fill box on the Gradient palette **2** or the Gradient button on the Toolbox.

3. *Optional:* Enter a different Angle for a linear gradient on the Gradient palette.

**TIP** Drag a gradient swatch or the Gradient Fill box over an unselected object to apply the gradient to that object.

**TIP** To apply a gradient to a Stroke, first apply Object menu > Path > Outline Path to convert the Stroke into a closed object (see page 101).

**TIP** To fill type with a gradient, you must first convert it into outlines (Type menu > Create Outlines).

**TIP** You can also use the Paint Bucket tool to apply a gradient to an object.

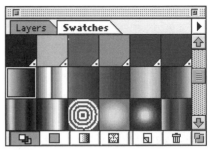

**1** *A gradient selected on the Swatches palette...*

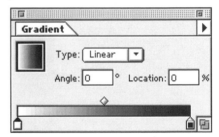

**2** *...and the same selected gradient displayed on the Gradient palette.*

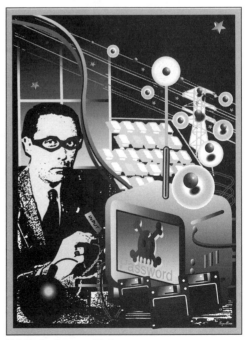

*Chris Spollen, **Internet Theft***

*Fill Object with a Gradient*

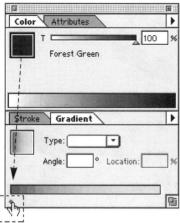

**1** *Drag a color from the Color palette to the far left side of the Gradient bar to define it as the starting color.*

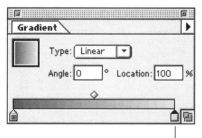

**2** *Next, mix a color for the right side of the Gradient bar using the Color palette to define it as the ending color.*

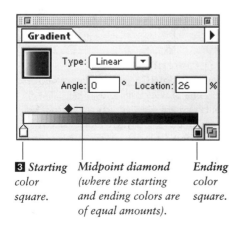

**3** *Starting*    *Midpoint diamond*    *Ending*
*color*    *(where the starting*    *color*
*square.*    *and ending colors are*    *square.*
     *of equal amounts).*

A gradient can be composed of CMYK and/or RGB process colors, one spot color in a mixture of tints, or multiple spot colors. When a gradient containing a mixture of color models is color separated, by default, all the colors are converted to CMYK process color.

### To create and save a two-color gradient:

1. Display the full Gradient palette, with its options panel.

2. Click the Color palette Color box. Mix the starting color using the Color palette, then drag the color to the far left side of the Gradient bar on the Gradient palette to create the starting color square **1**. You could also drag a swatch from the Swatches palette.
   *or*
   Click the starting color square on the Gradient palette, then Option/Alt click a swatch on the Swatches palette.

3. Repeat the previous step for the ending color square on the far right side of the Gradient bar **2**.

4. On the Gradient palette, choose Type: Linear or Radial.

5. *Optional:* Move the midpoint diamond (above the Gradient bar) to the right to produce more of the starting color than the ending color, or to the left to produce more of the ending color than the starting color (**3** on this page, **4**–**5** on the next page).

6. Selecting any other object or swatch now will cause the current gradient to be lost, if you don't first save it. To save the new gradient, drag the Gradient Fill box or the Toolbox Fill box onto the Swatches palette.
   *or*
   Click the New Swatch icon on the Swatches palette.
   *or*

*(Continued on the following page)*

Create a Two-Color Gradient

Option/Alt-click the New Swatch icon, type a new name for the gradient in the Swatch Name field, then press Return/Enter.

**TIP** To change a color in an an existing gradient, click an object that contains a gradient fill or click a gradient swatch on the Swatches palette that you want to edit, click a square below the Gradient slider for the color you want to edit on the Gradient palette, then choose a color from the Color palette. You can also drag from the Color palette or Swatches palette over a color square to change that square's color.

**TIP** To color separate a gradient containing more than one spot color, assign a different screen angle to each color using File menu > Separation Setup, and uncheck the Convert to Process box. Ask your service bureau for advice on printing spot colors.

You could also convert each spot color to process by clicking the spot color square on the Gradient bar and then choosing a process color model from the Color palette pop-up menu.

**TIP** To color separate a gradient from a spot color to white on one piece of film (one plate), create a gradient with the spot color and 0% tint of the same color.

**TIP** To swap the starting and ending colors or any other two color squares, Option/Alt-drag one square over the other.

**TIP** To delete a gradient swatch you saved, select the swatch and click the trash icon (Swatches palette).

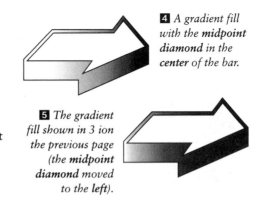

**4** *A gradient fill with the **midpoint** diamond in the center of the bar.*

**5** *The gradient fill shown in 3 ion the previous page (the **midpoint** diamond moved to the left).*

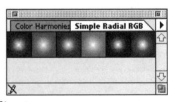

### More gradients
The Simple Radial RGB gradient library displayed above is one of several libraries of predefined gradients that are supplied with Illustrator. To open one of these libraries, choose Window menu > Swatch Libraries > Other Library, open Illustrator folder > Other Libraries > Gradients, highlight the library you want to open, then click Select. From the secondary Swatches palette containing those gradients that opens, drag swatches into your document's Swatches palette.

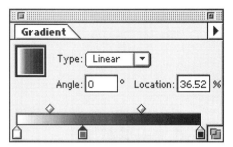

**1** *To add a color to a gradient, click under the Gradient bar to add a new square, then mix a process color on the Color palette or Option/Alt click a swatch on the Swatches palette.*

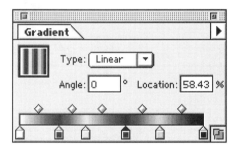

**2** *Four new shades of gray were added to this gradient.*

**3** *Multi-color gradients.*

A gradient can contain up to 32 colors. The colors can be changed and their quantities can be adjusted at any time.

## To create a multicolor gradient fill:

1. Follow steps on the previous two pages to produce a two-color gradient.
   *or*
   On the Swatches palette, click the gradient swatch that you want to modify.

2. Click on the bottom of the Gradient bar where you want the new color to appear, then use the Color palette to mix the new color.
   *or*
   Click the Color palette Color box, mix a color using the Color palette, then drag from the Color palette to the Gradient bar on the Gradient palette. A new color square will appear **1**.
   *or*
   Drag a swatch from the Swatches palette to the Gradient bar.

3. Do any of the following optional steps:

   Move the new square to the left or to the right to change its location.

   Move the midpoint diamond located above the Gradient bar to the left or right of the new color to change the location where the new color is equally mixed with either of the colors adjacent to it.

   Repeat step 2 to add more colors **2**–**3**.

   **TIP** To produce a sharp transition between colors, drag the midpoint diamond close to a color square or move the color squares close together.

   **TIP** To remove a color square, drag it downward out of the Gradient palette.

   **TIP** If you modify a gradient that's been saved as a swatch, the original gradient swatch won't change. If you want to keep the modified gradient, save it as a new swatch.

**Multicolor Gradient Fill**

Once an object is filled with a gradient, you can use the Gradient tool to manually change the direction of a linear fill or the location of the center of a radial gradient fill. You can also use this tool to apply a gradient across a series of objects (see the next page).

### To use the Gradient tool:

1. Apply a gradient fill to an object, and keep the object selected.

2. Choose the Gradient tool (G) .

**1** *Gradient tool.*

3. To modify a linear gradient fill, you can press and drag across the object in a new direction (right-to-left or diagonally) **2**–**3**. To blend the colors abruptly, drag a short distance; to blend the colors more gradually across a wider span, drag a longer distance.

   To modify a radial gradient fill, position the pointer where you want the center of the fill to be, then click or press and drag **4**–**5**.

**2** *A linear gradient fill applied using the Gradient or Swatches palette only.*

**TIP** If you're not happy with the results, drag in a different direction. Drag in the opposite direction to reverse the order of the fill colors.

**TIP** To save the new gradient, drag the Gradient Fill box from the Gradient palette to the Swatches palette.

**TIP** If you start to drag or finish dragging outside the edge of an object with the Gradient tool, the colors at the beginning or end of the gradient fill won't appear in the object.

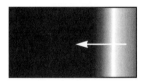

**3** *The Gradient tool dragged a short distance from right to left across the same gradient.*

**4** *A radial gradient fill before using the Gradient tool.*

**5** *After dragging the Gradient tool across the same radial gradient.*

Gradient Tool

**To spread a gradient across multiple objects:**

1. Select several objects, and fill them with a gradient **1**.

2. Choose the Gradient tool.

3. Drag across all the objects **2**. Hold down Shift while dragging to constrain the angle to the nearest 45°.

TIP Once multiple objects are filled with the same gradient, they shouldn't be combined into a compound path, because it may become too complex to print.

**1** *A gradient fill applied using the Swatches palette only. Each type object is filled with its own gradient.*

**2** *The gradient adjusted using the* **Gradient** *tool. The arrow shows the direction the mouse was dragged. A single gradient blends across all the type outlines.*

## To convert gradient shades into separate objects:

1. Select the object that contains the gradient .

2. Choose Object menu > Expand Fill.

3. *Optional:* A suggested number of steps for optimum screen and print output displays in the Estimates area and in the Number of Steps field. Enter a your own Number of Steps, if you want .

4. Click OK or press Return/Enter **3**–**4**.

**TIP** You could also apply this command to simplify a gradient fill that won't print.

**1** *This object contains Illustrator's Steel Bar gradient.*

**3** *After applying the Expand Fill command, the gradient is converted into a series of 12 separate rectangles grouped with a mask, each filled a different color or shade.*

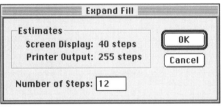

**4** *After deleting the resulting mask object. A few rectangle objects were pulled apart for illustration purposes.*

# PATTERNS 11

A pattern fill is an arrangement of adjacent rectangles, each containing the same shapes. You can fill an object with any of the patterns that are supplied with Illustrator or you can create your own patterns. In this chapter you will learn how to apply a pattern fill to an object, create and modify a pattern, create and apply a path pattern, and expand a pattern into a group of individual objects. Also included are tips for printing and transforming patterns.

## To fill with a pattern:

1. Select an object.

2. Click the Fill box on the Toolbox.

3. Click a pattern swatch on the Swatches palette. Patterns tile upward and rightward from the ruler origin.

   *or*

   Drag-and-drop a pattern swatch from the Swatches palette over an object **1**. The object doesn't have to be selected when you use this method.

**TIP** To copy patterns from another document's Swatches palette, choose Window > Swatches Libraries > Other Library, then locate and open the Patterns folder in the Other Libraries folder inside the Illustrator application folder. Additional patterns are contained on the Illustrator 7.0 CD-ROM. Pattern swatches on the Swatches palette will save with your document.

**TIP** To delete all unused patterns from a file, click the Pattern icon on the bottom of the Swatches palette to display only patterns, choose Select All Unused from the palette pop-up menu, then click the palette's trash icon.

**TIP** Don't apply a path pattern as a fill. A path pattern tile may contain unwanted, extraneous objects.

## Printing patterns

For a pattern to preview and print, the "Preview and Print Patterns" box must be checked in the Document Setup dialog box (File menu). Patterns can slow down screen redraw and printing, though, so uncheck this option when you don't need to preview or print your patterns.

If a document that contains a pattern fails to print altogether, try printing it with the Preview and print patterns box unchecked to see if the pattern is the culprit. If it is, try simplifying the pattern or grouping or uniting objects of the same color within the pattern. A document containing multiple patterns may be particularly problematic.

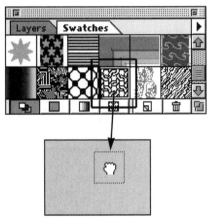

**1** *Drag-and-drop a pattern swatch over a selected or unselected object.*

**1** *Draw objects for the pattern.*

**2**

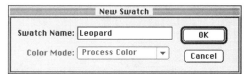

**3** *The New Swatch dialog box opens when the Define Pattern command is used.*

**4** *Draw a bounding rectangle around the objects, then send the rectangle to the back.*

**5** *An object filled with our Leopard pattern fill.*

**6**

## To create a pattern:

1. Draw an object or objects to be used as the pattern **1**. They may not contain a gradient, mask, or pattern. Simple shapes are least likely to cause a printing error.

2. *Strictly optional:* Apply the Roughen filter at a low setting to make the pattern shapes look more hand drawn.

3. Marquee all the objects with the Selection Tool (V).

4. Choose Edit menu > Define Pattern.
   *or*
   Drag the selection onto the Swatches palette **2**, then double-click the new swatch.

5. Type a name in the Swatch Name field **3**.

6. Click OK or press Return/Enter.

You can create a rectangle object to clearly define the amount of white space around the pattern or to crop parts of the objects that fall outside the rectangle.

## To create a pattern defined by a rectangle:

1. Draw objects to be used as the pattern.

2. Choose the Rectangle tool (M).

3. Draw a half-inch to one-inch square around the objects (use the Info palette to check). Fit the square closely around the objects if you don't want empty space to be part of the pattern **4**. If the pattern is complex, make the rectangle small (about a half inch square) to facilitate printing.

4. Choose Object menu > Arrange > Send to Back. The bounding rectangle must be behind the pattern objects.

5. Apply a fill and stroke of None to the rectangle.
   *or*
   Apply a fill color to be the background color in the pattern.

6. Follow steps 2–6 in the previous set of instructions **5**–**6**.

Create a Pattern

You can create a geometric pattern by arranging straight-sided objects around a common center point.

### To create a geometric pattern:

1. Create a geometric object . Use the Polygon, Spiral, or Star tool to create an object easily, if you wish *(see pages 58–63)*.

2. Choose a selection tool.

3. Option/Alt drag a copy of the object so it abuts the original. Also hold down Shift while dragging to constrain the movement horizontally or vertically. You can show the grid to help you align the objects *(see page 268)*.

4. Repeat step 3 with other objects to create a symmetrical arrangement .

5. *Optional:* Apply different fill colors to add variety to the pattern.

6. Choose the Rectangle tool.

7. Press and drag a rectangle around the objects. Make sure the symmetry is preserved .

8. With the rectangle still selected, choose Object menu > Arrange > Send to Back.

9. Follow steps 2–6 at the top of the previous page .

**TIP** You can use the Crop command to see exactly what the pattern tile will look like *(see page 99).*

**TIP** To create a pattern that repeats seamlessly, follow the instructions in the Illustrator User Guide.

**TIP** To reposition only the pattern within an object, hold down "~" and press and drag inside it with the Selection tool.

**1** *Draw a geometric object.*

**2** *Copy the object and arrange the copies symmetrically.*

**3** *Draw a bounding rectangle around the objects, then send the rectangle to the back. In order to produce a perfect repetitive pattern fill, the rectangle is aligned with the midpoints and edges of the geometric shapes.*

**4** *A geometric pattern fill.*

Create a Geometric Pattern

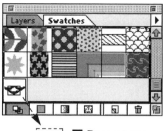

**1** *Drag a pattern swatch out of the Swatches palette to modify it.*

**2** *The pattern swatch dragged onto the page.*

**3** *A line added to the pattern.*

*The modified pattern.*

You can modify any pattern, including any pattern that's supplied with Illustrator. To change an existing pattern, first its swatch must be dragged back into a document. Objects already filled with the pattern in the document will update automatically if you save over the original.

## To modify a pattern:

1. Display a blank area in your document window, then drag the pattern swatch out of the Swatches palette **1**. The pattern is now a group with a bounding rectangle (with a fill and stroke of None) added behind it **2**.

2. Modify the pattern objects using the Direct Selection tool (A) to select the parts **3**.

3. Choose the Selection tool (V).

4. Click on any of the pattern objects to select the group.

5. Option/Alt-drag the selected pattern shapes over the original pattern swatch. Objects already filled with the pattern in the file will update automatically.

   *Note:* If you decide instead that you don't want to save over the original pattern, choose Edit menu > Define Pattern (or drag the selection onto the Swatches palette, then double-click the new swatch), enter a *new* name in the Swatch Name field, then click OK. A new swatch will be created—the original swatch won't change.

**TIP** To delete a pattern swatch, select it, then click the palette's trash icon.

**TIP** To retrieve a deleted pattern, choose Edit menu > Undo immediately. Or if the pattern was used as a fill in an object prior to being deleted, you can retrieve it by selecting the object and dragging the Fill box from the Toolbox onto the Swatches palette.

**Modify a Pattern**

The Path Pattern filter renders patterns along the edge of a closed or open path, and can be used to create custom frames, borders, or other decorative shapes. You can use up to three diferent-shaped tile pieces when you create a path pattern—a Side tile, an Outer Corner tile, and an Inner Corner tile—which will adapt to fit on the straight, or corner part of the path's contour, respectively. You can design your own tiles or use the pattern tiles that are supplied with Illustrator. Path pattern objects *can* be modified, even after they're applied to a path.

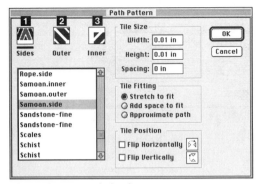

*The **Path Pattern** dialog box.*

### To place a pattern along the edge of a path:

1. Select the object to which you'd like to apply the pattern.

2. Choose Filter menu > Stylize > Path Pattern.

3. Click the Sides box **1**.

4. Choose a pattern name from the scroll list. For a round object, proceed to step 9. (See our tip regarding accessing pattern files and libraries.)

5. Click the Outer box **2**.

6. Choose the same pattern name again or choose a different pattern name from the scroll list. Choose None from the list if you don't want the pattern to appear on the corners of the path.

7. Click the Inner box **3**.

8. Choose the same pattern name again or choose a different pattern name from the scroll list.

9. *Optional:* Enter a new number in the Tile Size: Width or Height field to change the size of the pattern tile. The opposite dimension box will adjust automatically when you click OK or press Tab.

10. *Optional:* To add blank space between pattern tiles, enter an amount in the Tile Size: Spacing field.

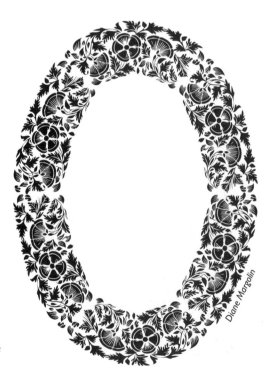

Diane Margolin

**Path Patterns**

*To create this pattern, Diane Margolin turned on the "Stretch to fit" option, and used Side, Outer Corner, and Inner Corner tile shapes.*

Diane Margolin

**11.** Click "Stretch to fit" to have Illustrator lengthen the tiles, where necessary, to fit on the path.
*or*
Click "Add space to fit" to have Illustrator add blank space between tiles, where necessary, to fit the pattern along the path, factoring in the Spacing amount, if one was entered. Choose this option if you want the original path's stroke color (or subsequently applied fill color) to show through blank spaces in the pattern.
*or*
For a rectangular path, if you click "Approximate path," the pattern tiles will be applied slightly inside or outside the path, rather than centered on the path, in order to produce even tiling.

**12.** *Optional:* To flip the pattern, check the Flip Horizontally and/or Flip Vertically box. This may not produce pleasing results in every pattern.

**13.** Click OK or press Return/Enter. The path pattern will appear on top of the original path, and will be separate from that path. You can recolor the original path, though in order to select it you may have to move the path pattern or send it to the back.

**TIP** A folder of path patterns is supplied with Illustrator. You'll find it in the Illustrator folder > Other Libraries > Path Patterns. Use Window menu > Swatch Libraries > Other Library to locate and open a path pattern library. The path pattern names have suffixes to designate which part of the path they are for: .side, .outer, and .inner. (More path patterns can be found in the Goodies folder on the Adobe Illustrator 7.0 CD-ROM.)

**Path Paterns**

### To manually resize individual path pattern tiles:

1. Select the path pattern, then choose Object menu > Ungroup (Command-Shift-G/Ctrl-Shift-G).

2. Deselect the path pattern.

3. Select any tile on the path.

4. Double-click the Scale tool, enter % values for the new tile size, then click OK or press Return/Enter.

5. Repeat steps 4 and 5 for any other tiles that you want to resize.

6. Choose the Selection tool.

7. Reselect the whole path pattern.

8. Choose Object menu > Group (Command-G/Ctrl-G).

You can create your own path pattern tiles from scratch or you can use an existing, applied path pattern as a starting point.

### To create path pattern tiles:

1. Draw closed path shapes for the side pattern tile. Try to limit your tile to about an inch wide—two inches at the most. You can resize them later in the Path Pattern dialog box.

*Note:* The Path Pattern filter places side tiles perpendicular to the path, so you should rotate any design that is taller than it is wide by following steps 2–4:

2. Choose the Selection tool, then select the shapes.

3. Double-click the Rotate tool.

4. Enter an Angle of 90, then click OK.

5. Draw separate shapes for the corner tiles, if necessary, to complete the design. Corner tiles should be the same height as the rotated side tile.

6. Choose the Selection tool, then select the side tile shapes.

7. Choose Edit menu > Define Pattern.
   *or*
   Drag the selection onto the Swatches palette, then double-click it.

### Creating a circular path pattern tile

*The path pattern tile and a circle.*

*The pattern tile applied to a circle. The width and height values were scaled to conform to the circle's diameter. A value of 1% of the circle's diameter worked for our pattern.*

*The resulting circle path pattern was selected, turned into a pattern tile, and applied via the Path Pattern filter to a rectangular path.*

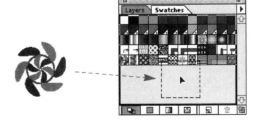

Path Patterns

**1** *The New Swatch dialog box opens when the Define Pattern command is used.*

**2** *The original pattern.*

*A detail of the pattern expanded (Artwork view).*

Diane Margolin

**3** *After applying the Expand command, releasing the mask, and applying the Transform Each command (moved .3" horizontally and -.3" vertically, rotated 17°, Random).*

**8.** Enter a name in the Swatch Name field, then click OK or press Return/Enter **1**.

**9.** Repeat steps 6 through 8 for the corner tile shapes. Type "outer" after the corner tile name.

**10.** Follow the steps on pages 146–147 to apply the new tiles to a path.

**TIP** While you don't *have* to use a bounding rectangle behind the shapes when you a create path pattern tile, you *can* do so if it helps you fit the tiles together. Apply a fill and stroke of None to the rectangle, and make sure nothing sticks out of it. It won't act as a cropping device as it would in a pattern fill. You could also include a rectangle with fill and/or stroke colors as part of the tile.

**TIP** Corner tiles will be rotated 90° for each corner of the path, starting from the upper left corner.

**TIP** Apply spot fill and stroke colors to the tile shapes, and name them appropriately so they can be readily associated with the tile. The tiles can then be easily recolored by changing the spot colors. You can also use the Adjust Color filter to adjust colors on an applied pattern.

**TIP** Apply the Roughen filter at a low setting to make geometric shapes look more hand drawn.

### To divide a pattern fill into individual objects:

**1.** Select an object that contains a pattern fill **2**.

**2.** Choose Object menu > Expand Fill (no dialog box will open). The pattern fill will be divided into the original shapes that made up the pattern tile, and these shapes will be inside a mask. You can now release the mask, alter the mask shape, or delete it.

**TIP** If you want to apply the Transform Each command with its Random option to an expanded pattern, first choose Objects menu > Masks > Release **3**.

**Expand Fill**

## Transforming fill patterns

If you transform (Move, Rotate, Scale, Reflect, or Shear) an object that contains a pattern fill, you can transform the pattern when you transform the object by checking the Patterns box in any transformation tool's dialog box **1**–**3** or by checking the Transform Pattern Tiles box in File menu > Preferences > General (Command-K/Ctrl-K). Checking or unchecking this option in one location automatically resets it in all other locations. Path patterns automatically transform, since they are objects, not fills.

To transform a pattern but not the object **4**, uncheck the Objects box in the transformation tool's dialog box. Or, choose the transformation tool, drag to position the point of origin, then hold down "~" and press and drag.

To open a transformation dialog box, double-click a transform tool or choose a transform command from the Object menu > Transform submenu. The transformation tools and commands are covered in depth in Chapter 16.

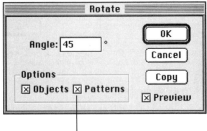

**1** *Check or uncheck the* **Patterns** *box in any transformation tool dialog box.*

**2** *The original pattern.*

**3** *The object and the pattern sheared.*

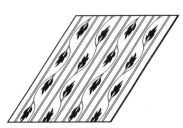

**4** *The pattern rotated; the object not rotated.*

# LAYERS 12

Each new object you draw in an illustration is automatically positioned on top of the previous object. This positioning is called the stacking order **1**. All new objects are stacked on a single, default layer which is created automatically when you create a new illustration. Using the Layers palette, you can add additional layers to an illustration, each of which can contain a stack of objects. You can change the stacking order of objects within a layer, and you can reorder whole layers. You can also group objects together so they can be moved as a unit. If you place objects on separate layers, you can selectively display/hide, edit/lock, and print them.

In this chapter you will learn to group and ungroup objects and to restack objects. Using the Layers palette, you will learn to create and reorder layers, move an object to a different layer, and hide/show, lock/unlock, print, and delete layers.

**1** *Imagine your illustration is built on transparent modular shelves. You can rearrange (restack) objects within the same shelf (layer), move an object to a different shelf, or rearrange the order of the shelves (layers).*

If you group objects together, you can easily select, cut, copy, paste, transform, recolor, or move them as a unit. When you group objects, they are automatically placed on the same layer (the layer of the frontmost object in the group). If you then apply Layers palette hide/show, lock/unlock, preview, and print options, they will affect the whole group.

## To group objects:

1. Choose the Selection tool.

2. Shift-click on each of the objects to be grouped **1**–**2**.
   *or*
   Position the pointer outside all the objects, then press and drag a marquee diagonally across them.

3. Choose Object menu > Group (Command-G/Ctrl-G) **3**.

**TIP** You can group multiple groups into a larger, parent group.

## To ungroup objects:

1. Choose the Selection tool.

2. Click on a group.

3. Choose Object menu > Ungroup (Command-Shift-G/Ctrl-Shift-G).

**1** *Select an object.*

**2** *Shift-click on additional objects.*

**3** *Choose Group from the Object menu.*

*Group; Ungroup*

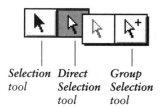

*Selection   Direct      Group*
*tool        Selection   Selection*
*            tool        tool*

**1** *Illustrator's selection tools.*

## To select grouped objects:

To select an entire group, click on any item in the group with the Selection tool (V) **1**.
*or*
To select individual anchor points or segments of an object within a group, use the Direct Selection tool (A).
*or*
To select multiple groups within a larger group in the order in which they were added to the group, use the Group Selection tool. Click once to select an object in a group **2**; click again on the same object to select the group that object is part of **3**; click again on the object to select the next larger group the first group is part of **4**, and so on.

**TIP** Hold down Option/Alt to quickly access the Group Selection tool when the Direct Selection tool is chosen.

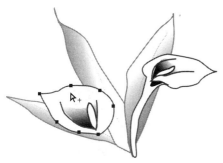

**2** *Click once with the **Group Selection** tool to select an individual object.*

**3** *Click a second time with the **Group Selection** tool to select the group that object is a member of.*

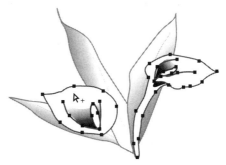

**4** *Click a third time with the **Group Selection** tool to select the next larger group the first group is a part of.*

**Select Grouped Objects**

Use the Bring To Front or Send To Back command to move an object or a group to the front or the back of its stack within its layer. If you restack an object within a group, it will move to the frontmost or backmost position in the same group.

### To place an object on the bottom of its stack:

1. Choose the Selection tool.
2. Click on the object or group.
3. Choose Object menu > Arrange > Send To Back (Command-Shift-[ / Ctrl-Shift-[ ) **1**–**3**.

**TIP** If you select only a portion of a path (a point or a segment) and then change its stacking position, the entire object will move.

### To place an object on the top of its stack:

1. Choose the Selection tool.
2. Click on the object or group.
3. Choose Object menu > Arrange > Bring To Front (Command-Shift-]/ Ctrl-Shift-]). The selected object or group will be placed on the top of its stack within the same layer.

### To move an object foward or backward within its stack:

1. Select an object.
2. Choose Object menu > Arrange > Bring Forward (Command-]/Ctrl-]) or Send Backward (Command-[/Ctrl-[) to shift the object one level at a time in its stacking order.

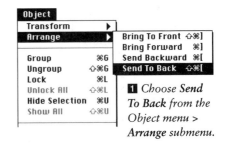

**1** *Choose* ***Send To Back*** *from the Object menu > Arrange submenu.*

**2** *The selected group.*

**3** *After choosing the* ***Send To Back*** *command.*

Restack an Object

**1** *The dark gray object was selected and then placed on the Clipboard via the Cut command.*

```
Edit
Undo Copy        ⌘Z
Redo             ⇧⌘Z
Cut              ⌘H
Copy             ⌘C
Paste            ⌘U
Paste In Front   ⌘F
Paste In Back    ⌘B
Clear
Define Pattern...
Select All       ⌘A
Deselect All     ⇧⌘A
Select           ▶
Publishing       ▶
Show Clipboard
```

**2** *Choose **Paste In Front** or **Paste In Back** from the **Edit** menu.*

**3** *The inner flower shape is selected. After choosing Paste In Back (Edit menu), the gray object is behind the inner flower shape.*

The Paste In Front and Paste In Back commands paste the Clipboard contents just in front of or just behind the currently selected object within the selected object's layer, in the same horizontal and vertical position from which it was cut.

### To restack an object in front of or behind another object:

1. Choose the Selection tool.

2. Click on an object **1**.

3. Choose Edit menu > Cut (Command-X/Ctrl-X) to place the object on the Clipboard.

4. Click on the object that you want to paste just in front of or just behind.

5. Choose Edit menu > Paste In Front (Command-F/Ctrl-F).
   *or*
   Choose Edit menu > Paste In Back (Command-B/Ctrl-B) **2–3**.

**TIP** To restack part of an object, use the Direct Selection tool to select it before choosing Cut.

**TIP** If no object is selected when you choose Paste In Front or Paste In Back, the object on the Clipboard will paste to the front or back, respectively, of the stack within the currently active layer (the highlighted layer on the Layers palette).

**TIP** You can use the Paste In Front or Paste In Back command to stack type outlines. For example, you can copy and Paste in Back a type outline with a stroke color and a fill of None, and then apply a wider stroke of a different color to the copy to create a two-tone stroke.

**TIP** If you cut an object, then use the Direct Selection tool to select an item in a group, and then choose the Paste In Front of or Paste In Back, the pasted object will be added to the group.

The first layer, Layer 1, is created automatically when you create a new document. You can add as many additional layers as you like.

To activate an individual layer to work on, simply click its name on the Layers palette. You can also reorder layers and lock, hide, or print individual layers. Any new object you create will be placed on the currently highlighted layer.

### To create a new layer:

1. Choose New Layer from the Layers palette pop-up menu ■.
   or
   Option/Alt-click the New Layer button.

2. Enter a name for the new layer ■.

3. *Optional:* Choose a different selection color for items on that layer from the Color drop-down menu. Selection colors help make it easier to tell which layer is which. The default order of colors, as they are assigned to new layers, is the order of colors as they appear on the Color drop-down menu.

4. *Optional:* Choose other layer options *(see page 160).*

5. Click OK or press Return/Enter.

**TIP** Click the New Layer button to create a new layer without opening the options dialog box. Illustrator will assign the next color on the Color drop-down menu to the new layer.

**TIP** To insert a new layer directly above the currently highlighted layer, Command-Option/Ctrl-Alt click the New Layer button.

**TIP** To insert a new layer directly below the currently highlighted layer, Command/Ctrl click the New Layer button.

*Selected object icon*

*Active layer icon*

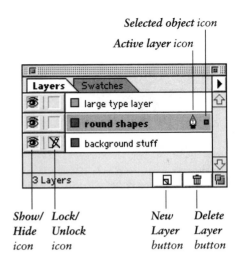

*Show/ Hide icon*   *Lock/ Unlock icon*   *New Layer button*   *Delete Layer button*

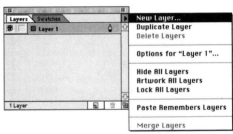

■ *Choose **New Layer** from the **Layers** palette pop-up menu or Option/Alt click the **New Layer** button.*

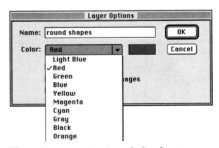

■ *In the **Layer Options** dialog box, type a Name and choose a Color.*

**Create a New Layer**

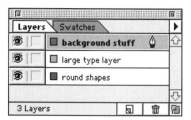

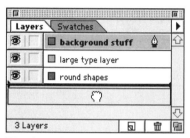

**1** *Press and drag a layer name upward or downward.*

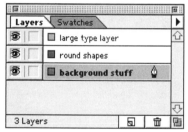

**2** *Release the mouse when the dark bar is in the desired position.*

**3** *The newly moved layer is now on the bottom, and objects on that layer are now in the back of the illustration.*

The order of names on the Layers palette matches the front-to-back order of layers in the illustration.

**To reorder layers:**

Press and drag a layer name up or down (the pointer will turn into a fist icon). Release the mouse when the dark bar is in the desired position **1**–**3**. The illustration will redraw.

**To select more than one layer to work on:**

Click a layer, then Shift-click another layer on the list. The layers you clicked on and all layers in between will be selected.
*or*
Command/Ctrl click non-contiguous layer names. Only the layers you clicked on will be selected.
*or*
Option/Alt click on or drag through a list of layer names. All the objects on the layers you clicked or dragged on will be selected (but not their layer names).

**TIP** Command/Ctrl click to deselect an individual layer when more than one layer is selected.

**TIP** Option/Alt click a layer name to select all the objects on that layer.

Duplicate a layer to copy that layer with all its layer options and all the objects contained on that layer.

*Note:* A mask that masks objects from more than one layer will duplicate as an object if its layer is duplicated, but the copy won't behave as a mask, and it will be given a stroke and fill of none.

### To duplicate a layer:

1. Select a layer to duplicate.

2. Choose Duplicate Layer from the palette pop-up menu.
   *or*
   Drag the layer name over the New Layer button **1**.

   A new layer will be created and the word "copy" will be added to the layer name. Objects from the original layer will appear in their same *x-y* location on the duplicate.

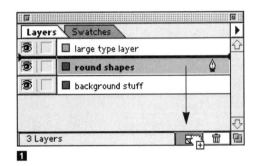

Any time your illustration contains more than one layer, you can select two or more of them and merge them into one. Their stacking order within the layer they're merged into will be the same order they were in prior to the merge.

*Note:* Before you apply the Merge Layers command, you might want to save a copy of the layered illustration using Save As if you think there's a chance you'll want to work with the individual layers again.

### To merge layers:

1. Select the layers you want to merge.

2. Choose Merge Layers from the palette pop-up menu **2**. The layers will merge into the currently active layer (the layer with the pen tip icon).

TIP If you merge any layer that contains a masked object, the effect of the mask may be released.

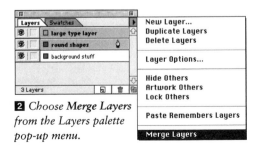

**2** *Choose Merge Layers from the Layers palette pop-up menu.*

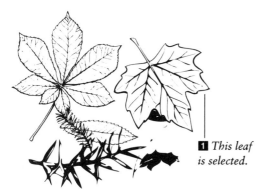

**1** *This leaf is selected.*

*The tiny colored square indicates which layer the currently selected object is on.*

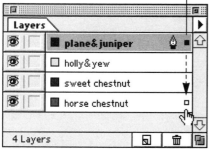

**2** *Move the little square for the selected object. Release the mouse when the temporary square is on the desired layer name. If you move to another layer an object that is part of a group or a mask, that object will be released from the group or mask.*

**3** *The object is now on a different layer.*

You can move an object to a different layer using the Layers palette alone (method 1) or using the Clipboard and the Layers palette (method 2).

### To move an object to a different layer (method 1):

1. Choose any selection tool, then click on the object or group you want to move **1**. The object's current layer will be highlighted on the Layers palette.

2. Drag the tiny colored square located to the right of the highlighted layer name upward or downward (the pointer will turn into a pointing hand icon) **2**, then release the mouse when the temporary square is on the desired layer name. The illustration will redraw with the object in its new layer **3**. (Option/Alt drag the square to *copy* the object to another layer.)

### To move an object to a different layer (method 2):

1. Choose the Selection tool, then click on the object you want to move.

2. Choose Edit menu > Cut.

3. Click on the name of the layer on the Layers palette to which you want the object to move. (Or select an object or a group that's on that layer.)

4. Choose Edit menu > Paste. The object will be placed at the top of the stack within the layer you highlighted.
   *or*
   If an object is selected, choose Edit menu > Paste in Front or Paste in Back to paste the object in its original position directly in front of or behind the selected object, respectively. If the selected object is in a group, the pasted object will join the group.

**TIP** If the object moves to the top of its stack rather than to a different layer, choose Paste Remembers Layers from the Layers palette pop-up menu to uncheck this option, or turn this option off in File menu > Preferences > General.

Move an Object to a Different Layer

The following options affect all the objects
on the currently highlighted layer.

### To choose layer options:

1. Double-click a layer name on the Layers
   palette.
   *or*
   Click a layer name on the Layers palette,
   then choose "Options for "[layer
   name]" from the palette pop-up menu.

2. Do any of the following:

   **Rename** the layer.

   Choose a different **Color** for selected
   objects on the layer.

   Check **Show** to display the layer;
   uncheck to hide it 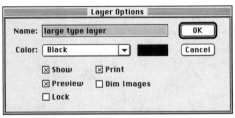. A hidden layer
   will not print.

   Check **Preview** to display the layer in
   Preview view; uncheck to display the
   layer in Artwork view.

   **TIP** Command/Ctrl click an eye icon to
   display that layer in Artwork view,
   regardless of the view chosen for
   the illustration. Command-Option/
   Ctrl-Alt click the eye icon to display all layers except that one in
   Artwork view.

   Check **Lock** to prevent all the objects
   on that layer from being edited;
   uncheck to allow objects to be edited.
   *Note:* Choosing the Layers palette
   option will not affect the status of the
   Object menu command, and vice versa.
   For example, choosing Lock from the
   Object menu will not cause the Lock
   option box in the Layers Option dialog
   box to be checked.

   Check to **Print;** uncheck to prevent
   all the objects on that layer from printing. Use to trouble-shoot a problem
   print job. Hidden layers don't print
   either.

   Check **Dim Images** to dim any placed
   images on that layer (useful for
   tracing); uncheck to display placed
   images normally.

**1** *In the Layer Options dialog box, check the*
***Show, Preview, Lock, Print,*** *or* ***Dim Images***
*boxes on or off.*

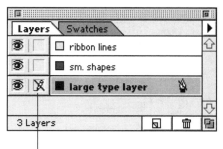

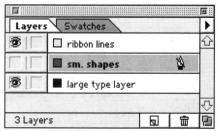

**1** *Click in the edit column to make a layer editable/non-editable. This layer is locked.*

If there is a crossed-out pencil icon next to a layer name, objects on that layer are currently locked (not editable).

### To make a layer uneditable (lock):

Click the edit column next to the layer name **1**. Objects in that layer cannot be selected or edited.

**TIP** To unlock the layer, click on the crossed-out pencil icon.

**TIP** Option/Alt click in the edit column to lock/unlock all other layers except the one you click on.

**2** *Click the eye icon or the empty space where the icon was to hide or show a layer. In this illustration, the "sm.shapes" layer is hidden and is uneditable.*

*Artwork view*

*Preview view*

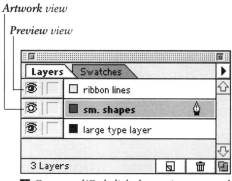

**3** *Command/Ctrl click the eye icon to toggle a layer between Artwork and Preview views.*

If an eye icon displays next to a layer name, that layer is currently displayed.

### To hide a layer:

Click the eye icon next to the layer name **2**. All objects on that layer will be hidden, whether or not they are selected.

*Note:* Hidden layers don't print. To make a visible layer non-printable, uncheck the Print box in the Layer Options dialog box.

**TIP** To redisplay the layer, click the column box where the eye icon was.

**TIP** To display a layer in Artwork view, Command/Ctrl click on the eye icon next to the layer name **3**. To redisplay the layer in Preview view, Command/Ctrl click the eye icon again.

**TIP** Option/Alt click in the eye column to hide/show all other layers except the one you click on.

Lock or Hide a Layer

**161**

**To hide or lock multiple layers:**

Drag upward or downward in the eye icon column or the edit column to quickly hide/show or lock/unlock the layers you drag through **1**.

**TIP** To quickly hide or lock one item at a time, choose Object menu > Hide or Lock. However, you cannot unlock or show individual items using the Object menu. Choosing Unlock All or Show All will affect all objects that were locked or hidden using the Object menu command, but it will not affect layers that were hidden or locked by clicking the Layers palette icon.

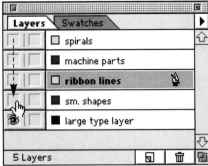

**1** *Drag in the eye icon column to quickly hide/show multiple layers. In this example, only the bottommost layer will remain visible. Note that the hidden layers are also uneditable, as indicated by the slash through the active layer (pen tip) icon.*

If you delete a layer, all the objects on that layer are removed.

**To delete a layer:**

1. Click the name of the layer you want to delete on the Layers palette.

2. Choose Delete "[layer name]" from the palette pop-up menu.
   *or*
   Drag the layer name onto the palette trash icon **2**.
   *or*
   Click the palette trash icon.

3. If there were any objects on the deleted layer, a warning prompt will appear. Click Yes.

**TIP** To retrieve the deleted layer and the objects on it, choose Edit menu > Undo Layer Deletion immediately.

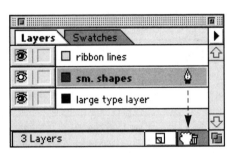

**2** *Click the name of the layer you want to delete, then drag it to the trash icon, or, just click the trash icon.*

# CREATE TYPE 13

*This chapter is an introduction to Illustrator's impressive type creation tools. You will learn how to create type that stands by itself, and you'll learn how to enter type inside an object or along a path. You'll also learn how to import type from another application, link type, copy type or a type object, and convert type into graphic outlines.*

*Typographic attributes are modified using the Character, Paragraph, and MM (Multiple Master) Design palettes, which are covered in the next chapter, along with methods for selecting type.*

Label by Louise Fili

**The Type Tools**

There are three basic type tools: The Type tool, the Area Type tool, and the Path Type tool. There are also three tools that create vertical type: The Vertical Type tool, the Vertical Area Type tool, and the Vertical Path Type tool. Some of these tools' functions overlap, but each of them has unique characteristics for producing a particular kind of type object.

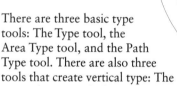

The **Type** tool is used to create a free-floating block of type, called **point** type, that is not associated with an object. You can also draw a rectangle with it and enter text inside the rectangle, or you can use it to enter type on the outside edge of an open path or inside a closed path. It's the most versatile of the type tools.

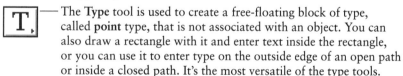

The **Area Type** tool is used to create type *inside* an open or closed path. Lines of type created with the Area Type tool automatically wrap inside the object.

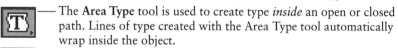

The **Path Type** tool is used to enter a line of type along the outside *edge* of an open or closed path.

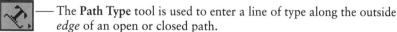

The **Vertical Type** tool has the same function as the Type tool, except that it's used to create type that reads vertically.

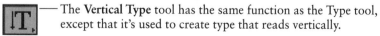

The **Vertical Area Type** tool is used to create vertical type *inside* an open or closed path. Vertical type reads from *right to left*, making it useful for typesetting text in languages that read in that direction.

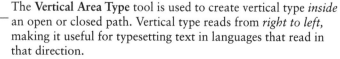

The **Vertical Path Type** tool is used to create vertical type along the outside *edge* of an open or closed path.

## A few things to know about fonts

The Helvetica, Courier, Symbol, and Times PostScript Type 1 fonts and two Multiple Master fonts are automatically installed into the Fonts folder located in the Illustrator program folder, which only Illustrator can access and utilize. Other fonts can be installed in this local folder, if desired. If the fonts in the local folder duplicate fonts that are already in your system, you can delete the local Fonts folder altogether.

Illustrator no longer utilizes Adobe Type Manager (ATM) to perform type rasterization and font-management. These functions are performed internally within Illustrator 7.

If you open a document containing type styled in a font whose suitcase is closed or is not available, that font won't display on screen. If you open a font suitcase using a utility, such as Suitcase or MasterJuggler, after launching Illustrator, the font will reappear on Illustrator's font list and the type should display correctly. If it doesn't, choose View menu > Artwork and then View menu > Preview to force the screen to redraw. Illustrator 7 supports ATM 4.0 Deluxe's activation and deactivation of fonts (see the Illustrator Read Me file).

Point type stands by itself—it's neither inside an object nor along a path. Use this tool to set a type block like a picture caption or a pull quote that doesn't need to be aligned with any neighboring type blocks.

### To create point type:

1. Choose the Type or Vertical Type tool **1**.
2. Click on a blank area of the Artboard where you want the type to start (not on an object). A flashing insertion marker will appear.
3. Enter type. Press Return/Enter when you want to start a new line **2**.
4. Choose a selection tool and click away from the type block to deselect it.
   *or*
   Click the Type tool again to complete the type block and start a new one.

### Choose type attributes first?

If you like to choose character and paragraph attributes before you create type, use the Character and Paragraph palettes. They're discussed in depth in the next chapter.

### Recolor after?

When type is entered inside an object or on a path, the object is filled and stroked with None. You can apply fill and/or stroke colors to the type object if you select it first with the Direct Selection tool (select only the edge). To recolor the type, first select it using a type tool or a selection tool (next chapter).

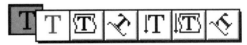

*Illustrator's type-tool lineup on the pop-out menu.*

*Type tool.*

*Vertical Type tool.*

'It spoils people's clothes to squeeze under a gate; the proper way to get in, is to climb down a pear tree.'

Beatrix Potter

**2** *Type created using the Type tool.*

## Type objects vs. graphic objects

Once you place type on or inside a graphic object, it becomes a type object, and can only be converted back into a graphic object via the Edit menu > Undo command. To preserve the original graphic object, make a copy of it and convert the copy into a type path. You can't enter type into a compound path or a mask object, nor can you make a compound path from a text object.

'It spoils people's clothes to squeeze under a gate; the proper way to get in, is to climb down a pear tree.'

**1** *Press and drag with the **Type** tool to create a rectangle, then enter type. The edges of the rectangle will be visible in Artwork view.*

**2** *Press and drag with the **Vertical Type** tool, then enter type. Type flows top to bottom and right to left.*

    C
    l
  a i
    m
  p b
  e
  a d
  r o
  t w
  r n
  e
  e
  .
  .
  .

'It spoils
people's
clothes to
squeeze
under a
gate; the
proper
way to
get in,
is to climb
down a
pear tree.'

**3** *The type rectangle reshaped using the **Direct Selection** tool. The edges of the rectangle will be hidden in **Preview** view.*

## To create a type rectangle:

1.  Choose the Type or Vertical Type tool (press "T" to cycle through the type tools).

2.  Press and drag to create a rectangle. When you release the mouse, a flashing insertion marker will appear in the upper left corner if you used the Type tool or in the upper right corner if you used the Vertical Type tool.

3.  Enter type. Press Return/Enter only when you need to create a new paragraph. The type will automatically conform to the rectangle **1**–**2**.

4.  Choose a selection tool and click away from the type block to deselect it.
    *or*
    Press Command/Ctrl (to temporarily access the last used selection tool) and click away from the type block to deselect it. Release Command/Ctrl, then click again to start a new type block.
    *or*
    Click the Type tool again to complete the type object and start a new one.

**TIP** Choose Artwork view if you want to see the edges of the rectangle.

**TIP** You can reshape a type rectangle using the Direct Selection tool. The type will reflow to fit the new shape **3**.

**TIP** To turn an object created with the Rectangle tool into a type rectangle, click on the edge of the path with either Type tool or Area Type tool, then enter text.

**TIP** If you save an illustration containing vertical type in the Illustrator PDF format, the vertical type will render the horizontal orientation when the PDF file is reopened in Illustrator. This may change in later versions of Illustrator and Acrobat.

*Create a Type Rectangle*

**165**

You can import text into a type rectangle or any other type shape from another application, such as Microsoft Word, WordPerfect, or SimpleText.

### To import type into an object using the Place command:

1. Choose the Type or Vertical Type tool, then drag to create a type rectangle.
   *or*
   Choose the Area Type or Vertical Area Type tool , then click on the edge of a graphic object to create a flashing insertion marker .

2. Choose File menu > Place.

3. Highlight the name of the text file you want to import **3**.

4. Click Place. The text file will flow into the object, with the same paragraph breaks, but not necessary the same line breaks **4**. (It may default to Courier.)

**TIP** If you click with the Type tool in a blank area rather than drag to create a rectangle, each paragraph of the imported text will appear on a separate, single line, and it may be harder to work with.

**TIP** You can also import type using File menu > Open or Place (with no object selected). The type will appear in a new text object, with paragraph breaks. (It may default to Courier.)

**TIP** Opening or placing a file in the Normal MS Word file format may cause some type styling to be lost. The Interchange RTF format preserves most type styling.

### Importing text in the EPS format

Create and style your text in a layout program, and then save the file in EPS format. If you then open the EPS file using Illustrator's Open command, you'll be able to manipulate it as you would any text in Illustrator. Beware, though, a new point type block will be created for every word in the imported text.

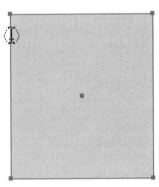

**1** *Area Type tool.*

*Vertical Area Type tool.*

**2** *The object will lose its fill and stroke colors as soon as you click on its edge with the* **Area Type** *tool.*

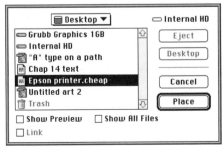

**3** *Highlight a text file you want to Place (import).*

Here was peace. She pulled in her horizon like a great fishnet. Pulled it from around the waist of the world and draped it over her shoulder.

*Zora Neale Hurston*

**4** *Text appears in the object.*

**1** *Rectangle tool.*

Here was peace. She pulled in her horizon like a great fish-net. Pulled it from around the waist of the world and draped it over

*The overflow symbol.*

**2** *Create a new rectangle with the Rectangle tool.*

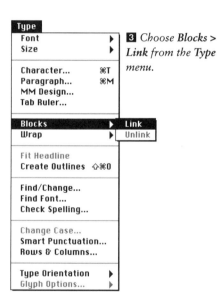

**3** *Choose Blocks > Link from the Type menu.*

Here was peace. She pulled in her horizon like a great fish-net. Pulled it from around the waist of the world and draped it over

her shoulder. So much of life in its meshes! She called in her soul to come and see.

**4** *Overflow type flows from the first object into the second object when the objects are linked.*

## What to do with overflow text

If a type rectangle isn't quite large enough to display all the type inside it, you can enlarge it using the Scale tool. First select only the rectangle—not the type—using the Direct Selection tool. Or you can enlarge the rectangle by dragging a segment using the Direct Selection tool (hold down Shift to constrain horizontally or vertically).

If you have a fair amount of overflow type, you can link its object to a second object, thus revealing the overflow type. Follow the instructions on this page to spill overflow type into a rectangular object. Follow the instructions on the next page to spill overflow type into a non-rectangular object.

### To link overflow type from one rectangular type object to another rectangle:

1. Choose the Rectangle tool **1**.

2. Press and drag diagonally to create a new rectangle **2**.

3. Choose any selection tool.

4. Shift-click or marquee both rectangles.

5. Choose Type menu > Blocks > Link **3**. Overflow type from the first rectangle will flow into the new rectangle **4**.

**TIP** To unlink two or more type objects, choose any selection tool and Shift-click or marquee both rectangles, or choose the Selection tool and click on one of the objects (all the linked objects will be selected), then choose Type menu > Blocks > Unlink. All the objects will unlink; the type in each object will no longer be part of a continuous text stream. To rejoin the text, copy and paste it back into the original object.

**TIP** To remove one type object from a series of linked objects but keep the text stream intact, choose the Direct Selection tool, Option/Alt click on the edge of the object to be removed (the type shouldn't be underlined), then press Delete. The type will reflow into the remaining objects.

**Link/Unlink Type**

## To link overflow type to a copy of an existing non-rectangular object:

1. Make sure your illustration is in Artwork view (Command-Y/Ctrl-Y to toggle between Preview and Artwork views).

2. Choose the Direct Selection tool .

3. Click away from the type object to deselect it.

4. Click on the edge of the type object. The type should not be underlined after you click.

5. Hold down Option/Alt and drag a copy of the type object away from the original object. To constrain the movement to a horizontal or vertical axis, hold down Option-Shift/Alt-Shift while dragging. Release the mouse, then release Option/Alt (and Shift, if used). The overflow type will appear inside the new object **2**.

6. *Optional:* Choose Object menu > Transform > Transform Again (Command-D/Ctrl-D) to create additional linked boxes.

**TIP** If both the type and the type object are selected when you drag, a copy of the object *and* the type will be created, but it will not be linked to the first object.

**TIP** To change the order in which type flows from one object to another, change one of the objects' stacking order in the document by shifting its layer frontward or backward. Or use the Object menu > Arrange > Send to Front, Send to Back, Send Forward, or Send Backward command.

## To add a type object to the end of a chain

Use the Group Selection tool to select the object you want to add and the object that you want to link it object to, then choose Type menu > Blocks > Link.

**1** *Direct Selection tool.*

The kiss of memory made pictures of love and light against the wall. Here was peace.

She pulled in her horizon like a great fish-net. Pulled it from around the waist of the world and

**2** *Overflow type from the first object appears in a copy of the object. (A paragraph indent was applied to the type to move it away from the edge of the objects.)*

**1** *Area Type* tool.

*Vertical Area Type tool.*

Use the Area Type or Vertical Area Type tool to place type inside a rectangle or an irregularly shaped object, or on an open path. The object you use will turn into a type path. You must click precisely on the edge of an object in order to enter type inside it.

**To enter type inside an object:**

1. Choose either Area Type tool if the object is an open or closed path, or choose either Type tool if the object is a closed path **1**.

2. Click on the edge of the object. A flashing insertion marker will appear, and any fill or stroke on the object will be removed.

3. Enter type. It will stay inside the object and conform to its shape **2**–**3**.
   *or*
   Import text using File menu > Place *(see page 166).*

4. Choose a selection tool and click away from the type object to deselect it.
   *or*
   Press Command/Ctrl (to temporarily access the last selection tool used) and click away from the type block to deselect it, then release Command/Ctrl and click on a new type object.
   *or*
   Click again on the type tool you used to complete the type object.

   (Vertical area type will flow from top to bottom and from right to left.)

This is text in a copy of a light bulb shape. You can use the Area-Type tool to place type into any shape you can create. When fitting type into a round shape, place small words at the top and the bottom. This is text in a copy of a light bulb shape. You can use

**2** *Area type.*

The kiss of memory made pictures of love and light against the wall. Here was peace. She pulled in her horizon like a great fish-net. Pulled it from around the waist of the world and draped it over her shoulder. So much of life in its meshes! She called in her soul to come and see.
ZORA NEALE HURSTON

**3** *Type in a circle.*

**Horizontal/vertical toggle**
With any type tool selected, press Shift to toggle between the vertical or horizontal equivalent of that tool.

Enter Type Inside an Object

Use the Path Type tool to place type on the inside or outside edge of an object. Type cannot be positioned on both sides of the same path, but it can be moved from one side to the other after it's created (see the next set of instructions). Only one line of type can be created per path.

**To place type on an object's path:**

1. Choose the Path Type or Vertical Path Type tool .

2. Click on the top or bottom edge of the object. A flashing insertion marker will appear.

3. Enter type. Do not press Return/Enter. The type will appear along the edge of the object, and the object's fill and stroke will revert to None –.

4. Choose a selection tool and click away from the type object to deselect it.
   *or*
   Click the Path Type tool again to complete the type object.

**To reposition path type:**

1. Choose the Selection tool.

2. Click on the path type object.

3. Press and drag the I-beam marker to the left or the right along the edge of the object **2**, move it inside the path. Or double-click the I-beam pointer.

**TIP** To shift *all* the characters slightly closer to or farther from the center of the path, but keep their orientation, choose the Selection tool and click or marquee the path. To shift *some* but not all of the characters, choose any type tool, and highlight the desired characters. Then choose a new number in the Baseline Shift area of the Character palette **5**–**6**. (If the Baseline Shift field isn't visible, keep double-clicking the Character tab until it appears.)

**1** *Path Type tool.*

*Vertical Path Type tool.*

*I-beam*

**2** *Horizontal path type entered on the edge of an oval.*

**3** *Horizontal path type.*

**4** *Vertical path type.*

V
E
R
T
I
C
A
L

**5** *Path type—default baseline position.*

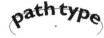
**6** *Path type—baseline shifted downward.*

## Italics into Photoshop

If you copy or drag-and-drop an italic type character in some fonts into Photoshop, the rightmost portion of the letter may become cropped. To prevent this from happening, convert the letter into an outline before copying it.

To test whether an italic letter will copy properly, select the letter with any Type tool. Any portion of the letter that extends beyond the highlight will be cropped.

To copy or move type with or without its object, use the Clipboard, a temporary storage area in memory. The Clipboard commands are Cut, Copy, and Paste. You can also use the drag-and-drop method to move a type object (see page 73).

### To copy type and its object between Illustrator documents or between Illustrator and Photoshop:

1. Choose the Selection tool.

2. Click on the edge of the object, on the type, or on the baseline of the type.

3. Choose Edit menu > Copy (Command-C/Ctrl-C).

4. Click in another Illustrator document window and choose Edit menu > Paste (Command-V/Ctrl-V). The type and its object will appear.
   *or*
   Click in a Photoshop document window, choose Edit menu > Paste, click Paste As Pixels, then click OK. The type and its object will appear on a new layer.

### To move type from one type object to another:

1. Choose any type tool.

2. Highlight the type.

3. Choose Edit menu > Cut (Command-X/Ctrl-X) **1**.

4. Choose any selection tool (or press Command/Ctrl) and click on the edge of another object to select it.

5. Choose a type tool whose attributes you want the type to have (such as area type or vertical type), then click on the edge of the newly selected object to create a flashing cursor.

6. Choose Edit menu > Paste. The type is now part of the new object. When type is cut from a path object, the object will still remain a type object.

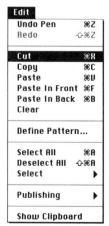

**1** *Choose **Cut** or **Copy** from the **Edit** menu, then later choose **Paste**.*

The Create Outlines command converts type into graphic objects. As outlines, the paths can be reshaped, transformed, used as a compound or a mask, or filled with a gradient or a pattern, like any other objects. Once type is converted into outlines, unless you Undo immediately, it can't be converted back into type again, and you can't change its typeface. An advantage to converting type into outlines is that if you import them into another application, like QuarkXPress, you won't need the printer fonts for the "characters" to print properly. Read the cautionary sidebar at right, though.

### To create type outlines:

1. Create type using any type tool. *All* the characters in the type object or on the path are going to convert into outlines.

2. Choose the Selection tool.

3. If the type isn't already selected, click on the type or on its baseline.

4. Choose Type menu > Create Outlines (Command-Shift-O/Ctrl-Shift-O) **1**–**3**. The characters' original fill and stroke attributes will be preserved, but the path object will be deleted.

**TIP** To create outlines, the Type 1 font (screen font and printer outlines) or TrueType font for the typeface you are using must be installed in your system or Illustrator's Font folder.

**TIP** Group multiple outline paths together using the Group command so they'll be easier to select and move.

**TIP** If the original character had an interior counter—as in an "A" or a "P"—the individual components (outside and inside shapes) will become a compound path after the Create Outlines conversion. If you want to divide the inside and outside parts of the type outline into separate objects, choose Object menu > Compound Paths > Release. To reassemble the components, select them both, then choose Object menu > Compound Paths > Make *(see page 216)*.

### Converter beware

The Create Outlines command is most suitable for creating logos or other large characters that require reshaping. This command is least suitable for smaller size text, like body text, because it causes a slight heavying of letterforms, making them harder to read, Compare printouts of your type before and after the conversion before you decide whether to use the outlines version. And don't apply a stroke to small type outlines.

**1** *The original type.*

**2** *Type converted into* ***outlines** (Artwork view).*

**3** *Type converted into* ***outlines** (Preview view).*

# STYLE & EDIT TYPE 14

In this chapter you will learn how to select type and apply character-based typographical attributes (font, size, leading, kerning, tracking, baseline shift, and horizontal and vertical scaling) using the Character palette; how to apply paragraph-based attributes (alignment, indentation, inter-paragraph spacing, and word and letter spacing) using the Paragraph palette; and how to use the new text orientation features.

You'll also learn to use Illustrator's word processing features to change case, check spelling, export text, find and replace fonts or text, create columns and rows, apply professional typesetter's marks, auto hyphenate, and apply tabs.

Before you can modify type, you must select it. If you use the **Selection** tool, both the type and its object will be selected **1**. If you use the **Direct Selection** tool, you can select the type object alone or the type object *and* the type **2**. If you use a **type** tool to select type, only the type itself will be selected, not the type object **3**.

If we
shadows
have
offended,
Think but
this—
and all is
mended—

If we
shadows
have
offended,
Think but
this—
and all is
mended—

If we
shadows
have
offended,
Think but
this—
and all is
mended—

*Shakespeare*

**1** *Type and type object selected with the Selection tool.*

**2** *Type object selected with the Direction Selection tool.*

**3** *Type (but not its object) selected with the Type tool.*

Use this selection method if you want to move, transform, restyle, or recolor a *whole* type *block*. To reshape or recolor a type *object*, use the selection method described at the bottom of this page. To edit type or to restyle or recolor *part* of a type *block*, use the selection method described on the next page.

### To select type and its object:

1. Choose the Selection tool .

2. Click on the edge of the type object. This may be easiest to do in Artwork view.
   *or*
   For point type, with your illustration in Artwork view, you can click on the little "x" before the first character **2–3**.
   *or*
   Click on the baseline of any character in the type object in any view.
   *or*
   With the Type Area Select option turned on (File menu > Preferences > Keyboard Increments), click on any part of the type to select it.

**TIP** To modify the paint attributes of type, use the Color palette *(see Chapter 9)*.

**TIP** To move, scale, rotate, shear, or reflect type, choose Object menu > Transform, or use any transform tool.

**1** *Selection tool.*

Think but this — and all is mended —

**2** *For point type in Artwork view, click on the "x."*

Baseline — Think but this — and all is mended —

**3** *The type and type object are both selected. If you select point type (type created with the Type tool or Vertical Type tool by clicking, then entering text) with the Selection or Direct Selection tool, the type will have a solid anchor point before the first character and each line will be underlined.*

Use this selection method if you want to reshape a type object (and thus reflow the type) or recolor a type object.

### To select a type object but not the type:

1. Choose the Direct Selection tool .

2. Click on the edge of the type object. This may be easiest to do in Artwork view **5–6**. Now, modifications you make will only affect the type object, and not the type.

**4** *Direct Selection tool.*

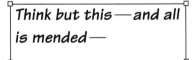

Think but this — and all is mended —

**5** *Only the type object is selected; the type is not.*

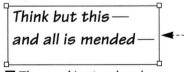

Think but this — and all is mended —

**6** *The type object is reshaped.*

Use this selection method if you want to edit all or a portion of a type block, or change its character, paragraph, or paint attributes.

## To select type but not its object:

1. Choose any type tool.

2. Drag horizontally (for horizontal type) with the I-beam pointer to select and highlight a word or a line of type **1**–**2**.
   *or*
   Drag vertically (for horizontal type) to select lines of type.
   *or*
   Double-click to select a word.
   *or*
   Triple-click to select a paragraph.
   *or*
   Click in the text block, then choose Edit menu > Select All (Command-A/Ctrl-A) to select all the type in the block or on the path, including any type to which it is linked.
   *or*
   Click where you want the selection to start, then Shift-click where you want the selection to end. (You can also extend a selection by Shift-clicking.)

3. After modifying the type, click on the selected type to deselect it and keep the flashing insertion marker in the type block for further editing.
   *or*
   Choose a selection tool and click away from the type object to deselect it.

**TIP** To select vertical type, with any type tool, drag vertically to select a line or drag horizontally to select lines.

---

*My line drawing is the purest and most direct translation of my emotion.*

**1** *The Type tool cursor will have a dotted outline until it is moved over type.*

*My line drawing is the purest and most direct* translation of *my emotion.*

Henri Matisse

**2** *Two words are selected. The I-beam cursor no longer has a dotted outline.*

**Select Type**

## Character palette

Use the Character palette (Command-T/ Ctrl-T) 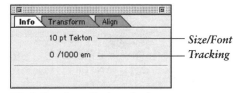 to modify font, type size, leading, kerning, and tracking values in one or more highlighted text characters. Choose Show Options from the pop-up menu at the upper right of the palette to expand the palette for baseline shift, and horizontal and vertical scale adjustments.

## Paragraph palette

Use the Paragraph palette (Command-M/ Ctrl-M)  to modify paragraph-wide attributes, like alignment and indentation. Choose Show Options from the pop-up menu at the upper right of the palette to adjust word and letter spacing, and to turn on auto hyphenation, hanging punctuation, repeated character processing (for Chinese, Japanese, or Korean (CJK) fonts, if installed), and line breaking.

If you want to change paragraph attributes of *all* the text in a type object or on a path, select the object or path with the Selection tool. To isolate a paragraph or series of paragraphs, select just those paragraphs with a type tool.

*Note:* A paragraph is created when the Return/Enter key is pressed within a type block. No on-screen, non-printing character symbol will display for a paragraph break in Illustrator.

## MM Design palette

Use the **Multiple Master** Palette 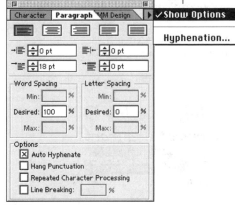 to modify the weight and width of characters in a multiple master (MM) font. The axes that can be adjusted depend on the MM font you are using. Choose Type menu > MM Design—when text in a document is set in a MM font and selected. Multiple Master fonts are useful when a type style is required that is slightly slimmer or heavier than an existing style. Two Multiple Master fonts are supplied with Illustrator 7—Nueva MM and Tekton MM—and they are installed by default.

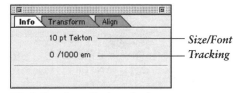

**1** *The Character palette.*

*Choose Show Options from the Character or Paragraph palette pop-up menu.*

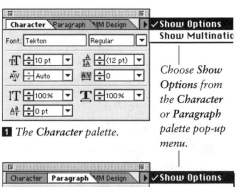

**2** *The Paragraph palette.*

**3** *The MM Design palette.*

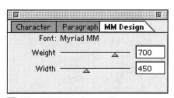

Size/Font
Tracking

*The Info palette displays the font name, size, and tracking values of type selected with a type tool. Choose Window menu > Show Info to open the Info palette. Attributes cannot be changed using this palette—it's for information only.*

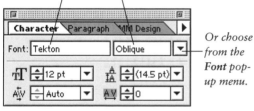

**1** *The Type tool.*

Art, like morality, consists of
drawing the line somewhere.

**2** *Select the type you want to modify.*

*Enter a font name and style.*

*Or choose from the Font pop-up menu.*

**3** *The Character palette.*

## To choose a font:

1. Choose any type tool **1**, then select the type you want to modify **2**.
   *or*
   Choose the Selection tool, then click on the type object.

2. On the Character palette, choose a font from the Font drop-down menu **3**. Choose from a submenu if the font name has an arrowhead next to it **4**.
   *or*
   Type the name of a font and the name of a style in the Font fields, then press Return/Enter. You need only enter the first few letters of the font name or style—the name or style with the closest spelling match will appear in the field **5**. If you want the Roman or Regular weight of a font, type only the font name (not the weight), then press Return/Enter.

   **TIP** You can also choose from the Type menu > Font pop-up menu or submenu.

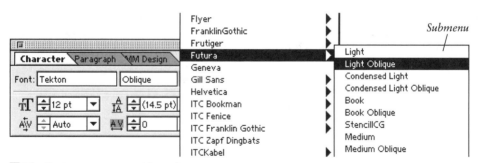

**4** *The Font pop-up menu with a submenu open.*

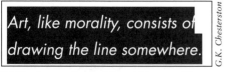

G.K. Chesterston

**5** *The font is changed from Tekton Bold Oblique to Futura Book Oblique.*

**Choose a Font**

## To resize type:

1. Select the type you want to modify.

2. On the Character palette, enter a point size between .1 and 1296 in the Size field, then press Return/Enter to apply, or press Tab to apply and highlight the next field **1**–**2**. You don't need to reenter the unit of measure. *Note:* If the type you have selected contains more than one point size, the Size field will be blank. Entering a size now will change all selected type to this size.

   *or*

   Choose a preset size from the Size drop-down menu or click the up or down arrow.

   *or*

   To resize type via the keyboard, hold down Command-Shift/Ctrl-Shift and press ">" to enlarge or "<" to reduce. The increment the type resizes each time you use this shortcut is specified in the Size/Leading field in File menu > Preferences > Keyboard Increments.

**TIP** You can also choose a preset size from the Type menu > Size submenu.

**TIP** You can scale selected type and its object using the Scale tool. Choose the Scale tool, then press and drag. Or click on a corner to set the origin for scaling, then press and drag on the opposite corner. Or double-click the Scale tool and enter a value in the Scale dialog box, then click OK. To scale type uniformly without condensing or extending it, click, then drag using the Scale tool with Shift held down.

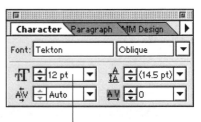

**1** *On the Character palette, enter a number in the Size field, or choose a preset size from the pop-up menu.*

# Origami

# Origami

**2** *Type enlarged.*

### Fitting type to its container

To track horizontal or vertical type outward to the edges of a text rectangle or type container, choose any type tool, highlight a one-line paragraph, then choose Type > Fit Headline **3**–**4**. When it's applied to a Multiple Master font, the Fit Headline command adjusts both the weight and tracking of the text.

**3** *The original, selected characters.*

# Fit Headline

**4** *After applying the Fit Headline command.*

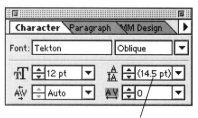

**1** On the **Character** palette, enter the desired leading in points in the **Leading** field, or choose Auto or a preset leading amount from the drop-down menu.

---

ACT III.

Scene I.

*The Wood. The* Queen of Fairies *lying*

*asleep.*

*Enter* QUINCE, SNUG, BOTTOM, FLUTE, SNOUT, *and* STARVELING.

*Bot.* Are we all met?

*Quin.* Pat, pat; and here is a marvellous convenient place for our rehearsal. This green plot shall be our stage, this hawthorn brake our tiringhouse; and we will do it in action, as we will do it before the duke.

*Loose* **Leading** *(8-point type; 12 point leading)*

**2**

---

ACT III.

Scene I.

*The Wood. The* Queen of Fairies *lying*

*asleep.*

*Enter* QUINCE, SNUG, BOTTOM, FLUTE, SNOUT, *and* STARVELING.

*Bot.* Are we all met?

*Quin.* Pat, pat; and here is a marvellous convenient place for our rehearsal. This green plot shall be our stage, this hawthorn brake our tiringhouse; and we will do it in action, as we will do it before the duke.

*Tight* **Leading** *(8-point type; 8.75 point leading)*

**3**

---

Leading is the distance from baseline to baseline between lines of type, and it is traditionally measured in points. Each line of type in a block can have a different leading amount. (To add space between paragraphs, follow the instructions on page 184.)

## To change leading:

1. Select the type you want to modify:

   Click anywhere in a type block with the Selection tool to change the leading of the entire block.
   *or*
   Highlight an entire paragraph with a type tool (triple-click anywhere in the paragraph) to change the leading of all the lines in that paragraph.
   *or*
   Highlight an entire line with a type tool (including the space at the end, if there is one) to change the leading of only that line.

2. On the Character palette:

   Enter a number in the Leading field, then press Return/Enter or Tab to apply **1**–**3**.
   *or*
   Choose a preset leading amount from the Leading drop-down menu or click the up or down arrow.
   *or*
   Choose Auto (always shown in parentheses) from the pop-up menu to set the leading to 120% of the largest type size on each line.

**TIP** Hold down Option/Alt and press the up arrow on the keyboard to decrease leading in selected horizontal text or the down arrow to increase leading. The increment the leading changes each time you use this shortcut is specified in the Size/Leading field in File menu > Preferences > Keyboard Increments.

Leading

Kerning is the adjustment of the space between *two adjacent* characters. All fonts have kerning pairs built into them, and body text sizes usually don't require manual kerning. Words or phrases set in larger sizes, on the other hand, like headlines or logos, usually require careful manual kerning to add or remove awkward spacing between character pairs. To kern a pair of characters, the cursor must be inserted between them.

Tracking is the simultaneous adjustment of the space between *three or more* characters. It's normally applied to a range of type— a paragraph or a line. To track type, first highlight the range of type you want to track using a type tool, or select an entire type block with a selection tool.

### To kern or track type:

1. Choose a type tool, then click to create an insertion point between the two characters you want to kern or highlight the range of text you want to track.
   *or*
   Choose the Selection tool, then click on a type object.

2. In the Kerning or Tracking field on the Character palette (Command-T/Ctrl-T), enter a positive number to add space between characters or a negative number to subtract space, then press Return/Enter or Tab to apply ■–■.
   *or*
   Choose a preset kerning or tracking amount from the drop-down menu or click the up or down arrow.
   *or*
   Hold down Option/Alt and press the right arrow on the keyboard to add space between letters or the left arrow to decrease space between letters. The amount of space that is added or removed each time you press an arrow is specified in the Tracking field in File menu > Preferences > Keyboard Increments. Add Command/Ctrl to the shortcut to track in larger increments.

### Spacing out

■ To adjust the overall word or letter spacing in a text block, use the Word Spacing and Letter Spacing fields on the Paragraph palette (see page 184).

■ Every font has built-in kerning pairs for improved inter-character spacing. To enable this feature, select the text you want to affect, then choose Auto from the Kerning drop-down menu on the Character palette (see the Figure ■ below). Choose or enter 0 to turn this feature off.

**1** *Kerning field and pop-up menu.*   *Tracking field and pop-up menu.*

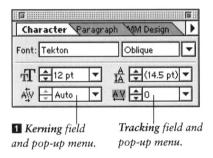

**2** *Normal type.*

**3** *Space added between the first two characters (kerning).*

**4** *Space removed between the last five characters (kerning or tracking).*

Kerning and Tracking

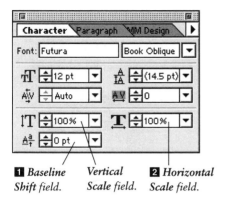

**1** *Baseline*   *Vertical*   **2** *Horizontal*
*Shift field.*   *Scale field.*   *Scale field.*

**3** *Characters on a path, baseline shifted downward.*

**4** *The "A" baseline shifted 9 points downward.*

**5** DANIELLE

*Normal type (no scaling).*

DANIELLE

*75% horizontal scale.*

DANIELLE

*125% horizontal scale.*

### Go for the real thing

You can stylize any typeface by using a scale command, but a Multiple Master typeface or a typeface that has been extended or condensed by its designer (i.e. Univers Extended or Helvetica Narrow) will look much better, because its weight, proportions, and counters (interior spaces) are adjusted specifically for that typeface.

The Baseline Shift option repositions characters above or below the baseline. You can use this command to offset curved path type from its path or to create superscript or subscript characters (there is no superscript or subscript type style in Illustrator).

### To baseline shift type:

1. Highlight the type you want to modify.
2. In the Baseline Shift field on the Character palette (choose Show Options from the pop-up menu if the field isn't visible), enter a positive number to baseline shift characters upward or a negative number to baseline shift characters downward, then press Return/Enter to apply **1**, **3**–**4**. Or choose a preset amount from the drop-down menu or click the up or down arrow.
   *or*
   Hold down Option/Alt and Shift and press the up arrow to shift highlighted characters upward, or the down arrow to shift characters downward. The amount type shifts each time you press an arrow is specified in the Baseline Shift field in File menu > Preferences > Keyboard Increments.

The Horizontal Scale option extends (widens) or condenses (narrows) type. The Vertical Scale option makes type taller or shorter. The default scale is 100%.

### To horizontally/vertically scale type:

1. Select the type you want to modify.
2. Enter a higher or lower percentage in the Horizontal or Vertical Scale field on the Character palette, then press Return/Enter or Tab to apply **2** and **5**. Or choose a preset amount from the drop-down menu or click the up or down arrow.

**TIP** You can also horizontally scale a selected type block using the Scale dialog box. Double-click the Scale tool, choose Non-Uniform from the pop-up menu, then enter a number other than 100 in the Horizontal or Vertical field.

Alignment, indent, and leading values affect whole paragraphs. To create a new paragraph (hard return) in a text block, press Return/Enter. Type preceding a return is part of one paragraph; type following a return is part of the next paragraph. Type that wraps automatically is part of the same paragraph. To create a line break (soft return) within a paragraph in non-tabular text, press Tab until the text is forced to the next line.

### To change paragraph alignment:

1. Select the paragraph or paragraphs you want to modify.

2. On the Paragraph palette, click the Align Left, Align Center, Align Right, Justify Full Lines, or Justify All Lines alignment icon **1**–**2**.
   *or*
   Use one of the keyboard shortcuts listed at right.

**TIP** The Justify Full Lines and Justify All Lines alignment options cannot be applied to path type or to point type (type not in an object or in a block), because there are no container edges to justify the type against.

### Paragraph alignment shortcuts

| | |
|---|---|
| *Left* | Command-Shift-L/Ctrl-Shift-L |
| *Center* | Command-Shift-C/Ctrl-Shift-C |
| *Right Justify* | Command-Shift-R/Ctrl-Shift-R |
| *Full Lines Justify* | Command-Shift-J/Ctrl-Shift-J |
| *All Lines* | Command-Shift-F/Ctrl-Shift-F |

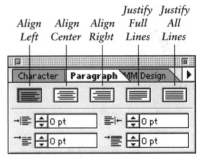

*Align Left*  *Align Center*  *Align Right*  *Justify Full Lines*  *Justify All Lines*

**1** *Click one of the five* **Alignment** *icons on the* **Paragraph** *palette.*

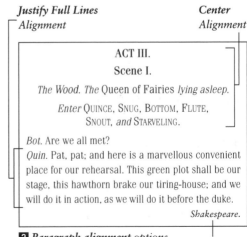

*Justify Full Lines Alignment*

*Center Alignment*

ACT III.

Scene I.

*The Wood. The* Queen of Fairies *lying asleep.*

*Enter* QUINCE, SNUG, BOTTOM, FLUTE, SNOUT, *and* STARVELING.

*Bot.* Are we all met?
*Quin.* Pat, pat; and here is a marvellous convenient place for our rehearsal. This green plot shall be our stage, this hawthorn brake our tiring-house; and we will do it in action, as we will do it before the duke.

*Shakespeare.*

**2** *Paragraph alignment options.*  *Right Alignment*

**Paragraph Alignment**

## How to select paragraphs for modification

If you want to change paragraph attributes of *all* the text in a type object or on a path, select the object or path with the Selection tool. To isolate a paragraph or series of paragraphs, select just those paragraphs with a type tool.

*Left Indent*          *Right Indent*

*First Line Left Indent*

**1** *The Indentation fields on the Paragraph palette. If you forget which one is which, rest the mouse over an icon—the tool tip will remind you.*

Both Left and Right Indentation values can be applied to area type. The type object can be an open or closed path of any shape. Only a Left Indent value can be applied to point type.

## To change paragraph indentation:

1. Choose a type tool, then select the para-graph(s) you want to modify.
   *or*
   Choose a selection tool, then select a type object.

2. Enter a new number in the Left and/or Right Indent fields on the Paragraph palette, then press Return/Enter or Tab to apply **1**–**2**.
   *or*
   Click the up or down arrow.
   *or*
   To indent only the first line of each paragraph, enter a number in the First Line Left Indent field.

**TIP** You can enter negative values in the Left Indent, First Line Left Indent, or Right Indent fields to expand the mea-sure of each line. The type will be pushed type outside its object, but it will still display and print **3**.

---

ACT II.

Scene I.

*A Wood near* Athens.

*Enter a* FAIRY *at one door, and* PUCK *at another.*

*Puck.* How now, spirit! whither wander you?

*Fai.* Over hill, over dale,
Thorough bush, thorough brier,
Over park, over pale,
Thorough flood, thorough fire,
I do wander everywhere,
Swifter than the moon's sphere;

**2** *Left Indentation.*

---

ACT III.

Scene I.

*The Wood. The* Queen of Fairies *lying asleep.*

*Enter* QUINCE, SNUG, BOTTOM, FLUTE, SNOUT, *and* STARVELING.

*Bot.* Are we all met?

*Quin.* Pat, pat; and here is a marvellous conve-nient place for our rehearsal. This green plot shall be our stage, this hawthorn brake our tiring-house; and we will do it in action, as we will do it before the duke.

*Shakespeare*

**3** *To create* **hanging indentation,** *as in the last paragraph in this illustration, enter a number in the* **Left Indent** *field and the same number with a minus sign in front of it in the* **First Line Left Indent** *field.*

**Paragraph Indentation**

Use the Space Before Paragraph field on the Paragraph palette to add or subtract space between paragraphs. Point type cannot be modified using this feature. (To adjust the spacing between lines of type *within* a paragraph (leading), follow the instructions on page 179.)

### To adjust inter-paragraph spacing:

1.  Select the type you want to modify. To modify the space before only one paragraph in a type block, select the paragraph with a type tool.

2.  Enter a number in the Space Before Paragraph field on the Paragraph palette **1**, then press Return/Enter or Tab to apply **2**.
    *or*
    Click the up or down arrow.

**TIP** To create a new paragraph (hard return), press Return/Enter. To create a line break within a paragraph (soft return), press Tab.

**TIP** To move paragraphs close together, enter a negative number in the Space Before Paragraph field.

### Word and letter spacing

To change the horizontal word or letter spacing for justified paragraphs, enter a higher or lower percentage in the Word Spacing or Letter Spacing fields, respectively: Minimum, Desired, or Maximum, on the Paragraph palette **3**–**5** (choose Show Options from the Paragraph palette pop-up menu if these options aren't visible). For non-justified type, you can only enter a value in the Desired fields. Headlines usually look better with reduced word spacing.

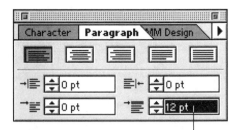

**1** *The Space Before Paragraph field on the Paragraph palette.*

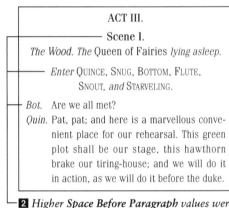

**2** *Higher Space Before Paragraph values were applied to these paragraphs to widen the space above them.*

---

Ocean

Body more immaculate than a wave,
salt washing away its own line,
and the brilliant bird
flying without ground roots.

*Pablo Neruda*

**3** *Normal word and letter spacing.*

---

Ocean

Body more immaculate than a wave,
salt washing away its own line,
and the brilliant bird
flying without ground roots.

**4** *Loose letter spacing.*

---

Ocean

Body more immaculate than a wave,
salt washing away its own line,
and the brilliant bird
flying without ground roots.

**5** *Tight word spacing.*

*Inter-Paragraph Spacing*

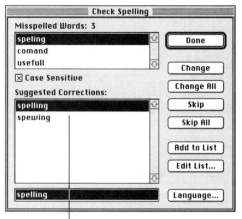

**1** *Double-click a word on the* **Check Spelling** *dialog box Suggested Corrections scroll list to make it replace a misspelled word in your document.*

### Check spelling in Dutch?

Click Language in the Check Spelling dialog box, highlight the dictionary you want to use in the Text Filters folder in the Plug-ins folder in the Adobe Illustrator 7 folder, then click Open.

*Note:* The Check Spelling command can be used only with roman fonts, not with CJK (Chinese, Japanese, and Korean) fonts.

The Check Spelling command checks spelling in your entire illustration using a built-in dictionary. You can also create and edit your own word list.

### To check spelling:

1. Choose Type menu > Check Spelling. Words not found in the application or user dictionary will appear on the Misspelled Words list **1**.

2. Leave the currently highlighted Misspelled Word selected or click a different word on the list. The misspelled word will be highlighted in your illustration.

3. *Optional:* Check the Case Sensitive box to display the Misspelled Word both ways if it appears in both upper and lower case (such as *Spelle* and *spelle*).

4. If the correctly spelled word appears on the Suggested Corrections list, double-click it. The command will proceed to the next mispelled word. Or to change all instances of the mispelled word instead, click the desired word, then click Change All.
   *or*
   If the correct word doesn't appear on the list, or no words appear at all (because there are no similar words in Illustrator's dictionary), type the correct word in the entry field at the bottom. Then click **Change** to change only the first instance of the highlighted

*(Continued on the next page)*

Check Spelling

Misspelled Word to the currently high-lighted Suggested Correction 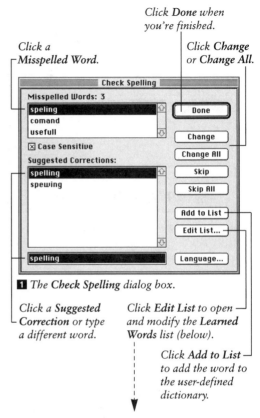, or click **Change All** to change all instances of the Misspelled Word.

For any word, you can click **Skip** to leave the current Misspelled Word unchanged or click **Skip All** to leave all instances of the Misspelled Word unchanged.

5. *Optional:* Click Add to List to add the currently highlighted Misspelled Word or Words to the Learned Words list (the AI User Dictionary file in the Text Filters folder inside the Plug-ins folder).

6. If you spell-check all the Misspelled Words, a prompt will appear. Click OK, then click Done.

**TIP** Click Edit List in the Check Spelling dialog box to open and modify the Learned Words list (user-defined dictionary). Click on a word in the list, retype it in the field at the bottom, then click Change; or click on a word, then click Remove; or type a completely new word, then click Add. Hyphenated words—like "pop-up"—are permitted **2**.

**TIP** Bug alert: The corrected word will take on the styling of the text preceding it and lose its original styling.

*Click a Misspelled Word.*

*Click Done when you're finished.*

*Click Change or Change All.*

**1** *The Check Spelling dialog box.*

*Click a Suggested Correction or type a different word.*

*Click Edit List to open and modify the Learned Words list (below).*

*Click Add to List to add the word to the user-defined dictionary.*

*Highlight a Learned Word, retype it below, then click Change.*

*Or highlight a Learned Word, then click Remove.*

**2** *Create your own word list using the Learned Words dialog box.*

*Or type a new word, in the bottom field, then click Add.*

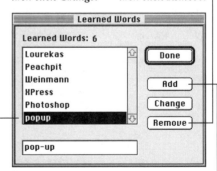

**Check Spelling**

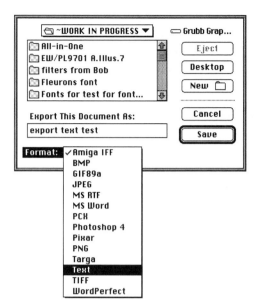

**1** *Choose a file format in which to save your selected text from the **Format** drop-down menu.*

Use the Export command to save Illustrator text in a format that can be imported into another application.

## To export text:

1. Select the text you want to export with a type tool or a selection tool.

2. Choose File menu > Export.

3. Choose a drive and folder in which to save the text file **1**.

4. Enter a name for the new file in the Export This Document As field.

5. Choose a file format from the Format (Macintosh) or Save as Type (Windows) drop-down menu.

6. Click Save.

7. If another dialog box opens, choose further options, then click OK.

The Find Font command can be used to generate a list of the fonts currently being used in an illustration. Or it can be used to replace fonts. The type color, kerning/tracking, and other attributes are retained.

## To find and replace a font:

1. Choose Type menu > Find Font.

2. Check any of the following Font List boxes to selectively display only fonts of those types on the scroll lists: Multiple Master, Standard, Type 1, Roman, TrueType, or CID. For Multiple Master fonts, you must also check the Type 1 box.

3. Leave the Font List: Document option chosen to display, on the Replacement Font List, only fonts currently being used in your document of the types checked in the previous step.
   *or*
   Choose Font List: System to display on the Replacement Font List all the fonts currently available in your system.

*(Continued on the following page)*

**4.** Click a font to search for on the Current Font List scroll list 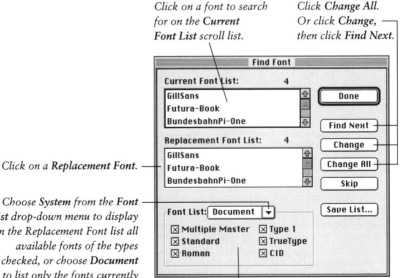.

**5.** Click a replacement font on the Replacement Font List scroll list.

**6.** Click **Find Next** to search for the next instance of the Current Font.
*or*
Click **Skip** to make no change and search for the next instance of the font in your document.
*or*
Click **Change** to change only the current instance of the Current Font.
*or*
Click **Change All** to change all instances of the Current Font. Once all the instances of the font are replaced, it is removed from the Current Font List.

**7.** *Optional:* To save a list of the fonts currently being used in the illustration as a text document, click Save List, enter a name, choose a location in which to save the file, then click Save. The text document can later be opened directly from the Desktop or imported into a text editing or layout application.

**8.** Click Done.

*Click on a font to search for on the **Current Font List** scroll list.*

*Click **Change All**. Or click **Change**, then click **Find Next**.*

*Click on a **Replacement Font**.*

*Choose **System** from the Font List drop-down menu to display on the Replacement Font list all available fonts of the types checked, or choose **Document** to list only the fonts currently being used in your illustration.*

**1** *The **Find Font** dialog box. Uncheck font types to narrow the selection.*

Use the Find/Change command to search for and replace characters without changing their paint or typographic attributes.

## To find and replace text:

1. *Optional:* Click with a Type tool to create an insertion point from which to start the search. If no text object is selected in your document, the search will begin from the most recently created object.

2. Choose Type menu > Find/Change.

3. Enter a word or phrase to search for in the "Find what" field 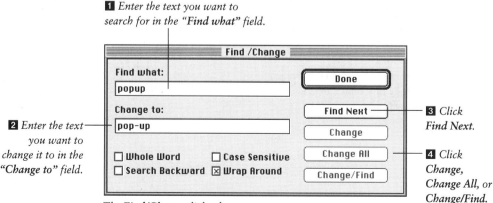.

4. Enter a replacement word or phrase in the "Change to" field ▇. Leave the "Change to" field blank to delete instances of the "Find what" text altogether.

5. *Optional:* Check the Whole Word box to find the "Find what" letters only if they appear as a complete word—not as part of a larger word.

6. *Optional:* Check the Case Sensitive box to find only those instances that match the exact uppercase/lowercase configuration of the "Find what" text.

7. *Optional:* Check the Wrap Around box to search from the current cursor position to the end of the text object or

string of linked objects and then continue the search from the most recently created object. With Wrap Around unchecked, the search will proceed only from the current cursor position forward to the end of that text object. You must click Find Next to resume the search.

8. *Optional:* Check the Search Backward box to search backward.

9. Click **Find Next** to search for the first instance of the "Find what" word or phrase or to skip over a word ▇.

10. Click **Change** to replace only the currently found instance of the "Find what" text.
*or*
Click **Change All** to replace all instances at once ▇.
*or*
Click **Change/Find** to replace the current instance and search for the next instance.

11. Click Done.

TIP Bug alert: The corrected word will take on the styling of the text preceding it and lose its original styling.

**Find and Replace Text**

▇ *Enter the text you want to search for in the "**Find what**" field.*

▇ *Enter the text you want to change it to in the "Change to" field.*

▇ *Click Find Next.*

▇ *Click Change, Change All, or Change/Find.*

*The **Find/Change** dialog box.*

**Find /Change**

Find what:
popup

Change to:
pop-up

☐ Whole Word    ☐ Case Sensitive
☐ Search Backward    ☒ Wrap Around

Done
Find Next
Change
Change All
Change/Find

The Rows & Columns command arranges text into columns and/or rows.

## To create linked text rows and columns:

1. Select a text object with the Selection tool.

2. Choose Type menu > Rows & Columns.

3. Check the Preview box to apply changes immediately 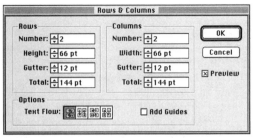.

**1** *The Rows & Columns dialog box.*

4. Click the left/right arrow or enter values in the fields to choose:

    The total number of Columns and Rows to be produced.
    *and*
    The Width of each Column and the Height of each Row.
    *and*
    The Gutter (space) between each Column and each Row.
    *and*
    The Total Width and Total Height of the entire block of Columns and Rows.

5. Click the Text Flow icon to control the direction of the text flow.

6. *Optional:* Check the Add Guides box to display a grid around the text blocks. Make sure the ruler origin is in the default location.

7. Click OK or press Return/Enter **2**–**3**.

**TIP** If you select the entire block of rows and columns with the Selection tool and then reopen the Rows & Columns dialog box, the current settings for that block will be displayed.

**TIP** With the Preview box checked, if you make a change in a field and it isn't immediately applied, press Tab.

Hey! diddle, diddle,
The cat and the Fiddle,
The cow jumped over the moon;
The little dog laugh'd
To see such sport,
And the dish ran away with the spoon.

**2** *One text object...*

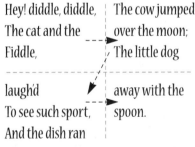

Hey! diddle, diddle,    The cow jumped
The cat and the       over the moon;
Fiddle,              The little dog

laugh'd          away with the
To see such sport,    spoon.
And the dish ran

**3** *...converted into two columns and two rows.*

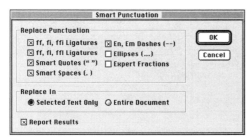

**1** *Check **Replace Punctuation** options in the **Smart Punctuation** dialog box.*

| Dialog box option | Keyboard | Smart punctuation |
|---|---|---|
| ff, fi, ffi Ligatures | ff, fi, ffi | ff, fi, ffi |
| ff, fl, ffl Ligatures | ff, fi, ffl | ff, fi, ffl |
| Smart Quotes | ' " | ' " " ' |
| Smart Spaces (one space after a period) | . T | . T |
| En [dashes] | -- | – |
| Em Dashes | --- | — |
| Ellipses | ... | ... |
| Expert Fractions | 1/2 | ½ |

The Smart Punctuation command converts keyboard punctuation into professional typesetting marks.

## To create smart punctuation:

1. *Optional:* Select text with the Type tool to smart-punctuate that text only. Otherwise, the command will affect the entire document.

2. Choose Type menu > Smart Punctuation.

3. Check any of the Replace Punctuation boxes **1**.

4. Click Replace In: Selected Text Only (if you selected text) or Entire Document.

5. *Optional:* Check Report Results to display a list of your changes.

6. Click OK or press Return/Enter **2**–**3**.

**TIP** To apply Ligatures and Expert Fractions, the Adobe Expert font set for the font you are using must be available in your system.

He supposed Miss Petiigrew might have leaned over the sugar bowl and said, "Mayor," which Daddy said was all she ever called him anymore, "I'd be pleased to have a chimpanzee." And Daddy supposed the mayor frumped himself up a little and muddied his expression and said, "Sister darling, your chimpanzee is just around the corner."

    "Louis!" Momma said. Daddy was hardly ever a very big hit with Momma.

**2** *Dumb punctuation: Straight quotes and two spaces after a period.*

He supposed Miss Petiigrew might have leaned over the sugar bowl and said, "Mayor," which Daddy said was all she ever called him anymore, "I'd be pleased to have a chimpanzee." And Daddy supposed the mayor frumped himself up a little and muddied his expression and said, "Sister darling, your chimpanzee is just around the corner."

    "Louis!" Momma said. Daddy was hardly ever a very big hit with Momma.

*T.R. Pearson*

**3** *Smart punctuation: Curly quotes and one space after a period.*

## To turn on auto hyphenation:

1. Auto hyphenation affects currently selected or subsequently created text only. If you want to hyphenate existing text, select it with a type tool now.

2. Check the Auto Hyphenate box on the Paragraph palette **1**. (If this option isn't visible, choose Show Options from the palette pop-up menu).

3. Choose Hyphenation from the pop-up menu at the upper right of the Paragraph palette.

4. In the "Hyphenate [ ] letters from beginning" field, enter the minimum number of characters to precede any hyphen **2**. Fewer than three letters before or after a hyphen can impair readability.

5. In the "Hyphenate [ ] letters from end" field, enter the minimum number of characters to carry over onto the next line following a hyphen **3**.

6. In the "Limit consecutive hyphens to [ ]" field, enter the maximum allowable number of hyphens in a row. More than two hyphens in a row impairs readability and looks unsightly.

7. Click OK or press Return/Enter.

**TIP** To hyphenate using rules of a different language for the current document only, choose Show Multinational from the pop-up menu at the Character palette's upper right, then choose from the Language drop-down menu. You can change the hyphenation language for the application in File menu > Preferences > Hyphenation Options, where you can also enter hyphenation exceptions or specify how particular words are to be hyphenated.

**TIP** To hyphenate a word manually: Command-Shift--(hyphen)/Ctrl-Shift--.

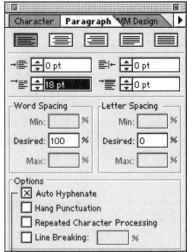

**1** *Check the **Auto Hyphenate** box on the **Paragraph** palette.*

**Sage** (Salvia)
Genus of annuals, biennials, perennials, and evergreen or semi-evergreen shrubs and sub-shrubs, grown for their tubular, 2-lipped, often brightly colored flowers and aromatic foliage. Leaves of some species may be used for flavoring foods. Fully hardy to frost tender, min. 41°F (5°C). Needs sun and fertile, well-drained soil. Propagate perennials by division in spring, perennials, shrubs, and sub-shrubs by softwood cuttings in mid-summer. Sow seed of half-hardy annuals under glass in early spring and of fully-hardy species outdoors in mid-spring.

*An overabundance of hyphens makes for tiring reading.* —

**2** *Minimum number of characters preceding a hyphen.*

**3** *Minimum number of characters after a hyphen.*

*Maximum number of hyphens in a row.* —

**Hyphenation Options**

Hyphenate [3] letters from beginning   [ OK ]
Hyphenate [3] letters from end   [ Cancel ]
Limit consecutive hyphens to: [2]

The Tab Ruler palette is used to set custom left, center, right, and decimal tabs in horizontal type, and top, center, bottom, and decimal tabs in vertical type. Default tab stops are half an inch apart.

## To insert tabs into text:

Press Tab as you input copy before typing each new column. The cursor will jump to the next tab stop.

*or*

To add a tab to already inputted text, click just to the left of the text that is to start a new column, then press Tab.

## To set custom tab stops:

1. Choose the Selection tool, then select a text object that contains tab characters.
   *or*
   Choose the Text tool and select text that contains tab characters.

2. Choose Type menu > Tab Ruler.

3. Click in the tabs ruler where the tab stop or stops are to occur. Text will align to the new stop immediately ■.

4. Click a tab alignment button in the top left corner of the palette.

**TIP** To delete a tab stop, drag the tab marker up and out of the ruler. As you drag it, the word *delete* will display on the palette.

**TIP** To move a tab stop, drag the marker to the left or the right. Shift-drag a marker to move all the markers to the right of it along with it.

| Basic Plaid Country Club | | | |
| --- | --- | --- | --- |
| | **Front 9** | **Back 9** | **Total** |
| Tiger | 38 | 44 | 82 |
| Jack | 34 | 36 | 70 |
| Lee | 42 | 48 | 90 |
| Hubie | 34 | 35 | 69 |

**1** *Text aligned using custom tab stops.*

*Check the **Snap** box to have a tab marker snap to the nearest ruler tick mark as you insert it or drag it. Or, to temporarily turn on the Snap feature when the Snap box is unchecked, hold down **Command/Ctrl** as you drag a marker.*

*The location of the currently selected tab marker. Tab Ruler measurements display in the currently chosen Artboard Units (File menu > Document Setup).*

*Click the **Alignment** box to realign the tabs ruler with the left margin of the selected text for horizontal type or the top margin for vertical type.*

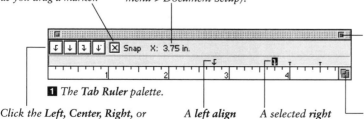

**1** *The Tab Ruler palette.*

*Click the **Left, Center, Right,** or **Decimal Alignment** button (or **Top** or **Bottom** button for vertical type).*

*A left align tab marker.*

*A selected right align tab marker.*

*Drag the **Extend Tab** ruler box to the right to widen the ruler.*

Tabs

The Change Case command changes selected text to all UPPER CASE, all lower case, or Mixed Case (initial capitals).

## To change case:

1. Highlight the text you want to modify with a type tool.

2. Choose Type menu > Change Case.

3. Click Upper Case (ABC), Lower Case (abc), or Mixed Case (Abc), in which the initial cap in every word is upper-case ■.

4. Click OK or press Return/Enter.

### Disappearing tracks

If you change case to uppercase and then undo, the letter tracking will remain for uppercase, not lowercase. Instead, choose Lower Case in the Change Case dialog box, and recapitalize, as needed.

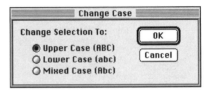

■ *Click an option in the* Change Case *dialog box.*

### Let it all hang out

To hang punctuation ■, select a paragraph, then check the Hang Punctuation option on the Paragraph palette (expand the palette, if necessary, by choosing Show Options from the pop-up menu.) This option works only with area type. It affects the period, comma, quotation mark, apostrophe, hyphen, dash, colon, and semicolon. Hang punctuation in type that is aligned left, right, or justified.

*Hanging*        *Left*
*punctuation*      *Alignment*

'Lo! all these trophies of affections hot,
Of pensiv'd and subdued desires the tender,
Nature hath charg'd me that I hoard them not,
But yield them up where I myself must render,
That is, to you, my origin and ender:
For these, of force, must your oblations be,
Since I their altar, you enpatron me.

*Shakespeare*

■ *Hanging punctuation looks pleasing because it keeps the edge of the paragraph uniform.*

# PLAY WITH TYPE

*Having learned how to create type (Chapter 13) and style type (Chapter 14), you might like to try some of the simple type exercises in this chapter. There are instructions for creating slanted type, shadow type, and type on a circle, and for wrapping type around an object.*

*Daniel Pelavin, **After Hours**, logo for Ziff-Davis*

## To slant a block of type:

1. Choose the Rectangle tool (M), then draw a rectangle.

2. Choose the Area Type tool (T).

3. Click on the edge of the rectangle, then enter type **3**.

4. With the rectangle still selected, double-click the Rotation tool.

5. Enter 30 in the Angle field, then click OK or press Return/Enter **4**.

6. Choose View menu > Artwork to display the rectangle's segments (or Command/Ctrl click on the dot in the eye column for the highlighted layer on the Layers palette).

7. Choose the Direct Selection tool (A), then drag the top segment diagonally to the right with Shift held down until the side segments are vertical **5**.

8. *Optional:* Drag the right segment of the rectangle a little to the right to enlarge the object and reflow the type.

9. Choose View menu > Preview **6**.

### Use the shears

You can use the Shear tool to slant a block of type **1**–**2**.

# SHEARING

**1** *The original type block.*

**2** *Select the type, click with the Shear tool on the center of the type, then drag upward or downward from the edge of the type block. (Hold down Shift to constrain vertically or horizontally.)*

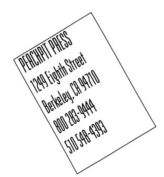

**3** *The original type object.*

**4** *Rotate the type 30°.*

**5** *Drag the top segment diagonally to the right.*

**6** *The reshaped type object (Preview view).*

**1** *Select a type block.*

**2** *Position the shadow close to the original type and send it to the back.*

## To create type with a shadow:

1. Create point type *(see page 164)* **1**.

2. *Optional:* Select the type with the Type tool, then track the characters out (Option/Alt right arrow).

3. Choose the Selection tool, then click on the type block.

4. Choose View menu > Preview.

5. Apply a dark fill color and a stroke of None.

6. Hold down Option/Alt and drag the type block by the baseline of the type or by its anchor point slightly to the right and downward. Release the mouse, then release Option/Alt.

7. With the copy of the type block still selected, apply a lighter shade of the original type.

8. *Optional:* Choose Object menu > Arrange > Send To Back **2**.

9. Reposition either type block—press any arrow key to move it in small increments.

**TIP** With the Type Area Select option on (File > Preferences > Keyboard Increments), it may be difficult to select the type block that's in the back. Either turn the option off or click just below any descender in that type block.

**Shadow Type**

SHADOW

*White on black.*

SHADOW

### A little more depth

Duplicate the type block again, then apply the background fill color to the middle type block. In the illustration above, the type on the top layer has a white fill, the type on the middle layer has a 20% black fill to match the background, and the type on the bottom has a 100% black fill.

## To create type with a slanting shadow:

1. Follow the steps on the previous page.

2. Choose the Selection tool.

3. Click on the baseline or anchor point of the shadow type (see our tip regarding Type Area Select on the previous page).

4. Double-click the Scale tool **1**.

5. Choose Non-uniform **2**, enter 100 in the Horizontal field, enter 60 in the Vertical field, then click OK.

6. With the shadow type still selected, double-click the Shear tool.

7. Enter 45 in the Shear Angle field **3**, click Axis: Horizontal, then click OK.

8. Use the arrow keys to move the baseline of the shadow text so it aligns with the baseline of the original text **4**–**5**. You might also need to move it to the right.

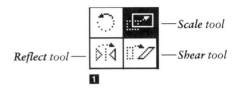

Reflect tool — / Scale tool — Shear tool

**1**

**2** Scale dialog box.

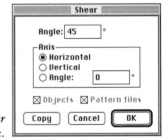

**3** Shear dialog box.

## Shadow slant variation:

1. Follow all the steps above.

2. Choose the Selection tool.

3. Click on the shadow type.

4. Double-click the Reflect tool.

5. Click Axis: Horizontal, then click OK or press Return/Enter.

6. Move the shadow block downward so it aligns with the baselines of the two blocks of letters **6**.

**TIP** If you cannot select the shadow type layer in the back, select the original type first, press the up arrow key to move it upward, then click on the baseline or anchor point of the shadow type.

# MARTINE

**4** The original type.

# MARTINE

**5** Reduce the shadow type, then Shear it.

# MARTINE

**6** After reflecting the shadow.

**1** *Create a 3–inch circle.*

**2** *Path Type tool*

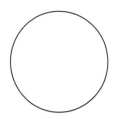

**3** *Create path type on the top of the first circle.*

**4** *Create path type on the bottom of the second circle.*

**5** *Drag the path type inside the circle.*

**6** *Baseline shift the path type on the second circle downward, and center it on the circle.*

## Exercise

### Create a logo—type on a circle

1. Start a new document, and open the Layers, Character, and Color palettes.

2. Choose File menu > Preferences > Units & Undo, then choose General: Inches.

3. Double-click Layer 1 on the Layers palette, then rename it "Circle type."

4. Choose the Ellipse tool (N), then click on the Artboard (don't drag).

5. Enter "3" in the Width field, click the word "Height," then click OK **1**.

6. On the Character palette, enter 24 in the Size field and choose a font.

7. Choose the Path-Type tool (T) **2**.

8. Click on the top of the circle.

9. Type "Type & Design" **3**.

10. Choose the Selection tool (V).

11. Drag the I–beam to the left.

12. Choose the Ellipse tool, click on the Artboard, then click OK (don't change the dimensions in the Oval dialog box).

13. Choose Path-Type tool (T).

14. Click on the bottom of new circle.

15. Enter the text "Form & Function" **4**.

16. Choose the Selection tool (V).

17. Drag the I–beam inside the circle **5**.

18. On the Character palette, enter -24 in the Baseline Shift field.

19. Move the path type to the left (move the I–beam). Don't cross over the edge of the circle **6**.

20. Apply a fill color and a stroke of None.

21. Apply the same fill color to the other type block using the Eyedropper tool.

22. Choose the Selection tool.

23. Choose View menu > Artwork.

*(Continued on the following page)*

24. Drag one circle over the other until their centers align perfectly. Press the arrow keys for precise positioning ■.

25. Choose View menu > Preview (Command-Y/Ctrl-Y).

26. Choose the Selection tool.

27. Marquee the circles.

28. Choose Object menu > Group (Command-G/Ctrl-G).

29. Double-click the Scale tool.

30. Choose Uniform, enter 125 in the Scale field, then click OK.

31. Choose Object menu > Transform > Transform Again (Command-D/Ctrl-D).

32. Save the document.

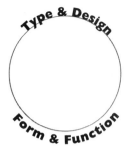

■ *Drag one circle over the other, then group both circles together.*

**To create point type for the center of the logo:**

1. Create a new layer called "Type Block" using the Layers palette.

2. Choose the Type tool.

3. Click on the Artboard, then type "Art," press Return/Enter, type "&," press Return/Enter, then type "Industry" ■.

4. Use the Type tool to select the type (Command-A/Ctrl-A).

5. Click the center alignment icon on the Paragraph palette.

6. On the Character palette, choose a font, point size, leading, and horizontal scale, and enter a Baseline shift value of 0.

7. Select the "A," choose a different font and point size, and change the fill color. Select the "I," then change the font, point size, and fill color ■.

8. Baseline shift the "A" and the "I" upward ■. Make any other style adjustments.

Art
&
Industry

■ *The original, unstyled type.*

■ *The type centered, recolored, and restyled.*

■ *The initial caps baseline shifted downward.*

Exercise: Logo

**1** *The ampersand cut and pasted into a separate type block, then resized and restyled. Place with the other type block.*

**2** *The final type block.*

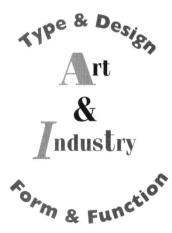

**3** *The type blocks moved inside the circle. Scale the type block, if necessary.*

**To make the "&" into a separate type block so you can resize, restack or reposition it easily:**

1. Choose the Type tool, Select the "&", then choose Edit menu > Cut.

2. Click the Type tool.

3. Click on the page to create an insertion point, then choose Edit menu > Paste.

4. Choose the Selection tool, then select the "&".

5. Choose a font, horizontal scale, fill color, and large point size **1**.

6. Drag the "&" into position with the other type block.

7. With the "&" still selected, choose Object menu > Arrange > Send to Back **2**.

8. Select the "&" and the type block, then choose Object menu > Group.

9. Save the document.

**To combine the type blocks for the logo:**

1. Choose the Selection tool.

2. Move the "ART" type block inside the circles.

**To resize the type block:**

1. Select the "ART" type.

2. Double-click the Scale tool.

3. Enter numbers in the Uniform or Non-uniform fields to enlarge or reduce the type block to fit nicely inside the circle.

4. Choose the Selection tool and adjust the position of the type block.

5. Save the document **3**.

## To add a backdrop to the logo:

1. Option/Alt click the New Layer icon on the Layers palette, enter the name "Gradient," then click OK.

2. On the Layers palette, drag the "Gradient" layer name below the other two layers.

3. Choose the Ellipse tool (N).

4. Option/Alt click on the center of the circles.

5. Enter 4.3 (inches) in the Width field, click the word "Height," then click OK.

6. Apply a gradient to the circle **1**.

## To wrap type around an object:

1. Create area type inside an object.

2. Choose the Selection tool.

3. Select the object the type is to wrap around **2**. It can be a placed image with a clipping path from Photoshop.

4. Choose Object menu > Arrange > Bring To Front.

5. Drag a marquee around both objects.

6. Choose Type menu > Wrap > Make **3**.

**TIP** Use the Direct Selection tool to move the object the type is wrapping around. To move multiple objects, first Shift-click them.

**TIP** To move the type away from the edge of the wrap object, enter values in the Left or Right Indentation fields on the Paragraph palette for the type.

**TIP** To undo the type wrap, select both objects using the Selection tool, then choose Type menu > Wrap > Release.

**TIP** To wrap type around part of a placed image (or any vector object), create an object with the desired shape for the wrap, and place that object between the type object and the placed image box. To tweak the wrap, move or adjust the object's anchor points using the Direct Selection tool.

**1** The logo further developed, with a radial gradient fill and a linear gradient fill.

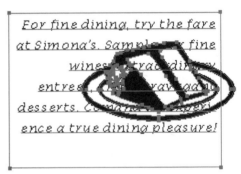

**2** Select a type object and the object the type is going to wrap around.

For fine dining, try the fare at Simona's. Sample our fine wines, scrumptious entrees, and extravagant desserts. Come and experience a true dining pleasure!

**3** The type wrap in Preview view.

# TRANSFORM

*This chapter covers the five individual transformation tools (Rotate, Scale, Reflect, Shear, and Blend), and the Transform Each command. The Transform palette is discussed on page 261 of the Precision Tools chapter.*

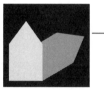 

The **Rotate** tool rotates an object around its center or around another specified point.

The **Scale** tool enlarges or reduces the size of an object proportionally or non-proportionally.

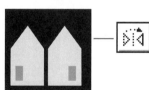

The **Reflect** tool creates a mirror image of an object across a specified axis.

The **Shear** tool slants an object in a specified direction.

The **Blend** tool transforms one object into another by creating a multi-step progression between them.

## How to use the transformation tools

The Rotate, Scale, Reflect and Shear tools transform objects from a user-defined point of origin **1**.

### Dialog box method

Select the whole object, double-click the Rotate, Scale, Reflect, or Shear tool to open the tool's dialog box (the default point of origin at the object's center will now be visible), then enter numbers in the tool dialog box.

To use a point of origin other than the object's center, select the object, choose one of the tools above, then Option/Alt click on or near the object to establish a new point of origin. A dialog box will open.

### Press-and-drag method

Select the whole object, choose the Rotate, Scale, Reflect, or Shear tool, position the cursor outside the object, then press and drag. The farther you drag, the greater the transformation.

To use a point of origin other than the object's center, select the object, choose a transformation tool, and click another location to establish a new point of origin. Reposition the mouse, then press and drag in any direction to complete the transformation **2**–**4**.

Hold down Option/Alt while dragging the arrowhead to transform a copy of the original. Release the mouse first, then release Option/Alt.

**TIP** After the point of origin is established, the cursor turns into an arrowhead. For more control, position the arrowhead far from the point of origin before dragging.

**TIP** The point of origin can also be moved by dragging it to another location.

### To repeat a transformation

Once you have transformed an object, you can transform it again using the same values by choosing Object menu > Transform > Transform Again (Command-D/Ctrl-D). If you make a copy of an object while transforming it and then apply the Transform Again command, a transformed copy of the last copy will be made. This command doesn't work with the Blend tool.

**1** *Point of origin indicator*

**2** *Click to establish a point of origin.*

**3** *Reposition the mouse.*

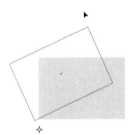
**4** *Press and drag to transform.*

Transformation Tool Methods

**204**

**1** *The shadow object is selected.*

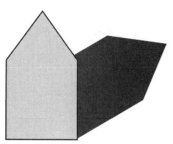

**2** *Rotate tool.*

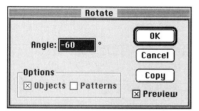

**3** *Enter a number in the **Angle** field in the **Rotate** dialog box. Click **Copy** to rotate a copy of the object.*

**4** *The shadow was rotated –60°, and then moved.*

## To rotate an object (dialog box method):

1. Select the object (or objects) **1**.
2. Double-click the Rotate tool in order to rotate the object around its center **2**.
   *or*
   Choose the Rotate tool, then Option/ Alt click near the object to establish a new point of origin.
3. Enter a number between 360 and –360 in the Angle field. Enter a positive number to rotate the object counterclockwise or a negative number to rotate the object clockwise **3**.
4. *Optional:* If the object contains a pattern fill and you check the "Patterns" box, the pattern will rotate with the object. (This option can also be turned on or off in File menu > Preferences > General.)
5. *Optional:* Click Copy to rotate a copy of the original (not the original object) and close the dialog box.
6. *Optional:* Check the Preview box to preview the rotation before closing the dialog box.
7. Click OK or press Return/Enter **4**.

**TIP** To transform type, see page 196. To transform patterns, see page 150.

## To rotate an object by dragging:

1. Select the object (or objects).
2. Choose the Rotate tool.
3. Press and drag around the object to use the object's center as the point of origin.
   *or*
   Click to establish a new point of origin (the cursor will turn into an arrowhead), reposition the mouse, then drag to rotate the object. Option/Alt drag to rotate a copy of the object (release the mouse before you release Option/Alt).

**TIP** Hold down Shift while dragging to rotate in 45° increments. Release the mouse before you release Shift.

**Rotate**

## To scale an object (dialog box method):

1. Select the object (or objects).

2. To scale the object from its center, double-click the Scale tool .
   *or*
   Choose the Scale tool, then Option/Alt click near the object to establish a new point of origin.

3. To scale the object **proportionally**:
   Choose Uniform from the drop-down menu **2**. In the Scale field, enter a number above 100 to enlarge the object or a number below 100 to reduce it.

   *Optional:* Check the "Scale line weight" box to also scale the Stroke thickness by the same percentage.
   *or*
   To scale the object **non-proportionally**: Choose Non-Uniform from the drop-down menu. In the Horizontal and/or Vertical fields, enter a number above or below 100 to enlarge or reduce that dimension **3**. Enter 100 to leave the dimension unchanged. Line weights won't scale.

4. *Optional:* Click Copy to scale a copy of the original (not the original object) and close the dialog box.

5. *Optional:* If the object contains a pattern fill and you check the "Patterns" box, the pattern will rescale with the object.

6. Click OK or press Return/Enter **4**–**6**.

 **1** *Scale tool.*

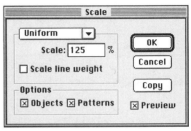

**2** *In the Scale dialog box, choose* **Uniform** *(default) to scale proportionally, then enter a Scale percentage.*

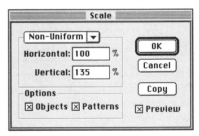

**3** *To scale non-proportionally, choose* **Non-Uniform** *and enter different* **Horizontal** *and* **Vertical** *percentages.*

Scale

**4** *The original object.*

**5** *The object and pattern scaled* **Uniformly** *(125%).*

**6** *The object and pattern scaled* **Non-uniformly** *(100% Horizontal, 135% Vertical).*

## To scale an object by dragging:

1. Select the object (or objects).

2. Choose the Scale tool.

3. Click near the object to establish a point of origin **1** (the cursor will turn into an arrowhead), reposition the mouse **2**, then press and drag away from the object to enlarge it or drag toward the object to shrink it **3**. Option/Alt drag to scale a copy of the object. It will remain selected when you release the mouse **4**.

   *or*

   To scale from the object's center, press and drag (without clicking first) away from or toward the object.

**TIP** Hold down Shift while dragging diagonally to scale the object proportionally. Release the mouse before you release Shift.

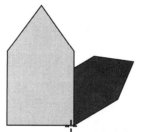

**1** *Click to establish a point of origin.*

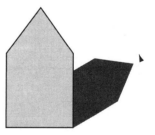

**2** *Reposition the mouse, then...*

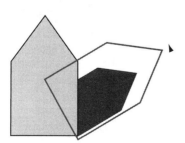

**3** *...press and drag away from the object.*

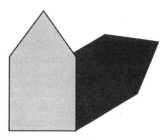

**4** *The shadow object is enlarged.*

**Scale**

207

## To reflect (flip) an object (dialog box method):

1. Select the object (or objects).

2. To reflect from the object's center, double-click the Reflect tool .
   *or*
   Choose the Reflect tool, then Option/Alt click near the object to establish a new point of origin.

3. Click the Axis: Horizontal or Vertical (the axis the mirror image will flip across) **2**.
   *or*
   Enter a number between 360 and –360 in the Angle field. Enter a positive number to rotate the object counterclockwise or a negative number to rotate the object clockwise. The angle is measured from the horizontal (x) axis.

4. *Optional:* If the object contains a pattern fill and you check the "Patterns" box, the pattern will also reflect with the object.

5. *Optional:* Click Copy to reflect a copy of the original (not the original object) and close the dialog box.

6. Click OK or press Return/Enter **3**–**4**.

## To reflect an object by dragging:

1. Select the object (or objects).

2. Choose the Reflect tool.

3. Click near the object to establish a new point of origin (the cursor will turn into an arrowhead).

4. Reposition the mouse, then press and drag towards the point of origin. The object will flip across the axis you create by dragging. (Option/Alt drag to reflect a copy of the object.)

**TIP** Hold down Shift while dragging to mirror the object in 90° increments. Release the mouse before you release Shift.

**1** *Reflect tool.*

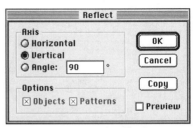

**2** *In the Reflect dialog box, click Horizontal, Vertical, or Angle, and enter a number in the Angle field, if desired.*

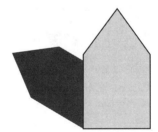

**3** *The original objects.*

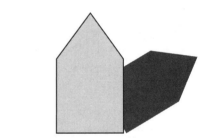

**4** *The shadow reflected across the Vertical Axis at the default angle of 90°.*

### Mirror, Mirror...

The default Horizontal angle is 0°, the default Vertical angle is 90°. The default starting point for measuring the degree of an angle is the horizontal (x) axis (3 o'clock position).

**Reflect**

**1** *The shadow object is selected.*

 **2** *Shear tool*

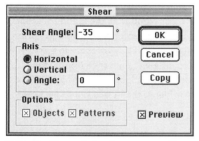

**3** *In the Shear dialog box, enter a Shear Angle, then click an Axis button.*

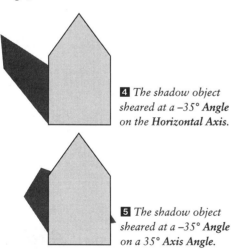

**4** *The shadow object sheared at a −35° Angle on the Horizontal Axis.*

**5** *The shadow object sheared at a −35° Angle on a 35° Axis Angle.*

## Get the numbers

Instead of entering random numbers in the dialog box, shear manually by the dragging method to get the shape you want (or close to it), then double-click the Shear tool. The exact values for that transformation will display in the dialog box.

## To shear (slant) an object (dialog box method):

1. Select the object (or objects) **1**.
2. To shear the object from its center, double-click the Shear tool **2**.
   *or*
   Choose the Shear tool, then Option/Alt click near the object to establish a new point of origin.
3. Enter a number between 360 and −360 in the Shear Angle field **3**.
4. Click the Horizontal or Vertical button (the axis along which the object will be sheared) **4**.
   *or*
   Click the Axis Angle button, then enter a number in the Axis Angle field. The angle will be calculated relative to the horizontal *(x)* axis **5**.
5. Optional: Check the Patterns box to shear a pattern fill with the object.
6. Optional: Click Copy to shear a copy of the original (not the original object) and close the dialog box.
7. Click OK or press Return/Enter.

## To shear an object by dragging:

1. Select the object (or objects).
2. Choose the Shear tool.
3. Click near the object to establish a new point of origin, reposition the mouse, then press and drag. Hold down Option/Alt while dragging to shear a copy of the object.
   *or*
   Position the cursor outside the object, then (without clicking first) press and drag away from the object. The object will slant from its center in the direction that you drag.

**TIP** To shear the object in 45° increments, start dragging, then hold down Shift. Release the mouse, then release Shift.

**Shear**

The Blend tool creates a multi-step progression between two objects. The objects can have different shapes and different fill and stroke attributes. You can blend two open paths—like lines—or two closed paths, but you can't blend an open and a closed path.

*Note:* To only blend colors between objects—not object shapes—use a Blend filter (see page 131).

## To blend (transform) one object into another:

1. Position two different-shaped open or two closed paths (objects) to allow room for the transition objects that will be created between them. You can apply different colors to them.

2. Choose the Selection tool.

3. Marquee both objects.

4. Choose the Blend tool .

5. Click an anchor point on the first object.

6. Click a corresponding anchor point on the second object ❷. For example, if you clicked on the bottom left corner of the first object, click on the bottom left corner of the second object. If the objects are open paths, click a corresponding endpoint on each.

7. Enter a number in the Steps field for the number of transition objects between the two original objects ❸. Try a low number first. (See the sidebar at right.)

8. *Optional:* Press Tab to modify the First and Last default percentages. Use differing percentages to vary where the first or last transition shape's color begins.

9. Click OK or press Return/Enter. The transition objects will be selected and grouped ❹.

## Blending steps

Illustrator automatically inserts a suggested number of steps in the Blend dialog box based on the difference in CMYK component percentages between the two objects and the assumption that the output device will be high-resolution (1200 dpi or higher). To produce a smooth transition between objects, use the suggested step number or greater—up to 1000. To output on a lower resolution printer or to produce a noticeable, banded transition, enter a lower number. Read more about this topic on page 277.

Illustrator's Gradient fill feature may produce a smoother color blend than the Blend tool, since gradients are designed for high-resolution printing. Banding is more likely to occur in a color blend if it spans a wide distance (more than seven inches). Use Adobe Photoshop to create a wide color blend, then place it into Illustrator.

❶ *Blend tool.*

*...then click here* ✕

*Click here...* ✕

❷ *Click corresponding anchor points on two selected objects.*

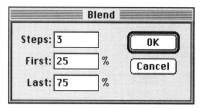

**3** *In the Blend dialog box, enter a number of transition* **Steps.**

## Process or spot?

If one of the original objects contains a process color and the other object contains a spot color, the transition objects will be painted with process colors. If you blend two tints of the same spot color, the transition objects will be painted with graduated tints of that color. To blend between a spot color and white, apply 0% of the spot color to the white object.

**TIP** After producing a blend, group the original objects and the transition objects together so you can select and move them easily.

**TIP** If you don't like the blend, press Delete while the transition objects are still selected—the original objects will remain. Select the original objects again and redo the blend.

**TIP** If you click with the Blend tool on non-corresponding points of similar objects (such as the top of one shape and the bottom of the other), the transition objects will flip or twist.

**TIP** If one object has more points than the other, rather than selecting entire objects (steps 2 and 3 on the previous page), you can use the Direct Selection tool to select the same number of similarly located points on each object.

**TIP** The transition objects will be clearly delineated if the original objects have a stroke color.

**TIP** If the blend shapes are too close together or too far apart, reposition the two outermost (original) objects and redo the blend.

**Blend Objects**

**4** *A military plane transformed into a bird by entering 3 steps in the Blend dialog box and leaving First and Last fields unchanged.*

### To make the edge of an object look three-dimensional:

1. Select the object **1**.
2. Apply a medium color fill and a stroke of None.
3. Double-click the Scale tool.
4. Choose Uniform from the drop-down menu.
5. Enter a number between 60 and 80 in the Scale field, click Copy, then click OK or press Return/Enter.
6. With the copy still selected, choose a lighter or darker variation of the original fill color **2**. (For a process color, you can hold down Shift and drag a process color slider on the Color palette to lighten or darken the color.)
7. Choose the Selection tool.
8. Marquee or Shift-click both objects.
9. Choose the Blend tool.
10. Click on an anchor point on one object.
11. Click on a similarly located anchor point on the other object.
12. Enter a number between 30 and 60 in the Steps field **3**.
    *or*
    Leave the suggested number of steps.
13. Click OK or press Return/Enter **4**.

**TIP** Make sure the smaller object is in front of the larger object before blending in order to see the blend.

**TIP** To create a 3D surface modeling effect that follows the contour of all or part of an object, create a line in the desired shape, copy it to a new location, reshape the copy, if desired, and recolor it. Select both lines, click the same end-points on each with the Blend tool, enter a number of steps, and click OK.

**1** *The original object.*

**2** *A reduced-size copy of the object is created, and a darker fill color is applied.*

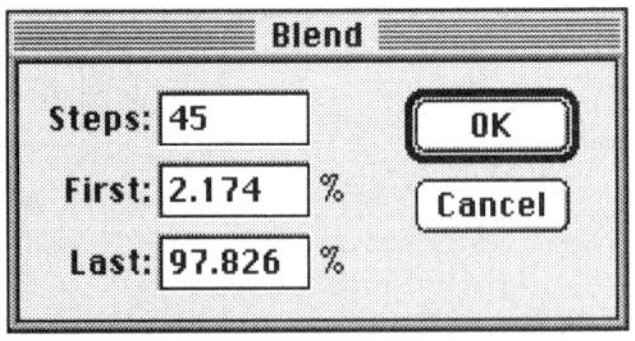


**3** *In the **Blend** dialog box, enter a number of transition **Steps**.*

**4** *The two objects are blended together.*

The original formation.

The formation rotated 15° via the Rotate tool.

The formation rotated 15° via the Transform Each command (Random box unchecked).

**1** The **Transform Each** command vs. the **Rotate** tool.

**2** Choose **Transform Each** from the Transform submenu under the Object menu.

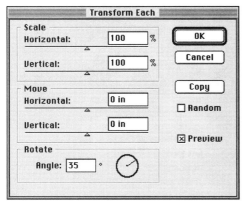

**3** The **Transform Each** dialog box.

The Transform Each command modifies one or more selected objects relative to their *individual* center points. The transformation tools, in contrast, transform multiple objects relative to a single, *common* center point **1**. To make your illustration look less regular and more hand drawn, apply the Transform Each command to multiple objects with the Random box checked.

## To apply several transformation commands at once:

1. Select one or more objects.
2. Choose Object menu > Transform > Transform Each **2**.
3. Check the Preview box **3**.

   **Perform any or all of steps 4–7:**
4. Move the Scale sliders to change the object's horizontal and/or vertical dimensions.
5. Choose a higher or lower Horizontal Move amount to move the object to the right or left, or a higher or lower Vertical Move amount to move the object up or down, respectively.
6. Enter a number in the Rotate Angle field, or rotate the dial.
7. *Optional:* Check the Random box to have Illustrator apply random transformations within the range of the slider values you've chosen in the Scale, Move, and/or Rotate fields. For example, if you set the Rotate Angle to 35°, Illustrator will use different angles between 0° and 35° for each selected object.
8. Click OK or press Return/Enter.

**TIP** Objects are scaled horizontally or vertically from their center points.

*(Illustrations on the next page)*

Transform Each

**213**

Transform Each

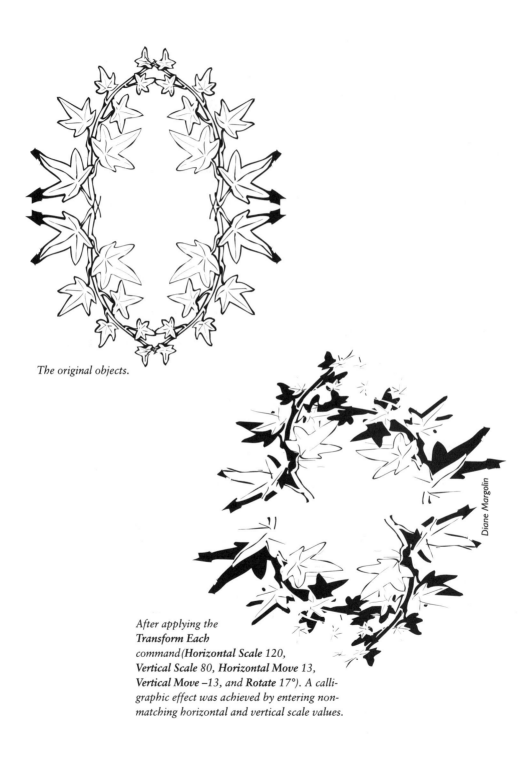

*The original objects.*

Diane Margolin

*After applying the*
**Transform Each**
*command(**Horizontal Scale** 120,*
**Vertical Scale** *80,* **Horizontal Move** *13,*
**Vertical Move** *–13, and* **Rotate** *17°). A calli-*
*graphic effect was achieved by entering non-*
*matching horizontal and vertical scale values.*

# COMPOUNDS 17

The compound path command joins two or more objects into one object. Where the original objects overlapped, a transparent hole is created, through which shapes or patterns behind the object are revealed.

In this chapter, you will learn to create a compound path using the Make Compound Paths command or the Minus Front command, to release a compound path, and to recolor parts of a compound path. The Divide command is also discussed because it can be used to create cutouts or translucent effects.

*The gray bar behind shows through the transparent areas in the compound.*

DANIEL PELAVIN

Regardless of their original paint attributes, all the objects in a compound path are painted with the attributes of the backmost object, and they're grouped.

### To create a compound path:

1. Arrange the objects you want to see through in front of a larger shape . (For these instructions, you might want to display the illustration in two windows, one in Artwork view and the other in Preview view.)

2. Choose the Selection tool.

3. Marquee or Shift-click all the objects.

4. Choose Object menu > Compound Paths > Make (Command-8/Ctrl-8) . The frontmost objects will "cut" through the backmost object –.

**TIP** Areas where the frontmost objects originally overlapped each other and parts of the frontmost objects that originally extended beyond the edge of the backmost object will be painted with the color of the backmost object.

**TIP** Use the Selection tool to select or move a whole compound path; use the Direct Selection tool to select and move a part of a compound path.

**TIP** Regardless of the layers the objects were originally on, the final compound path will be placed on the frontmost object's layer.

**TIP** Only one fill color can be applied to a compound path.

**TIP** To add an object to a compound path, select the compound path and the object you want to add to it, then choose Object menu > Compound Paths > Make.

**1** Several objects are placed on top of a larger object, and all the objects are selected.

**2** Choose **Make** from the **Compound Paths** submenu under the **Object** menu.

**3** The objects converted into a compound path.

**4** A background object is placed behind the compound path (and a white Stroke is applied).

Create a Compound Path

**1** *Click on the compound path.*

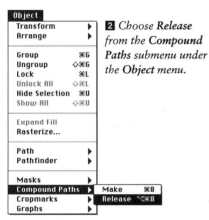

**2** *Choose Release from the Compound Paths submenu under the Object menu.*

**3** *The released compound path. The buttonholes are no longer transparent.*

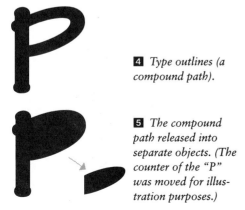

**4** *Type outlines (a compound path).*

**5** *The compound path released into separate objects. (The counter of the "P" was moved for illustration purposes.)*

You can revert a compound path back into individual objects.

## To release a compound path:

1. Choose the Selection tool.

2. Click on the compound path **1**.

3. Choose Object menu > Compound Paths > Release (Command-Option-8/Ctrl-Alt-8) **2**. All the objects will be selected and painted with the attributes from the compound path **3**.

**TIP** If you release a type outline compound path that has a counter (interior shape), the counter will become a separate shape with the same paint attributes as the outer part of the letterform **4**–**5**.

**TIP** To remove an object from a compound path without releasing the compound, select the object with the Direct Selection tool, then press Delete. Or, cut and paste the object if you want to save it.

**TIP** All objects released from a compound path will have the same stroke and fill, not their pre-compound colors. It may be difficult to distinguish overlapping objects if your illustration is in Preview view; they will be easier to distinguish in Artwork view. The objects will also stay on the same layer, regardless of which layer they were on before being assembled into a compound.

**Release a Compound Path**

**217**

You can remove the fill color of any shape in a compound and make the object transparent, or vice versa, by flicking the Reverse Path Direction switch on the Attributes palette.

### To reverse an object's fill in a compound path:

1. Choose Direct Selection tool.

2. Click on the object in the compound path whose color you want to reverse ▣.

3. Choose Window menu > Show Attributes.

4. Click the Reverse Path Direction On icon ▣ or the Reverse Path Direction Off icon ▣–▣, whichever isn't highlighted.

**TIP** If neither of the Reverse Path Direction icons are highlighted, you have selected the whole compound path. Be sure to select only one path within the compound instead.

▣ *Click on an object in the compound path.*

▣ *Reverse Path Direction Off icon*    ▣ *Reverse Path Direction On icon*

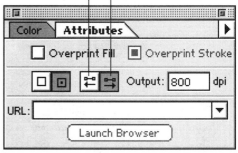

*On the **Attributes** palette, click the Reverse Path Direction Off icon or the Reverse Path Direction On icon to alter the fill of the object.*

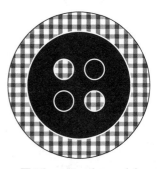

▣ *The color of two of the buttonholes has been reversed.*

**1** *The frontmost object does not extend beyond the edge of the black square.*

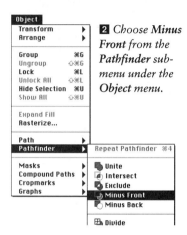

**2** *Choose **Minus Front** from the **Pathfinder** sub-menu under the Object menu.*

**3** *The box is a compound path.*

**4** *The lines extend beyond the box.*

**5** *After applying the **Minus Front** command, the box is divided into three separate objects, and is no longer a compound path.*

## To create a compound path using the Minus Front command:

1. Arrange the objects you want to combine in the compound path. Make sure the frontmost objects do not extend beyond the edge of the backmost object, otherwise you won't create a compound path **1**.

2. Choose the Selection tool.

3. Select all the objects.

4. Choose Object menu > Pathfinder > Minus Front **2**. The frontmost objects will "cut through" the backmost object **3**.

**TIP** If objects extend beyond the edge of the backmost object before you apply the Minus Front command, the backmost object will be divided into separate objects, and the overhanging objects will be deleted **4**–**5**. The result will not be a compound path, but you can create interesting effects by applying different fill colors to the separate objects.

**TIP** You can arrange smaller objects behind a larger object and then apply the Minus Back command. The smaller objects will cut through the frontmost object.

**TIP** If the frontmost object is a line, choose Object menu > Path > Outline Path to convert it into a closed path before applying the Minus Front command. Using a line in a compound path may produce irregular cutout shapes. Illustrator will automatically "fill" the line shape before using it to cut the background shape.

**Minus Front Command**

The Divide command does not create a compound path, but it can be used to a create a compound-like effect, an illusion of translucency, or a cutout.

### To apply the Divide command:

1. Arrange objects so they at least partially overlap .

2. Choose the Selection tool.

3. Marquee all the objects.

4. Choose Object menu > Pathfinder > Divide. Each area where the original objects overlapped will become a separate object.

5. Click away from all objects to deselect them.

6. Choose the Direct Selection tool.

7. Click on any of the objects and apply new fill colors or apply a fill of None to make an object transparent **2**. Or move or remove individual objects to create cutouts.

**TIP** The object's original stroke color, if any, will remain.

**1** *The original objects.*

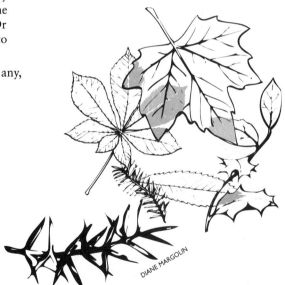

**2** *After applying the **Divide** command. Unlike in a compound path, the areas where the original objects overlapped are now separate objects. A gray fill was applied to the divided parts of the leaves to achieve an illusion of semi-transparency.*

*Divide Command*

# MASKS 18

A mask is also called a clipping path, because it clips away the parts of other shapes that extend beyond its border. Only parts of objects that are within the confines of the mask will show. Masked objects can be moved, restacked, reshaped, or repainted. In this chapter you will learn how to create a mask, how to restack, add, delete, or repaint masked objects, how to unmask an object, and how to release a mask.

Daniel Pelavin (icon appears courtesy of DFS Group, Ltd.)

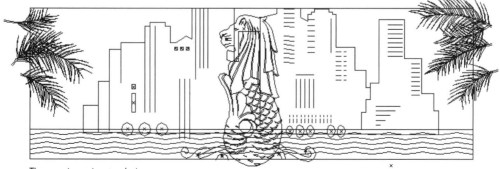

The same image in artwork view.

*Note:* To use a group of objects or use multiple type outline shapes as a single mask, you must first convert them into a compound path (choose Object menu > Compound Paths > Make).

## To create a mask:

1. *Optional:* Follow the instructions on the next page to place the masking object and the objects to be masked on one layer before you create the mask so you can easily reposition them using the Layers palette.

2. Arrange the objects to be masked **1**. The masking object can be an open or a closed path.

3. Select the masking object, then choose Object menu > Arrange > Bring to Front (Command-Shift-]/Ctrl-Shift-]) or move the object to the top layer using the Layers palette **2**.

4. Choose the Selection tool.

5. Select all the objects, including the masking object.

6. Choose Object menu > Masks > Make (Command-7/Ctrl-7) **3**. The mask will have a stroke and fill of None and all the objects will be selected. You can move masked objects individually using the Selection or Direct Selection tool. If the mask was made from a compound, use the Direct Selection tool to move individual objects.

**TIP** If the mask is too complex, it may not print. Don't make a mask out of a complex shape that contains hundreds of points or out of an intricate compound path. And don't use more than seven or eight type outline characters per compound path if you plan to then make the compound into a mask.

**TIP** To copy a masked object, drag it with Option/Alt held down. The copy will also be masked.

**1** *Arrange the objects to be masked.*

**2** *Place the masking object in front of the other objects.*

**3** *The black strokes aren't visible beyond the edge of the mask. As an extra step for this illustration, a stroke color was applied to the mask.*

Create a Mask

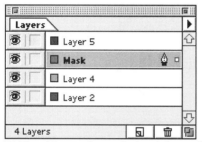

**1** *The current selection square from Layer 2 being moved up to the layer called "Mask."*

**2** *The objects to be masked and the mask are on the same layer.*

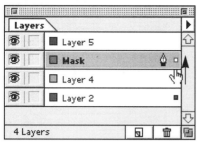

**3** *An object in a mask is selected.*

**4** *The object is brought forward.*

If the mask and objects that you select to be masked are on more than one layer, any unselected object between the backmost object in the mask and the masking object will also be masked. Follow these steps to move the objects you want to mask to their own layer, which will prevent other objects from being masked inadvertently.

### To position the objects to be masked on one layer:

1. On the Layers palette, Option/Alt click the New Layer button, enter a name ("Mask"), then click OK.

2. Choose the Selection tool.

3. Shift-click on the masking object and the objects to be masked.
   *or*
   Drag a marquee over the masking object and all the objects to be masked.

4. On the Layers palette, drag the current selection squares up or down to the new layer **1**–**2**.

5. Follow the instructions on the previous page to create a mask.

**TIP** You can also select all the objects (step 4) and then group them, which will automatically put them on one layer.

Stacking is explained in Chapter 12.

### To restack a masked object:

1. Choose the Selection tool.

2. Select the object to be restacked.

3. Choose Object menu > Arrange > Bring Forward (Command-]/Ctrl-]) or Send Backward (Command-[/Ctrl-[) **3**–**4**.
   *or*
   Choose Edit menu > Cut, select another masked object, then choose Edit menu > Paste In Front or Paste In Back.

**Re-Layer or Re-Stack Masked Objects**

## To select mask objects:

To select the mask *and* the masked objects, choose the Group Selection tool (or hold down Option/Alt with the Direct Selection tool), then double-click on any of the objects.

To select *one or more* individual masked objects, use the Selection tool.

If you haven't applied a Fill or Stroke color to the mask, it will be invisible in Preview view. To select *only* the mask when your illustration is in Preview view, choose the Selection tool, then drag across where you think the edge of the mask is. If your illustration is in Artwork view, choose the Selection tool, then click on the edge of the mask.

To select *all* the masks in your illustration, deselect all objects, then choose Edit menu > Select > Masks. Shift-click with the Selection tool on any mask you don't want selected.

**TIP** To convert a gradient or a pattern into a grouped set of masked objects, select an object that contains a gradient or pattern fill, then choose Object menu > Expand Fill.

## To add an object to a mask:

1. Choose the Selection tool.
2. Select the object to be added.
3. Move the object over the mask **1**.
4. Choose Edit menu > Cut.
5. Click on a masked object.
6. Choose Edit menu > Paste In Front (Command-F/Ctrl-F) or Paste In Back (Command-B/Ctrl-B). The new object will be masked and will be stacked in front of or behind the object you selected **2**.

**TIP** Follow the instructions on the previous page if you want to change the stacking position of the newly pasted object.

## Is it a mask?

To find out whether an object is a mask, select the object, then choose File menu > Selection Info. Choose Objects from the Info drop-down menu. If the Masks entry has the number 1 after it, then the object is a mask.

**1** *Move the object you want to add over the mask.*

**2** *The object is added to the mask.*

**1** *Select the object you want to unmask.*

**2** *The object is now unmasked.*

## To unmask an object:

1. Choose the Selection tool.

2. Click on the object you want to unmask **1**.

3. Choose Edit menu > Cut (Command-X/Ctrl-X).

4. *Optional:* If the mask and masked objects are on different layers, highlight a layer on the Layers palette that is above or below those layers.

5. Choose Edit menu > Paste (Command-V/Ctrl-V). The pasted object will now be independent of the mask. Reposition it, if you like **2**.

**TIP** To unmask an object another way, select the object, then, on the Layers palette, drag the current selection square to a different layer.

**TIP** To unmask an object and delete it from the illustration, select it, then press Delete.

When you release a mask, the complete objects are displayed again. If no fill or stroke was applied to the masking object, that object will not display in Preview view.

## To release a mask:

1. Choose the Group Selection tool (press "A" to toggle between the Direct Selection and Group Selection tools).

2. Double-click on the mask or click on the masking object.

3. Choose Object menu > Masks > Release (Command-Option-7/Ctrl-Alt-7) **3**.

**3** *The mask is released.*

To apply a fill and/or stroke color to a mask for the first time, you must use the Fill & Stroke for Mask filter. Once you have done so, you can then recolor the mask as you would any other object.

*Note:* To recolor a masked object, just use the Color and Tools palettes.

### To fill and/or stroke a mask:

1. Choose the Group Selection tool and select the whole mask **1**.

2. Choose Filter menu > Create > Fill & Stroke for Mask. The filter produces a CMYK gray fill and a CMYK black stroke, each of which is a separate object. The fill object will be behind the masked objects. The stroke object will be in front of, but not part of, the mask.

3. Select the fill or the stroke object with the Selection tool and repaint it using the Fill and Stroke boxes on the Toolbox and the Color palette **2**–**4**.

4. If the masked objects are on the same layer, the fill object will be masked. If the masked objects are on more than one layer, the fill object will not be masked.

5. *Optional:* To group the stroke object with the mask, choose the Selection tool, press and drag a marquee across the mask and the stroke object, then choose Object menu > Group (Command-G/Ctrl-G).

**1** *The original mask.*

**2** *A Black fill was applied to the mask. The masked objects were also repainted.*

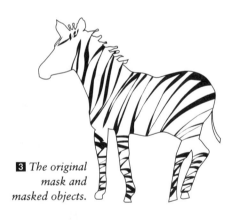

**3** *The original mask and masked objects.*

**4** *The repainted mask and masked objects.*

# FILTERS 19

This chapter covers many of Illustrator's powerful
and easy-to-use object reshaping and bitmap image
enhancing filters.

*The **last-used filter**
(Command-E/Ctrl-E).
Choose to reapply the fil-
ter using the same settings.*

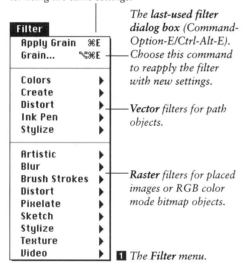

*The **last-used filter**
dialog box (Command-
Option-E/Ctrl-Alt-E).
Choose this command
to reapply the filter
with new settings.*

*—**Vector** filters for path
objects.*

*—**Raster** filters for placed
images or RGB color
mode bitmap objects.*

**1** *The **Filter** menu.*

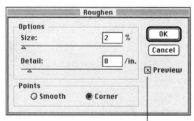

**2** *Many filter dialog boxes have a **Preview**
option. Turn it on to preview the filter
effect in your illustration while the dialog
box is open. Press **Tab** to preview after
entering a new amount in an entry field.*

Some of Illustrator's filters **1** are designed
primarily for use with path objects, and
they are grouped in five submenu categories:
Color, Create, Distort, Ink Pen, and Stylize.
Several of these filters are discussed in the
pages that follow.

Other Illustrator filters are designed for use
with bitmap images or rasterized objects,
and they are grouped in nine submenus
categories at the bottom of the Filter menu:
Artistic, Blur, Brush Strokes, Distort,
Pixelate, Sketch, Stylize, Texture, and
Video. If you're a Photoshop user, you may
already be familiar with them. The raster
filters are discussed and illustrated in the
latter part of this chapter.

For a filter to be accessible in Illustrator, it
must be in Illustrator's Plug-ins folder when
the application is launched.

You can also apply Photoshop-compatible
filters to placed images and to objects rasterized in Illustrator. To make them accessible in Illustrator, copy the filters (or aliases
of the filters) into a new folder in the
Photoshop Filters folder inside Illustrator's
Plug-ins folder.

Some filters are applied simply by selecting
the filter name from a submenu. Other
filters are applied via a dialog box in
which special options are chosen **2**. You'll
probably also want to memorize the two
keyboard shortcuts listed at left.

Some Illustrator filters are covered in
other chapters. Look in the index for page
locations.

The Object Mosaic filter breaks up a raster image into a grid of little squares, each of which is a separate object that can be moved individually.

### To apply the Object Mosaic filter:

1. Click on a rasterized object, or on a PICT, TIFF, or parsed (non-linked) EPS bitmap image.

2. Choose Filter menu > Create > Object Mosaic.

3. *Optional:* The Current Size field displays the width and height of the image in points 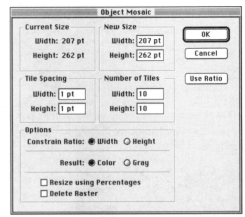. Enter new numbers in the New Size: Width and/or Height fields. (If you want to enter the dimensions in percentages relative to the original, first check the Resize using Percentages box.)
   *or*
   Enter a new Width (or Height), click Constrain Ratio: Width (or Height) to lock in that dimension, then click Use Ratio (right size of the dialog box) to have Illustrator automatically calculate the opposite dimension proportionate to the object's original dimensions.

4. Enter the Number of Tiles to fill the width and height dimensions. If you clicked Use Ratio, the Number of Tiles will be calculated automatically.

5. *Optional:* To add space between each tile, enter numbers in the Tile Spacing: Width and Height fields.

6. *Optional:* When it's applied to a bitmap image, the Object Mosaic filter affects a copy of the image that's made automatically, and the original is left unchanged. Check the Delete Raster box if you want the original image to be deleted.

7. Click Result: Color or Gray.

8. Click OK or press Return/Enter **2**–**4**.

**1** *In the* **Object Mosaic** *dialog box, enter numbers in the* **New Size** *and* **Number of Tiles** *fields.*

**2** *The original PICT.*

**3** *The* **Object Mosaic** *filter applied with the Width or Height unchanged.*

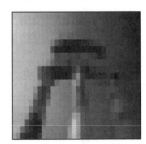

**4** *The* **Object Mosaic** *filter applied,* **Use Ratio** *option not clicked and the Height value changed.*

**1** *The original object.*

**2** *Drag any corner points of the rectangle in the Free Distort dialog box.*

**3** *After applying the Free Distort filter.*

## To apply the Free Distort filter:

1. Select an object or objects **1**.

2. Choose Filter menu > Distort > Free Distort.

3. Drag any corner point or points of the rectangle that surrounds the object(s) in the dialog box **2**. You can drag it beyond the edges of the dialog box.

4. Check the Show Me box to preview the shape in the dialog box.

5. *Optional:* Click Reset if you want to restore the original object and its surrounding rectangle in the preview window.

6. Click OK or press Return/Enter **3**–**5**.

**TIP** If the object is complex, it may not render accurately in the preview box, but it will be drawn accurately in the illustration.

**TIP** To apply the Free Distort filter to type, you must first convert the type to outlines (select it using a selection tool, then choose Type menu > Create Outlines).

**Free Distort Filter**

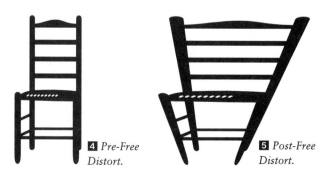

**4** *Pre-Free Distort.*

**5** *Post-Free Distort.*

## To scribble or tweak:

1. Select an object or objects.

2. Choose Filter menu > Distort > Scribble and Tweak.

3. Check the Preview box **1**.

4. Choose Scribble or Tweak from the drop-down menu. Scribble moves points randomly, Tweak moves points the exact amounts you specify.

5. Choose Horizontal and Vertical amounts (calculated as a percentage of the longest segment of the object) to specify how much an anchor point or a segment can be moved (Scribble) or will actually move (Tweak).

6. Check the Anchor Points, "In" Control Points or "Out" Control Points boxes to choose which points on the path will be moved.

7. Click OK or press Return/Enter **2**–**3**. Direction lines will be added automatically to the corner points of paths that have straight sides. How these new direction lines are moved depends on the "In" and "Out" options you chose.

**TIP** The greater the number of anchor points on the path, the greater the Scribble filter effect. To add points to an object, apply the Add Anchor Points command (Object menu > Path).

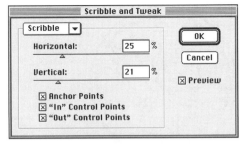

**1** *The Scribble and Tweak dialog box.*

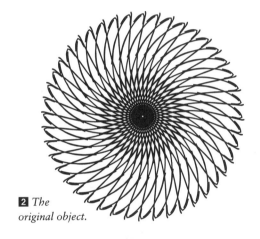

**2** *The original object.*

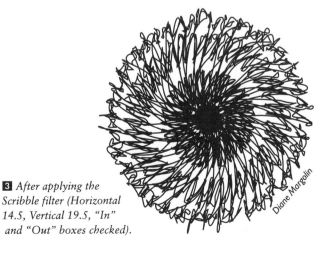

**3** *After applying the Scribble filter (Horizontal 14.5, Vertical 19.5, "In" and "Out" boxes checked).*

Diane Margolin

**1** *The **Roughen** dialog box.*

**2** *The original object.*

**3** *After applying the **Roughen** filter (or seeing a dog).*

The Roughen filter makes an object look more hand drawn by adding anchor points and then moving them.

### To rough up a shape:

1. Select an object or objects, and choose View menu > Hide Edges (Command-H/Ctrl-H), if you like, to make previewing easier.

2. Choose Filter menu > Distort > Roughen.

3. Check the Preview box **1**.

4. Move the Size slider (a percentage of the object's longest path segment) to specify how far points can be moved. Try a low number first.

5. Move the Detail slider (how many points will be added to each inch of the path segments).

6. Click Smooth to produce soft edges or click Corner to produce Sharp edges.

7. Click OK or press Return/Enter **2**–**3**.

**4** *The original objects.*

**5** *The objects twirled together, Angle 1000°.*

**6** *The **Twirl** filter applied to **5**, Angle 3000°.*

### To twirl path points around an object's center (dialog box method):

1. Select an object or objects **4**. If two or more objects are selected, they will be twirled together.

2. Choose Filter menu > Distort > Twirl.

3. Enter a number between -3600 and 3600 in the Angle field. Enter a positive number to twirl the paths clockwise; enter a negative number to twirl them counterclockwise.

4. Click OK or press Return/Enter **5**–**6**.

**TIP** To add points to a path and heighten the Twirl filter effect, choose Object menu > Path > Add Anchor Points before applying the Twirl filter.

Roughen Filter; Twirl Filter

Like the Twirl filter, the Twirl tool twirls points around an object's center, but its effect is usually subtler.

### To twirl points around an object's center (mouse method):

1. Select an object.

2. Choose the Twirl tool (press "R" to toggle between the Rotation and Twirl tools) .

3. *Optional:* Click if you want to establish the center of the twirl.

4. Move the mouse slightly away from the center point (if one was established), then drag clockwise around the object to twirl it clockwise or drag counter-clockwise to twirl the object counter-clockwise. Repeat to intensify the twirl effect ▨–▨.

**TIP** To open the Twirl dialog box, Option/Alt click in the document window with the Twirl tool.

**TIP** Neither the Twirl tool nor the Twirl filter will affect a pattern or a gradient fill—they will only twirl an object's outer shape. To twirl a pattern or gradient fill, apply the Object menu > Expand Fill command to the object first to break the pattern or gradient up into discrete shapes. A document containing numerous expanded and twirled objects will be large in size, though, and may not print easily.

**1** *The Twirl tool.*

**2** *The original objects.*

**3** *After twirling.*

**4** *Before twirling.*          **5** *After slight twirling.*

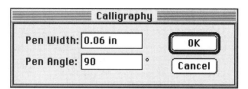

**1** *Enter numbers in the **Pen Width** and **Pen Angle** fields in the **Calligraphy** dialog box.*

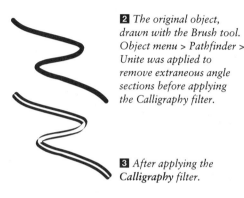

**2** *The original object, drawn with the Brush tool. Object menu > Pathfinder > Unite was applied to remove extraneous angle sections before applying the Calligraphy filter.*

**3** *After applying the **Calligraphy** filter.*

The Calligraphy filter produces a thick-and-thin line like the Brush tool produces when used with its Calligraphic option. Unlike the Brush tool, however, the Calligraphy filter can be applied to an object after it's drawn.

**To create calligraphic edges:**

1. Select any object except a type object.
2. Choose Filter menu > Stylize > Calligraphy.
3. Enter a number between .02 and 55.55 in. in the Pen Width field (the width of the thickest part of the stroke) **1**.
4. Enter a number in the Pen Angle field.
5. Click OK or press Return/Enter **2**–**7**. The Calligraphy filter will convert an open path—like a line—into a closed path. If the object is a filled, closed path, the filter will remove its center area and create a thick-and-thin, ribbon-like fill along its edge. To retain the fill, work on a copy of the path.

**4** *The original object. This flower was drawn with the Pencil tool.*

**6** *The original object.*

**5** *After applying the **Calligraphy** filter.*

**7** *After applying the **Calligraphy** filter.*

Calligraphy Filter

**233**

Drop shadow objects that the Drop Shadow filter creates are colored in a darker shade of the object's fill and stroke colors. (To produce a shadow by copying an object, see page 197.)

### To create a drop shadow:

1. Select one or more objects . The filter can be applied to type.

2. Choose Filter menu > Stylize > Drop Shadow.

3. Enter a number in the X Offset field (the horizontal distance between the object and the shadow) and a number in the Y Offset field (the vertical distance) **2**.

4. In the Intensity field, enter the percentage of black to be added to the object's fill color to produce the shadow color. 100% will produce solid black.

5. *Optional:* Check the Group Shadows box to group the object with its shadow.

6. Click OK or press Return/Enter **3**. You can recolor the shadow.

**TIP** If the objects are type outlines and you check the Group Shadows box, each character will be grouped individually with its shadow. Instead, you can select the original type shapes with the Selection tool, group them, apply the Drop Shadow filter with the Group Shadows box unchecked, and then group the shadow letters by themselves.

*The original object.*

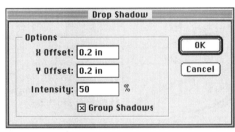

**2** *In the* **Drop Shaadow** *dialog box, enter* **X** *and* **Y** *Offset values and the percentage the shadow color will be* **Darker** *than the object's fill color.*

**3** *With a drop shadow.*

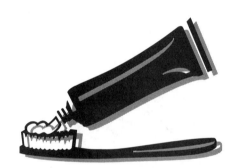

### Texturize the shadow

Apply the Drop Shadow filter with the "Group shadows box" unchecked. Select the shadow shapes, apply Object menu > Rasterize, then apply Filter menu > Artistic > Rough Pastels (Stroke Length: around 13, Stroke Detail: around 3, Texture: Sandstone, Scaling: 100%, Relief: 36, Light Dir: Top Left. Click Preview). As an optional step, apply Filter menu > Distort > Glass (Smoothness: 1–2, Distortion: 1–2, Texture: Frosted, Scaling: 125%) **4**.

*Drop Shadow Filter*

**gothic horror**

**1** *The original objects (type outlines).*

**2** *After applying the Punk filter.*

**3** *The original objects (type outlines).*

**4** *After applying the Punk filter.*

## To punk or bloat an object:

1. Select an object or objects **1** and **3**.

2. Choose Filter menu > Distort > Punk & Bloat.

3. Check the Preview box.

4. Move the slider to the left to Punk (anchor points move outward and curve segments move inward, or move the slider to the right to Bloat (anchor points move inward and curve segments move outward).

5. Click OK **2** and **4**.

**TIP** To add points to the path and intensify the Punk or Bloat effect, choose Object menu > Path > Add Anchor Points before applying the filter. See also Figures **1**–**3** on page 80.

### And a couple of third-party filters...

*A fish is selected.*

```
┌─────── Gefilte ───────┐
│                       │
│  Number: [1        ]  │
│                       │
│    ⊠ Bitter herbs     │
│                       │
│   ( Cancel )  [ OK ]  │
│                       │
└───────────────────────┘
```

*The **Gefilte** dialog box.*

*An amphibian is selected.*

```
┌─────── Evolution ───────┐
│  ○ Amphibian            │
│  ○ Neanderthal          │
│  ⊙ Sensitive male       │
│  Sensitivity:           │
│  Coarse    △     Fine   │
│   ( Cancel )   [ OK ]   │
└─────────────────────────┘
```

*The **Evolution** dialog box.*

*Sensitive male.*

**235**

The Ink Pen filter creates an amazing assortment of line work patterns by turning an object into a mask and then creating line work shapes behind the mask. You can choose from 25 preset pen patterns—called hatch styles—that you can use as is or further modify using a wide variety of options. You can also create a new hatch style from scratch from an Illustrator object.

### To apply the Ink Pen filter:

1. Select an object.

2. Choose Filter menu > Ink Pen > Effects.

3. Check the Preview box. If you find the preview slows things down too much, uncheck it.

4. Choose a predefined effect from the topmost drop-down menu **1**.

   If you're satisfied with the pattern, click OK. To further modify it, follow any of the remaining steps.

5. Choose a predefined hatch style from the Hatch drop-down menu.

6. Move the Density slider to adjust the number of hatches in the fill. You can click a tone on the vertical bar on the right side of the dialog box to change the hatch density.

7. For any of the following options, choose an option from the bottommost drop-down menu. Choose a setting other than None from the drop-down menu on the right side, and move one or both of the sliders.

   Dispersion increases/decreases the amount hatch shapes are scattered **2**.

   Thickness increases/decreases the line thickness of the hatch shapes. This property is only available for hatch styles that are composed of lines (Cross, Crosshatch 1, Vertical Lines, and Worm) **3**.

   Rotation increases/decreases the amount the hatch shapes are rotated **4**.

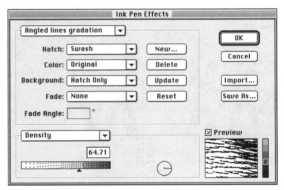

**1** The **Ink Pen Effects** dialog box showing hatch settings.

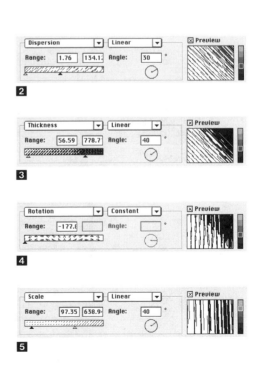

Ink Pen Filter

## The hatch style drop-down menu options

*None:* No effect.

*Constant:* Effect repeats without changing across the entire shape.

*Linear:* Effect changes from one side of the fill shape to the other in a straight-line progression.

*Reflect:* Effect changes starting from the center of the fill shape outward.

*Symmetric:* Like Linear, but more proportionate and even.

*Random:* Effect changes in a random, haphazard fashion across the fill shape.

The Linear, Reflect, Symmetric and Random options have two sliders each, and their position determines the range of choices for that option. The wider the distance between a pair of sliders, the wider the range of possibilities for that option. Enter a value in the Angle box to specify an axis for the change. Press Tab to preview an Angle change.

## Big hairy monster?

Ink Pen Fills can be quite complex, and their direction lines and line endpoints may extend way beyond the edge of the original object. To prevent accidentally selecting an Ink Pen Fill, put the Ink Pen object on its own layer and then lock that layer.

If your Ink Pen fill doesn't print, try reducing the object's Output resolution (see page 275). Also, don't apply the Ink Pen filter to an object that already contains an Ink Pen fill—it will demand too much from your output device.

Scale increases/decreases the size of the hatch shapes **5**.

8. From the Color drop-down menu, choose whether the hatch will keep its original color or will match the currently selected object's fill color.

9. From the Background drop-down menu, choose whether the object will retain its fill color or will have a fill of None.

10. From the Fade drop-down menu, choose whether the hatch style will fade To Black or To White across the fill shape. If the object's fill was a gradient, choose Use Gradient to color the hatch style with the gradient. If you like, you can enter an angle for the axis along which the fade will occur. Press Tab to preview the angle effect.

11. Click OK or press Return/Enter.

**TIP** To save properties or style changes to a separate custom hatch set file that can be imported into other documents, click Save As, enter a name in the Hatch Set Name field, choose a location in which to save the file, then click Save.

**TIP** To import hatch settings, click Import, locate and highlight the hatch file, then click Select.

**TIP** To save any properties and style options changes to a custom settings variation, click New, enter a name in the Settings Name field, then click OK.

**TIP** Click Delete to delete an existing Settings variation. Warning: This can't be undone by the Undo command or by pressing Cancel in the Ink Pen Effects dialog box and then performing another operation.

**TIP** Click Update to save the current property and style options to the current Settings variant. Warning: Update overwrites existing variant settings.

**TIP** To adjust the density of the hatch style a different way, click a different gray on the grayscale bar next to the preview window.

**Ink Pen Filter**

The hatch is the underlying pattern tile that is used by the Ink Pen filter.

### To create a new hatch style pattern:

1. Create a small object or objects to use as the pattern.

2. Select the object or objects.

3. Choose Filter menu > Ink Pen > Hatches.

4. Click New.

5. Enter a Name for the hatch, then click OK or press Return/Enter.

6. The new pattern will display in the preview window if you check the Preview box. Click OK or press Return/Enter to close the Ink Pen Edit dialog box. The hatch will save with the current document.

**TIP** Click Delete to remove the currently chosen hatch style from the Hatch drop-down menu. This can't be undone.

**TIP** Click Save as to save the hatch in a separate file that can be imported into other documents by clicking Import in the Ink Pen Effects dialog box.

### To modify an existing hatch style pattern:

1. Scroll to a blank area of the Artboard, and deselect.

2. Choose Filter menu > Ink Pen > Hatches.

3. Choose the pattern you want to edit from the Hatch drop-down menu.

4. Click Paste.

5. Click OK or press Return/Enter. The hatch pattern objects will be selected. Zoom in, if you need to.

6. Modify the hatch pattern.

7. Reselect the hatch pattern object.

8. Follow steps 3–6 in the previous set of instructions (and reread the tips).

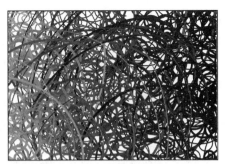

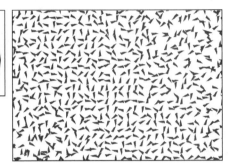

*A spiral hatch with a Fade to white.*

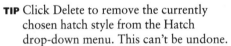

*Using the hatch in the small illustration at left.*

*Vertical lines with Fade to white.*

*Worm hatch with symmetric settings.*

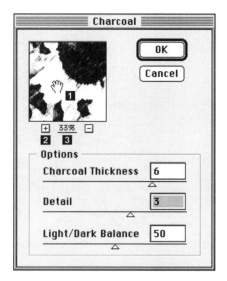

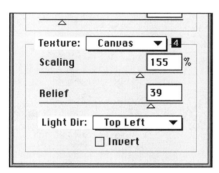

**5** *Rough Pastels filter, Burlap texture.*

## The raster filters

Illustrator's raster filters can be applied to rasterized objects or placed bitmap images (both in the RGB color space). Some of these filters introduce an element of randomness or distortion that would be difficult to achieve by hand. Others, like the Artistic, Brush Strokes, Sketch, and Texture filters, are designed to make an image look a little less machine-made, and more hand rendered.

## Using a raster filter dialog box

Raster filter dialog boxes have a Preview window. Drag in the preview window to move the image inside it **1**.

Click the "+" button to zoom in on the image in the preview box, or click the "–" button to zoom out **2**.

A flashing line below the preview size percentage indicates the filter effect is still rendering in the preview window **3**.

Hold down Option/Alt and click Reset to reset the slider settings to what they were when the dialog box opened.

When a raster filter is applied to a large, high resolution bitmap image, a progress bar displays while the filter is processing. Click Stop or press Return/Enter to cancel a filter in progress.

In some filter dialog boxes, like Rough Pastels, Grain, and Fresco, there are texture and/or relief setting options. Choose a texture type from the Texture pop-up menu **4**–**5**, move the Scaling slider to enlarge or reduce the size of the texture pattern, and move the Relief slider, if there is one, to adjust the depth and prominence of the texture on the image's surface. In some dialog boxes you'll also have the option to load in a bitmap image saved in Photoshop format to use instead of a preset texture. To do this, choose Load Texture from the Texture drop-down menu, highlight the name of the bitmap file you want to use, then click Open.

**Raster Filters**

## *The raster filters illustrated*

### Artistic filters

Original image

Colored Pencil

Cutout

Dry Brush

Film Grain

Fresco

Neon Glow

Paint Daubs

Palette Knife

Artistic Filters

## Artistic filters

Original image

Plastic Wrap

Poster Edges

Rough Pastels

Smudge Stick

Sponge

Underpainting

Watercolor

## Blur filter

Original image

Radial Blur

## Brush Strokes filters

Original image

Accented Edges

Angled Strokes

Crosshatch

Dark Strokes

Ink Outlines

## Brush Strokes filters

Spatter

Sprayed Strokes

Sumi-e

## Distort filters

Original image

Diffuse Glow

Glass

Ocean Ripple

**243**

## Pixelate filters

Original image

Color Halftone

Crystallize

Mezzotint (Short Strokes)

Mezzotint (Medium Dots)

Pointillize

## Stylize filter

Original image

Glowing Edges

## Sketch filters

Original image

Bas Relief

Chalk & Charcoal

Charcoal

Chrome

Conté Crayon

Graphic Pen

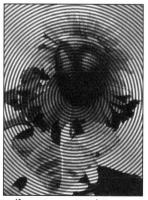

Halftone Pattern (Circle)

Halftone Pattern (Dot)

## Sketch filters

Original image

Note Paper

Photocopy

Plaster

Reticulation

Stamp

Torn Edges

Water Paper

# Texture filters

Original image

Craquelure

Grain Enlarged

Grain Horizontal

Mosaic Tiles

Patchwork

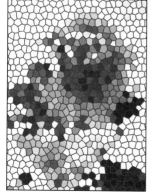

Stained Glass

Texturizer

**Texture Filters**

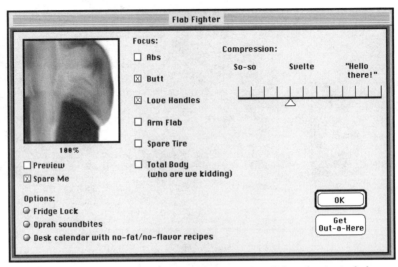

*Flab Fighter filter from Mend-Your-Ways Software, Inc. Other plug-ins include: Stop Smoking and Rediscover Your Furniture, OS Installation Suicide Rescue Line, and Life Beyond Computers.*

### Stuff you can do to a placed image

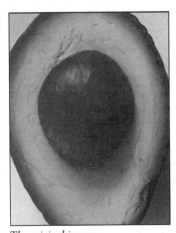

*The original image.*

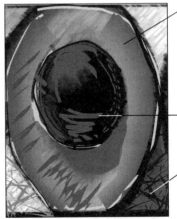

*After applying the Sketch > Chalk & Charcoal filter to the placed image. Colors > Adjust Color was also used to lighten the image and convert it to grayscale.*

*A blend was created between two different-colored lines to create a shading effect.*

*The Pencil and Paintbrush tools were used to draw strokes.*

*The Ink Pen > Effects filter was used in this corner and in the lower left corner.*

# GRAPHS 20

Nine different graph styles can be created in Illustrator: Column, stacked column, bar, stacked bar, line, area, scatter, pie, and radar. Explaining Illustrator's elaborate graphing features in depth is beyond the scope of this book. However, this chapter contains learn-by-example instructions for creating a simple grouped column graph and then customizing the graph design. Also included are general guidelines for creating other types of graphs. Alternate design and graph style variations are discussed in the Tips.

See the Illustrator User Guide for more information about creating graphs. Also, check out the files in the Adobe Illustrator folder > Sample Files > Graphs & Graph Design, which contain graph examples and artwork for custom graph designs.

*The nine graph style tools.*

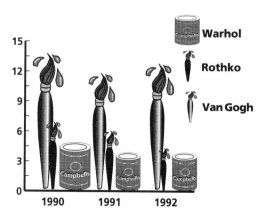

## The basic graph-making steps

1) Define the graph **area**
2) Enter graph **data** and **labels**
3) Choose **graph style** options
4) Add custom **design** elements

A graph created in Illustrator is a group of objects. As long as a graph remains grouped, its data and/or style can be changed. As with any group, individual elements in a graph can be selected using the Direct Selection or Group Selection tool and then modified without having to ungroup the whole graph.

**249**

## To define the graph area:

Choose the Graph tool , then press and drag diagonally.

*or*

Choose the Graph tool, click on your page, enter numbers in the Width and Height fields, then click OK **2**. The Graph data dialog box will open automatically.

**TIP** You can use the Scale tool to resize the whole graph later on.

The Graph Data dialog box is like a worksheet, with rows and columns for entering numbers and labels. Most graphs are created in an x/y axis formation. The y-axis (vertical) is numerical and shows the data in quantities. The x-axis (horizontal) represents information categories.

## To enter graph data:

1. For this exercise, enter the data shown in **3** into the cells in the Graph data dialog box. Be sure to enter quotation marks with the dates in the first column. If you enter any letters with the numbers, no quotes are needed. (For other graphs, you can click the Import button to import a tab-delineated text file or a file from a spreadsheet application.)

   Click a cell, type the entry, then:

   Press Tab to move across a row.
   *or*
   Press Return to move down a column.
   *or*
   Click on any row or column cell.
   *or*
   Press any arrow key.

2. On the top row of the worksheet, enter the labels. These will appear next to the legend boxes in the graph.

3. Click the close box **4**.

   **TIP** If you make a mistake when entering data, click on the incorrect data cell, correct the error in the highlighted entry line, then press Tab or Return/Enter to accept the correction.

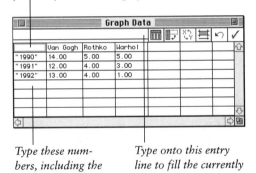

**1** *Graph tool.*

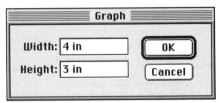

**2** *Enter **Width** and **Height** dimensions for a new graph in the **Graph** dialog box.*

*Do not enter any data in this first cell for a Column graph.*

| | Van Gogh | Rothko | Warhol |
|---|---|---|---|
| "1990" | 14.00 | 5.00 | 5.00 |
| "1991" | 12.00 | 4.00 | 3.00 |
| "1992" | 13.00 | 4.00 | 1.00 |

*Type these numbers, including the quotaton marks.*

*Type onto this entry line to fill the currently highlighted cell.*

**3** *The **Graph data** dialog box.*

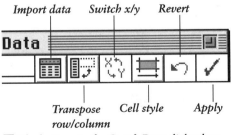

Import data   Switch x/y   Revert

Transpose row/column   Cell style   Apply

**4** *The buttons in the **Graph Data** dialog box.*

**1** *Drag this line to the right to make the second column wider.*

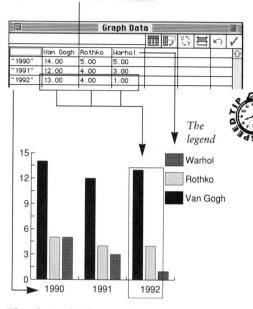

*The relationship between data on the worksheet and the parts of the graph.*

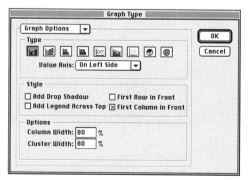

**2** *The Graph Type dialog box with Graph Options displayed.*

**TIP** To make a column wider to accommodate a long label name, drag the vertical column line to the right **1**.

**TIP** To make a legend name appear on two lines, enter "|", which you get with this keystroke: Shift-\ (backslash) in the line where you want the name to break.

**TIP** To preview the new graph while the Graph data dialog box is open, click the Apply (check mark) button. Move the dialog box to the side if you need to.

The Graph Type dialog box contains three different option screens: graph choice (Graph Options), vertical axis (Value Axis) and horizontal axis (Category Axis).

### To style the graph:

1. Select the whole graph (use the Selection tool), then choose Object menu > Graphs > Type (or double-click the Graph tool).

2. For this exercise, click the Column (first) icon **2**. This graph type is a good choice if you want to compare two or three entities over several time periods.

3. Enter 80 in the Options: Column Width field to make the individual columns narrower. With a Cluster Width of 80%, the three column shapes will spread across only 80% of the horizontal area allotted for each *x*-axis category.

4. For this exercise, choose On Left Side from the Value Axis drop-down menu. The Value Axis options affect how and where the *x/y* axis appears.

5. To style the vertical axis, choose Value Axis from the top drop-down menu. For this exercise, leave the default Override Calculated Values box checked. Illustrator will scale the *y*-axis automatically based on the largest and smallest numbers entered on the worksheet. (Uncheck this box to enter your

(Continued on the following page)

**Style the Graph**

**251**

own maximum and minimum values and number of divisions for the *y*-axis.)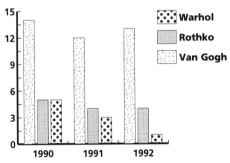

6. The middle part of the dialog box is used for styling the vertical axis tick lines (the small lines perpendicular to the axis lines). For this exercise, choose Short from the Length drop-down menu and enter 2 in the "Draw…tick marks per division" field to add an extra tick mark between each *y*-axis number.

7. Click OK **2**.

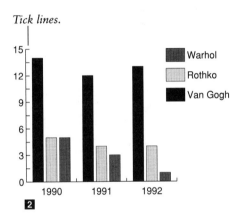

**1** *The Graph Type dialog box with Value Axis options displayed. Choose Tick Values (size of axis), Tick Marks, and Add Label options for the vertical axis.*

## To customize the graph

You can move, transform or modify the fill and/or stroke of an individual object in a graph if you select it first with the Group Selection tool.

**TIP** To restack part of a graph, select a whole group (i.e., the bars and their legend or an axis and its tick marks) with the Group Selection tool, then choose Object menu > Arrange > Bring To Front or Send To Back.

### To recolor the columns/legend:

*(In this "Artists Graph": Warhol, Rothko, Van Gogh)*

1. Choose the Group Selection tool.

2. Double-click on a legend rectangle to select the legend and its three related columns.

3. Change the fill and/or stroke for the legend—the related column objects will also change **3**. Repeat for the other rectangles.

**TIP** You can also click on a column with the Group Selection tool to select it, click a second time to add its related columns to the selection, then click a third time to add its legend to the selection. Or, use the Direct Selection tool with Option/Alt held down instead of using the Group Selection tool.

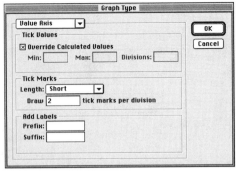

**2**

**3** *To restyle this column graph, new fill patterns were applied to the legend rectangles and their related columns, a heavier stroke weight was applied to the axes, and the type in the graph was changed.*

Customize a Graph

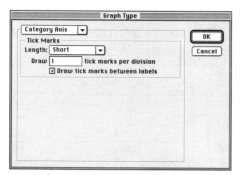

## Don't forget the horizontal axis

This is the Graph Type dialog box with the Category Axis options displayed. Choose a Length option and enter a value for the number of tick marks for the x-axis.

*Click on the line (not the square marker) to select the legend and its line bar.*

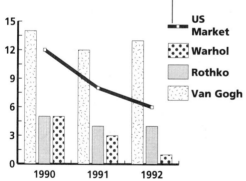

**1** *The Column style and Line style are combined this "Artist's Graph." A new legend name and a column of new data was entered in the fourth column in the Graph Data dialog box. The new legend box and its bars were selected, then the Line icon was selected in the Graph Type dialog box. The new line and the legend were selected with the Goup Selection tool (two clicks) and Object menu > Arrange > Bring to Front was chosen.*

## To change the type in a graph:

1. Choose the Group Selection tool.

2. Click once on the baseline of a type block to select just that block.
   *or*
   Click twice to select all the type in the legends or all the labels.
   *or*
   Click three times to select all the type in the graph.

3. Modify the type as usual.

**TIP** To switch the row and column data, choose Object menu > Graphs > Data, then click the Transpose row/column (second) button.

## To combine different styles in one graph:

1. Choose the Group Selection tool.

2. Click twice on the legend box for the category you want to have in a new style.

3. Choose Object menu > Graphs > Type.

4. Choose a new Graph type and modify the options for that type. For this exercise, click the Line graph (fifth) button.

5. Check Options: Draw Filled lines box and enter 6 in the Line Width field.

6. Choose On Left Side from the Value Axis drop-down menu.

7. Click OK **1**.

**TIP** To select the line bar in the graph, click twice with the Group Selection tool on the small line bar in the legend (not on the small square marker), or click on the line bar segments in the graph.

**TIP** To modify the marker squares (the points on the line), double-click on the square marker in the legend with the Group Selection tool.

You can replace the rectangles in a graph with graphic objects.

### To create a custom graph design:

1. Create a graphic object. Draw a rectangle around the object. Apply a fill and stroke of None (unless you want the rectangle to display in the graph). With the rectangle selected, choose Object menu > Arrange > Send To Back.

2. Choose the Selection tool, and press and drag a marquee over the rectangle and the graphic object. Group the objects, if desired, and leave them selected.

3. Choose Object menu > Graphs > Design.

4. Click New Design 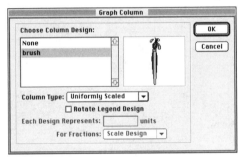.

5. Enter a name for the graphic object. For this exercise, click Rename, type "Brush," click OK, then click OK again.

6. Click three times on a legend box with the Group Selection tool (the legend and its bars should be selected).

7. Choose Object menu > Graphs > Column.

8. Choose a column design, and choose from the Column Type drop-down menu 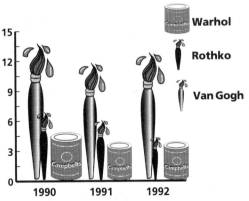. The selected type will preview in a thumbnail. For the "Artists Graph," we chose Uniformly scaled to keep the brush wide and we unchecked the "Rotate legend design" box. Click OK 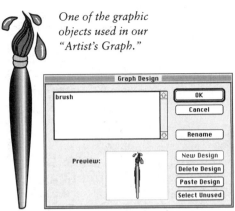.

Choose the "Vertically scaled" option to stretch the entire design object.

Choose the "Repeating" option to create a stacked column of design objects. The top of the stack can be scaled or cropped (for the Fractions options) to fit the numeric value of that column. To keep the design object from becoming too small, enter a larger number in the "Each design represents" field.

Choose the "Sliding" option to stretch the design object across a section you designate. *(See page 264 of the Adobe Illustrator 7.0 User Guide.)*

*One of the graphic objects used in our "Artist's Graph."*

**1** The **Graph Design** dialog box.

**2** The **Graph Column** dialog box.

**3** *Custom design elements in a Column graph (Column type: Uniformly scaled). In the Graph Type dialog box, we increased the Column width value to further widen the brush (we chose 100%). You can also use the Scale tool to resize a selected graph object.*

Customize a Graph

# PRECISION TOOLS 21

There are many tools that you can use to position or move objects more precisely. In this chapter you will learn how to use rulers, guides, and grids to align and position objects. How to move an object a specified distance via the Move dialog box. How to use the Measure tool to calculate distances between objects. How to use the Transform palette to reposition, resize, rotate, or shear an object. And how to use the Align palette to align or distribute objects.

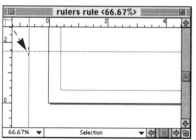

**1** *Press and drag diagonally away from the intersection of the rulers.*

*(Double-click the intersection of the rulers if you want to restore the default ruler origin.)*

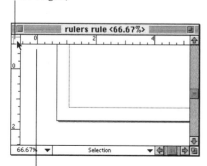

**2** *Note the new position of the zeros on the rulers after dragging the ruler origin.*

## The ruler origin

The rulers are located on the top and left edges of the document window. The ruler origin is the point from which all measurements are read—the point where the zero is on each ruler. By default, the ruler origin is positioned at the lower left corner of the page, but it can be moved to a different location in any individual document.

To move the ruler origin, make sure the rulers are displayed (choose View menu > Show Rulers or use the Command-R/Ctrl-R shortcut), then drag the square where the two rulers intersect to a new position **1**–**2**. To restore the ruler origin to its default position, double-click where the two rulers intersect at the upper left corner of the document window.

*Note:* If you move the ruler origin, the position of a pattern fill in a newly created object may differ from the position of the same pattern in an existing object.

Follow these instructions to change the ruler units for the current document only. Choose a unit of measure for the current *and* future documents in the Preferences > Units & Undo dialog box (File menu).

### To change the ruler units for the current document only:

1. Choose File menu > Document Setup (Command-Shift-P/Ctrl-Shift-P).

2. Choose Units: Picas, Points, Inches, Millimeters, or Centimeters 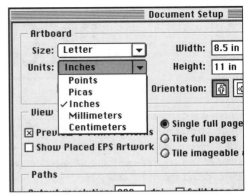.

3. Click OK. The ruler unit you chose will also be used in dialog boxes.

**TIP** The larger the view size, the finer the ruler increments. The current location of the pointer is indicated by dotted lines on the rulers.

*Choose **Units: Points, Picas, Inches, Millimeters,** or **Centimeters** in the **Document Setup** dialog box.*

Guides are non-printing dotted lines that you can use to mechanically align or arrange objects. If Snap to Point is turned on in File menu > Preferences > General, as you drag an object within two pixels of a guide, the black pointer will turn white and the part of the object under the pointer will snap to the guide. You can create a guide by dragging from the horizontal or vertical ruler or you can turn any object into a guide.

### To create a ruler guide:

1. *Optional:* Create a new layer for the guides.

2. If the rulers are not displayed, choose View menu > Show Rulers.

3. Drag a guide from the horizontal or vertical ruler onto your page 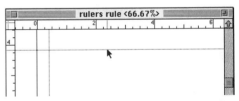. The newly created guide will be locked.

**TIP** Choose View menu > Hide Guides or Show Guides (Command-;/Ctrl-;) to hide or display guides.

*Press and drag a **guide** from the horizontal or vertical ruler.*

### To turn an object into a guide:

1. Select an object or a group of objects .

2. Choose View menu > Make Guides (Command-5/Ctrl-5) 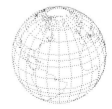.

 *The original object.*  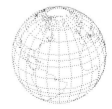 *The object turned into a guide.*

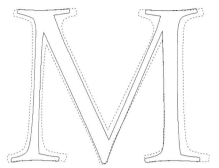

*Typeface designer Jonathan Hoefler uses guides created from outline text characters as a reference for creating new characters. In this example, a character in the text version of the Mazarin typeface that he designed for GQ magazine was turned into guides and served as a reference for creating a new version of the typeface for larger display sizes.*

By default guides are locked. To select or move guides, they must be unlocked.

### To unlock guides:

1. Choose View menu > Lock Guides (Command-Option-;/Ctrl-Alt-;) to deselect the command. All the guides will unlock.

2. *Optional:* Select any unlocked guide with the Selection tool, then move it or press Delete to remove it.

**TIP** To lock an individual guide, unlock all guides, select the individual guide, then choose Object menu > Lock.

### To turn a guide back into an object:

1. Choose View menu > Lock Guides to unlock all guides, if necessary.

2. Choose the Selection tool and select the guide. (To release multiple guides, use the Selection tool to marquee or Shift-click them).

3. Choose View menu > Release Guides (Command-Option-5/Ctrl-Alt-5). The guide will turn into a selected object with its former fill and stroke.

### See it from a new angle

Choose File menu > Preferences > General, then enter a new number in the Constrain Angle field (0° is the default). Any new object that you draw in a new or existing document will rest on the new axes, and any new object that you move or transform with Shift held down will snap to the new axes. This tool also affects text objects, and the Rectangle, Ellipse, Graph, Scale, Reflect, and Shear tools, as well as the arrow keys, the grid, and Info palette readouts.

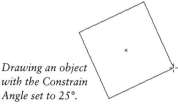

*Drawing an object with the Constrain Angle set to 25°.*

Grids are non-printing lines, displayed or hidden, that can be used to help align objects in exact geometric schemes. Objects can snap to the grid. To change the grid style (lines or dots), color, or spacing, see page 268.

### To view the default or current grid:

Choose View menu > Show Grid (Command-"/Ctrl-"). Choose this command again to hide the grid.

### To force objects to snap to the grid:

Choose View menu > Snap to Grid (Command-Shift-"/Ctrl-Shift-"). The snap function works even when the grid is not displayed. Choose the command again to turn it off.

## To place guides around an object or create evenly spaced guides:

1. Choose the Selection tool, then select an existing rectangle. *Warning:* If you use a non-rectangular shape, the shape will revert to a rectangle!
   *or*
   Choose the Rectangle tool, then drag a rectangle to define the guide area 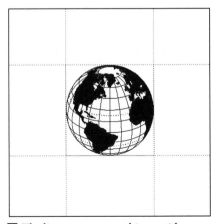.

2. Make sure the ruler origin is in the default location.

3. Choose Type menu > Rows & Columns.

4. Make sure the Preview box is checked 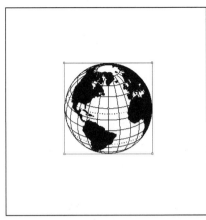, and check the Add Guides box.

5. Choose the desired number of Columns or Rows, Column Width, Row Height, and Gutters. To encircle the object with guides without dividing it, leave the number of Columns and Rows as 1.

6. Click OK or press Return/Enter 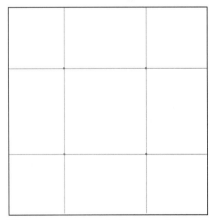.

7. Choose the Selection tool.

8. Shift-click on the rectangle or rectangles to deselect them so they are not affected by the next step.

9. Choose View menu > Make Guides . If you like, you can now delete the rectangles that were used to create the guides.

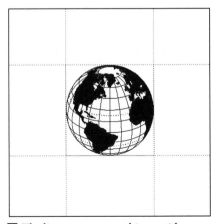

**1** *A rectangle is drawn around the globe to define the guide area.*

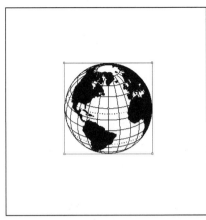

**2** *Choose rows and columns specifications.*

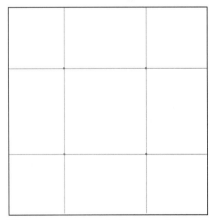

**3** *Lines are automatically created around the rectangle.*

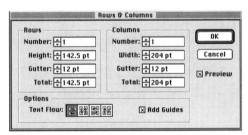

**4** *The lines are converted into guides.*

*Guides Around an Object; Evenly Spaced Guides*

You can precisely reposition an object by entering values in the Move dialog box. Move dialog box settings remain the same until you change them, move an object using the mouse, or use the Measure tool, so you can repeat the same move as many times as you like using the Transform Again shortcut (Command-D/Ctrl-D).

## To move an object a specified distance:

1. Choose the Selection tool.
2. Select the object you want to move.
3. Choose Object menu > Transform > Move **1**.
   *or*
   Double-click the Selection tool.
4. Enter a positive number in the Horizontal and/or Vertical field to move the object to the right or upward, respectively. Enter a negative number to move the object to the left or downward **2**. Enter 0 in either field to keep the object from moving along that axis. (You can use any of these units of measure: "p", "pt", "in", "mm", or "cm")
   *or*
   Enter a positive Distance amount and a positive Angle between 0 and 180 to move the object upward. Enter a positive Distance amount and a negative Angle between 0 and –180 to move the object downward. The other fields will change automatically.
5. Check Preview to preview the move.
6. *Optional:* Click Copy to close the dialog box and move a copy of the object (not the object itself).
7. Click OK or press Return/Enter.

TIP If you move an object that contains a pattern fill manually or using the Move dialog box and the Patterns box is unchecked in the Move dialog box, the pattern won't move with the object. If the Patterns box is checked, but the Objects box is not, only the pattern will move, not the object.

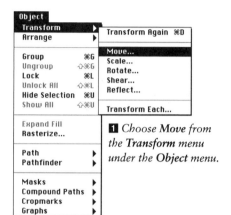

**1** *Choose* **Move** *from the* **Transform** *menu under the* **Object** *menu.*

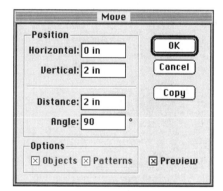

**2** *In the* **Move** *dialog box, enter numbers in the* **Horizontal** *and* **Vertical** *fields, or enter a* **Distance** *and* **Angle** *you want the object to move.*

**Move an Object a Specified Distance**

You can use the Measure tool to calculate the distance and/or angle between two points in an illustration. When you use the Measure tool, the amounts it calculates are displayed on the Info palette, which opens automatically.

The distances calculated using the Measure tool, as displayed on the Info palette, also become the current values in the Move dialog box, so you can use the Measure tool as a guide to judge how far to move an object first, then open the Move dialog box and click OK.

### To measure a distance using the Measure tool:

1. Choose the Measure tool (U) .

2. Click the starting and ending points spanning the distance or angle you want to measure 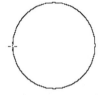–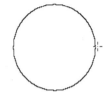.
   *or*
   Press and drag from the first point to the second point.

   Measurements will be displayed in the "D:" area on the Info palette 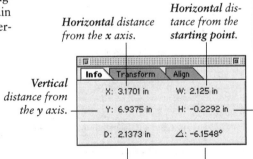.

**TIP** Hold down Shift while clicking or dragging with the Measure tool to constrain the measurement to a horizontal or vertical axis.

**2** *Click a starting point. The Info palette will open.*

**3** *Click an ending point. The distance between clicks will display on the Info palette.*

**1** *Measure tool.*

*Vertical distance from the starting point.*

*Horizontal distance from the starting point.*

*Horizontal distance from the x axis.*

*Vertical distance from the y axis.*

*Total distance from the starting point.*

*Angle from the starting point.*

**4** *The Info palette after clicking a starting and ending point with the Measure tool. The x and y positions are measured from the ruler origin.*

## Let the palette do the math

In the W or H field on the Transform palette, you can perform simple math to resize an object. Type an asterisk, then a percentage value. For example, click to the right of the current value, then type "*50%." Or replace the entire field with "50%" to reduce the current size value by half (i.e., 4p becomes 2p). Or type "75%" to reduce the W or H to three-quarters of it's current value (i.e., 4p becomes 3p). Or enter a positive or negative number to the right of the current number, like "+2" or "-2", to increase or decrease, respectively, the current value by that amount. Press Tab to apply the math and advance to another field, or press Return/Enter to exit the palette.

Use the Transform palette to reposition, resize, rotate, or shear an object or objects based on exact values or percentages.

## To reposition, resize, rotate, or shear an object using the Transform palette:

1. If the Transform palette isn't open, choose Window menu > Show Transform.

2. Select an object or objects.

3. Choose the reference point from which you want the transformation to be measured by clicking a handle on the Reference Point Options icon on the left side of the palette **1**.

4. Press Return (to exit the palette) or press Tab (to highlight the next field) to apply any of these new values:

   To **move** the object horizontally, enter a new value in the X field. (Enter a higher value to move the object to the right.)

   To **move** the object vertically, enter a new value in the Y field. (Enter a higher value to move the object upward.)

   To change the **width** and/or **height** of the object, enter new values in the W (width) and/or H (height) fields.

   To **rotate** the object counterclockwise, enter a positive value in the Rotate field. Enter a negative value to rotate it clockwise.

   To **shear** an object to the right, enter a positive number in the Shear field. To shear an object to the left, enter a negative number in the Shear field.

*The x and y axes location of the currently selected reference point. Enter new values to move the object.*

*The selected object's **Width**.*

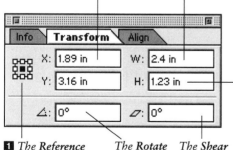

*The selected object's **Height**.*

**1** *The Reference Point Options icon (the part of the object the Transform palette amounts are calculated from).*

*The Rotate field for rotating the object.*

*The Shear field for shearing the object.*

*The Transform palette.*

## To align or distribute objects:

1. To align, select two or more objects. To distribute, select three or more objects.

2. On the Align palette, click an Align icon **1**–**3**.
   *and/or*
   Click a Distribute icon. Objects will distribute evenly between the two objects that are farthest apart.

**TIP** If you'd like to apply a different alignment or distribution option, first use the Undo command to undo the last one.

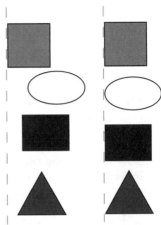

**1** *The original objects.*

*The objects horizontally aligned left and vertically distributed from their bottom edges.*

**2** *The original objects.*

*The objects aligned by centers (horizontal and vertical align center icons clicked).*

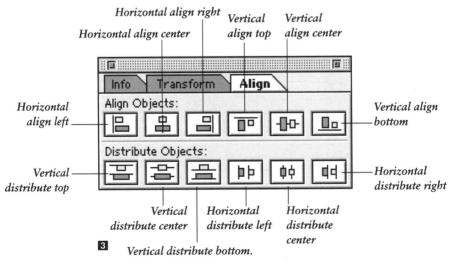

*Horizontal align right*
*Horizontal align center*
*Vertical align top*
*Vertical align center*
*Horizontal align left*
*Vertical align bottom*
*Vertical distribute top*
*Vertical distribute center*
*Horizontal distribute left*
*Horizontal distribute center*
*Horizontal distribute right*

**3** *Vertical distribute bottom.*

# PREFERENCES 22

In this chapter you will learn to choose default settings for many features, tools, and palettes. You will learn how to create a startup file containing colors, patterns, gradients, and document settings that you work with regularly so they will automatically be part of any new document you create. Using the File > Preferences submenu dialog boxes, you can set tool behavior, keyboard increments, units, undos, guides, grid, hyphenation, plug-ins folder, scratch disk, and many other preferences for the current and future documents.

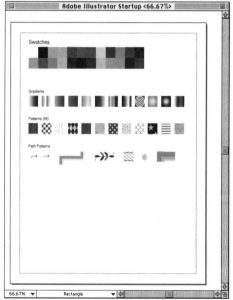

**1** *The Adobe Illustrator* **Startup** *file.*

## Don't overdo it

A startup file with a lot of custom components may cause Illustrator to launch slowly. To reduce the number of elements in the startup file, delete any patterns, gradients, or solid color swatches that you don't need.

## To create a custom startup file:

1. In the Finder, duplicate the existing Adobe Illustrator Startup file (Macintosh) or Startup.ai file (Windows) (it's in the Plug-ins folder in the Illustrator application folder), and move the copy to another folder.

2. Double-click the default Adobe Illustrator Startup file **1**.

3. Do any of the following:

   Create new colors, patterns, or gradients, apply them to individual objects in the file (plain rectangles are fine), and add these new items to the Swatches palette.

   Copy swatches from other Swatch libraries to the Swatches palette—spot color libraries or files from the Other Libraries folder in the Illustrator folder.

   Choose Document Setup or Page Setup options.

   Choose ruler and page origins.

   Choose a view size, document window size, scroll positions.

   Create new view settings.

4. Delete any elements that you *don't* want in the startup file.

5. Choose File menu > Save.

## General Preferences

*Choose File menu > Preferences > General*

### Tool behavior

**Constrain Angle**

The angle for the *x* and *y* axes. The default setting is 0° (parallel to the edges of the document window). Tool and dialog box measurements are calculated relative to the current Constrain angle (see page 257).

**Corner Radius**

The amount of curvature in the corners of objects drawn with the Rounded Rectangle tool. 0 produces a right angle. Changing this number updates the same value in the Rectangle tool dialog box, and vice versa.

**Curve Fitting Tolerance**

The value (between 0 and 10) that determines whether many or few anchor points will be created when you draw an object using the Pencil tool. 1 will produce many points on a line; 10 will produce fewer points. The Curve Fitting Tolerance also affects how many points will be created on a path rendered by the Auto Trace tool.

**Auto Trace Gap**

The exactness with which the Auto Trace tool traces the contour of a bitmap image (0–2). The lower the gap, the more closely an image will be traced, and the more anchor points will be created.

### Options

**Snap to Point**

When checked, the part of an object that is under the pointer will snap to a guide or an anchor point on another object if it's moved within two pixels of it. (Drag from the edge of an object to snap to that edge.)

**Transform Pattern Tiles**

When checked, if you use a transformation tool on an object that contains a pattern fill, the pattern will also transform. (You can also turn this option on or off for an individual transformation tool in its own dialog box or in the Move dialog box.)

**Use Precise Cursors**

The drawing and editing tool pointers display as a crosshair icon.

**Paste Remembers Layers**

Whether an object cut or copied to the Clipboard can be pasted onto a different layer from where it originated (unchecked), or can only be pasted back onto its current layer (checked). Paste Remembers Layers can also be turned on or off from the Layers palette pop-up menu.

**AI 6.0 Tool Shortcuts**

For stubborn Illustrator 6.0 diehards. Check this box to use Illustrator 6 keyboard shortcuts in place of the current shortcuts.

*(Continued on the following page)*

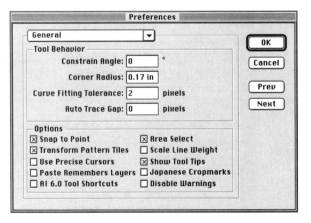

## Fast route to the Preferences

Use the shortcut that opens the General Preferences dialog box (Command-K/Ctrl-K), then choose the desired preferences dialog box from the drop-down menu.

### Area Select

When checked, you can click with a selection tool on an object's fill when your illustration is in Preview view to select the whole object.

### Scale Line Weight

Check this box to scale an object's stroke weight when you use the Scale tool. (You can also turn this option on or off in the Scale tool dialog box.)

### Show Tool Tips

Check this box to see an on-screen display of the name of the tool or icon currently under the cursor.

### Japanese Cropmarks

Check this box to use Japanese style cropmarks when printing separations. Preview this style in the Separation Setup dialog box.

### Disable Warnings

Check this box to prevent Illustrator from displaying an alert dialog box when a tool is used incorrectly.

## Keyboard Increments Preferences

*Choose File menu > Preferences > Keyboard Increments*

### Cursor Key

The distance a selected object moves when a keyboard arrow is pressed.

### Size/Leading, Baseline Shift, Tracking

The amount selected text is altered each time a keyboard shortcut is executed for the respective command.

### Greek Type Limit

The point size at or below which type displays on the screen as gray bars rather than as readable characters. Greeking speeds up screen redraw, but it has no effect on how a document prints.

### Anti-alias Type

Pixels are added to soften the edges of type.

### Type Area Select

When checked, you can select type by clicking with a selection tool anywhere within a type character.

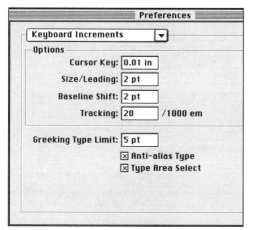

*The Preferences > Keyboard increments dialog box.*

## Units & Undo Preferences

*Choose File menu > Preferences > Units & Undo*

### Units

#### General

The unit of measure for the rulers and all dialog boxes for the current document and all new documents (see the instructions on page 256 to change Ruler units for an individual document). The value in the Units field in the Document Setup dialog box matches the Units & Undo setting, unless you alter the Document Setup units for the current document. Dialog boxes will then reflect the Document Setup unit of measure.

#### Type

The unit of measure used on the Character and Paragraph palettes.

### Undo

#### Min. Undo Levels

Normally, you can undo/redo up to 200 operations, depending on available memory. If additional RAM is required to perform illustration edits, the number of undos will be reduced to the specified minimum.

## Hyphenation Options Preferences

*Choose File menu > Preferences > Hyphenation Options*

#### Default Language

Choose the language dictionary Illustrator will use when inserting hyphen breaks. Choose a hyphenation language dictionary for the current document from the Language drop-down menu on the Character palette.

#### Exceptions

Enter words that you want to be hyphenated in a particular way. Type the word in the New Entry field, inserting hyphens where you would want them to appear. Enter a word with no hyphens to prevent Illustrator from hyphenating it. Click Add. To remove a word from list, highlight it, then click Delete.

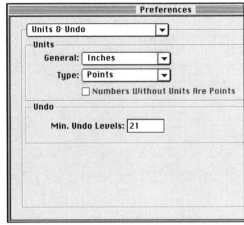

*The Preferences > **Units & Undo** dialog box.*

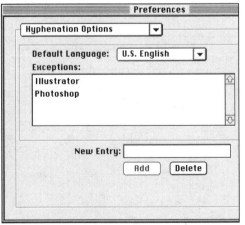

*The Preferences > **Hyphenation Options** dialog box.*

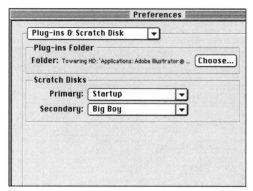

*The Preferences > **Plug-ins & Scratch Disk** dialog box.*

## Plug-ins & Scratch Disk Preferences

*Choose File menu > Preferences > Plug-ins & Scratch Disk*

### Plug-ins folder

*Note:* for changes made in this dialog box to take effect, you must quit/exit and re-launch Illustrator.

### Folder

Illustrator contains core and add-on plug-in files that provide additional functionality to the main application. These plug-in files are placed in the Plug-ins folder in the Illustrator folder. If, for some reason, you need to change the location of the Plug-ins folder, you must use this Preferences dialog box to tell Illustrator the new location of the folder.

The current Plug-ins folder location is listed to the left of the Choose button. To change the plug-ins location, click Choose, locate and highlight the new folder name, then click the Select button at the bottom of the open dialog box. The new location will now be listed.

### Scratch Disks

### Primary

The primary (and optional Secondary) Scratch Disk is used when available RAM is insufficient for image processing. Choose an available hard drive, preferably your largest and fastest, from the Primary drop-down menu. Startup is the default.

### Secondary

As an optional step, choose an alternate Secondary hard drive to be used as extra work space, when needed. If you have only one hard drive, of course you'll only have one scratch disk.

**TIP** To see how much of Illustrator's memory allotment is currently available, choose Free Memory from the Status line pop-up menu at the bottom of the document window.

## Guides & Grid Preferences

*Choose File menu > Preferences > Guides &*
*Grid.*

### Guides

### Color

Choose a color from the Color drop-down
menu. Or choose Other from this menu or
double-click the color square to open the
system color picker to mix your own color.
Click OK to accept the new color and close
the color picker.

### Style

Choose a style from the Style drop-down
menu. Choosing Dots style will help differentiate guide lines from grid lines.

### Grid

### Color

Choose a color from the Color drop-down
menu. Or choose Other from this menu or
double-click the color square to open the
system color picker to mix your own color.
Click OK to close the color picker.

### Style

Choose a grid style. Subdivision lines do
not display when the Dot style is chosen.

### Gridline every

Enter a distance value for the spacing
between the main, heavier grid lines.

### Subdivision

The number of subdivision lines to be
drawn between the major grid lines.

### Grids in Back

Check the Grids in Back box to have the
grid display behind all objects. With the
grid in back, you can easily tell which
objects have a fill of None, because the grid
will be visible underneath them.

**TIP** Guides will snap to grid lines if View
menu > Snap to Grid is turned on.

**TIP** If Snap to Grid and Snap to Point are
both turned on at the same time, it
may be hard to tell whether an object
is snapping to the grid or to a guide,
especially if the grid isn't displayed.

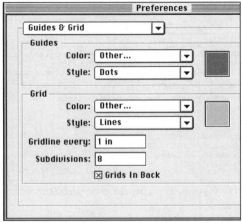

*The **Guides & Grid** Preferences dialog box.*

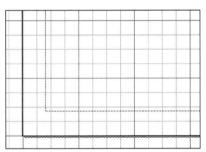

*Grid lines with four subdivisions.*

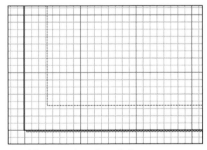

*Grid lines with eight subdivisions.*

# OUTPUT 23

*Illustrator objects are described and stored as mathematical commands. But when they are printed, they are rendered as dots. The higher the resolution of the output device, the finer and sharper the rendering of lines, curves, gradients, and continuous-tone images. In this chapter you will learn to print an illustration on a PostScript black-and-white or composite color printer, to create crop or trim marks, to print an oversized illustration, to troubleshoot printing problems, and to produce smooth blends. You'll also learn how to save a file in a variety of formats for export to other applications, and how to prepare a file for the World Wide Web. (To produce color separations, read the next chapter.)*

Michael Bartalos, **Downloading Files**, for In Magazine

### To print on a black-and-white or color PostScript printer:

1. Macintosh users: Select the Chooser, click the LaserWriter icon, click on the desired printer name, then close the Chooser. Windows users: Choose a printer from the Print Setup dialog box in the Document Setup dialog box.

2. In Illustrator, choose File menu > Document Setup.

3. Macintosh users: Click Page Setup. Windows users: Click Print Setup, click Properties, then click the Paper tab.

4. Choose a size from the Paper pop-up menu 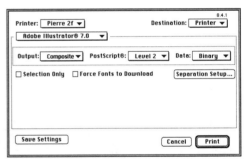.
   *and*
   Make sure the correct Orientation icon is selected (to print vertically or horizontally on the paper), then click OK.

5. Click OK or press Return/Enter.

6. Choose File menu > Print (Command-P/Ctrl-P).

7. Mac users: Choose Adobe Illustrator 7.0 from the pop-up menu. Mac and Win users: Choose PostScript®: Level 1 or Level 2 (depending on your printer and printer driver) 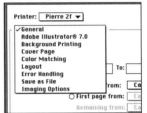–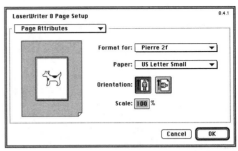.

8. Mac users: Choose Color Matching. Mac and Win users: Choose Color/Grayscale so colors will print in color on a color printer or in shades of gray on a black-and-white printer. For a color printer, choose the appropriate color options.

9. Mac users: Choose General. Mac and Win users: Enter the desired number of Copies 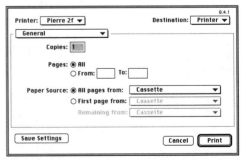.

10. To print a single full page document or a Tile imageable areas document, leave the Pages: All button selected.
    *or*
    To print selective tiled pages, enter starting and ending page numbers in the From and To fields.

11. Mac users: Click Print. Win users: click OK.

**■ In the Page Setup dialog box for a black-and-white printer, choose a Paper size from the Paper pop-up menu.**

**② On Macintosh, choose the various option areas from the Print dialog box pop-up menu.**

**③ In the Illustrator area of the Print dialog box, choose the PostScript Level 2 option.**

**④ In the Print dialog box, enter a number of Copies and the Pages you want to print.**

*Print Black & White or Color*

## Smoother halftones

If your printer has halftone enhancing software, choose the Imaging Options area in the Print dialog box, then click On for PhotoGrade and/or FinePrint (Macintosh). Or, choose Properties from the Print Setup dialog box and turn on the enhancement option under the Graphics tab or the Device Options tab (Windows). Click OK. Next, check the Use printer's default screen option in the Document Setup dialog box. This will enable the printer's halftone method and disable Illustrator's built-in halftone method.

**1** *Rectangle tool.*

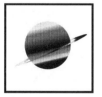

**2** *A rectangle is drawn.*

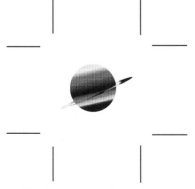

**3** *After choosing the Make Cropmarks command.*

Crop marks are short perpendicular lines around the edge of a page that a print shop uses as guides for trimming the paper. Illustrator's Cropmarks command creates crop marks around a rectangle that you draw, and they become part of your illustration.

### To create crop marks:

1. Choose the Rectangle tool (M) **1**.

2. Draw a rectangle to encompass some or all of the objects in the illustration **2**.

3. With the rectangle still selected, choose Object menu > Cropmarks > Make. The rectangle will disappear, and crop marks will appear where the corners of the rectangle were **3**.

**TIP** If you don't create a rectangle before choosing Object > Cropmarks > Make, crop marks will be placed around the full page. If Tile full pages is selected (Document Setup), then crop marks will be created for only one page.

**TIP** Only one set of crops can be created per illustration using the Cropmarks command. To create more than one set of crop marks in an illustration, apply the Trim Marks filter (instructions are on the next page).

**TIP** If you apply Object > Cropmarks > Make a second time, new marks will replace the existing ones.

### To remove crop marks created with the Cropmarks command:

Choose Object menu > Cropmarks > Release. The selected rectangle will reappear, with a fill and stroke of None. You can repaint it or delete it.

**TIP** If the crop marks were created for the entire page, the released rectangle will be the same dimensions as the printable page (and the same size as the Artboard, if the Artboard dimensions match the printable page dimensions).

The Trim Marks filter places eight trim marks around a selected object or objects. You can create more than one set of Trim Marks in an illustration.

### To create trim marks:

1. Select the object or objects to be trimmed.

2. Choose Filter menu > Create > Trim Marks. Trim marks will surround the smallest rectangle that could be drawn around the object or objects **1**.

**TIP** Group the trim marks with the objects they surround so you can move them as a unit.

**TIP** To move or delete trim marks, select them first with the Selection tool.

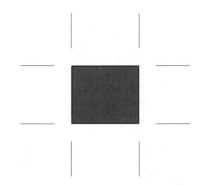

**1** *After applying the* **Trim Marks** *filter.*

### To print (tile) an illustration that is larger than the paper size:

1. Choose File > Document Setup.

2. Choose the appropriate Artboard dimensions (Width and Height) for the illustration **2**.

3. Click "Tile imageable areas."

4. *Optional:* Change the Orientation in the Page Setup/Print Setup dialog box to change the orientation of the tiles.

5. Click OK or press Return/Enter.

6. Double-click the Hand tool (H) to display the entire Artboard.

7. *Optional:* Choose the Page tool (H) **3**, then press and drag the tile grid so it divides the illustration into better tiling breaks. The grid will redraw **4**.

8. Follow steps 6–11 on page 270 to print.

**TIP** On a Tile imageable areas document, only tile pages with objects on them will print. If a direction line from a curved anchor point extends onto a blank tile, that page will also print.

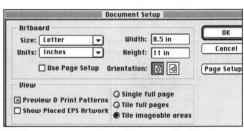

**2** *Choose or enter the appropriate* **Artboard** *dimensions and turn on* **Tile imageable areas** *in the* **Document Setup** *dialog box.*

**3** *The Page tool.*

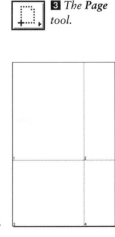

**4** *The tile grid.*

## Send me a letter

On Windows, the File menu also contains the Send command. Use this command to send the current illustration file directly to a selected system device (i.e., mail, fax).

## How to solve printing problems

*When things don't go as smoothly as you'd like...*

### Patterns

■ By default, patterns preview and print. If a document containing patterns doesn't print, uncheck the "Preview and print patterns" box in the Document Setup dialog box (File menu) and try printing again. If the document prints, the patterns are the likely culprit.

■ Try to limit the number of pattern fills in an illustration.

■ Make the original bounding rectangle for the pattern tile no larger than one-inch square.

■ Use the Path Pattern filter to stroke a path. Use a PostScript Level 2 printer when printing elaborate patterns.

■ Don't apply a pattern fill to a compound path.

### Complex paths

Sometimes a file containing complex paths with many anchor points won't print—a limitcheck or VM error message will appear in the print progress window. To help prevent a limitcheck error, limit the number of complex objects in your illustration. If you do get such a message, first manually delete excess anchor points from long paths using the Delete-anchor-point tool 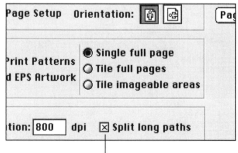 and try printing again.

**1** *Delete-anchor-point tool.*

If that doesn't work, check the "Split long paths" box in the Document Setup dialog box **2** and try printing again. Complex paths will be split into two or more separate paths, but their overall path shapes won't change. The "Split long paths" option does not affect stroked paths, compound paths, or masks. You can also split a stroked path manually using the Scissors tool. (To preserve a copy of the document with its non-split paths, before checking the "Split long paths" box, save the document under a new name using Save as.) To rejoin split paths, choose Object menu > Pathfinder > Unite.

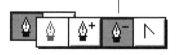

**2** *Check the Split long paths box in the Document Setup dialog box.*

### Additional troubleshooting tips

■ Masks may cause printing problems, particularly those created from compound paths. A document containing multiple masks may not print altogether. For a complex mask, consider using the Knife tool to cut all the shapes in half—including the mask object itself—before you create the mask. Select and mask each half separately, then move them together.

■ As a last resort you can lower the output resolution of individual objects to facilitate printing *(see the following page)*.

■ Choose Object menu > Path > Cleanup to delete any Stray Points (inadvertent clicks on the Artboard), Unpainted Objects, or Empty Text Paths ■.

■ Try reducing the number of fonts used in the file if you receive a VM error, or convert large text into outlines (Type menu > Create Outlines) so fewer fonts need to be downloaded.

■ Use a Pathfinder command—like Divide or Minus Front—to produce the same effect as a compound.

■ On the Layers palette, double-click the name of the layer the object is on, and make sure the Print box is checked.

■ To improve gradient fill printing on a PostScript Level 1 imagesetter and some PostScript clone printers, check the "Compatible gradient printing" box in the Document Setup dialog box (File menu), then re-save the file. Don't check this option if your gradients are printing well, as it may slow printing, or if you're using a PostScript Level 2 imagesetter.

■ If you're creating an illustration using complex elements like compounds and masks, print the file in stages as you add complex elements so you'll be able to pinpoint where a problem is if one of the versions doesn't print. Or, place a complex object on its own layer and uncheck the print option for that layer, then try printing again.

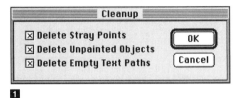

■

The degree to which Illustrator renders an object precisely is determined by the object's output resolution. Different objects within an illustration can be rendered at different resolutions. If a complex object doesn't print, lower its output resolution and try printing again.

*Note:* The output resolution setting controls the amount of flatness in a curve. The lower the output resolution, the less precisely a printed curve segment will match the original mathematically defined curve segment.

### To lower an object's output resolution to facilitate printing:

1. Choose any selection tool, then click on the object that did not print or you anticipate may not print.

2. Show the Attributes palette.

3. Enter a lower number in the Output field **1**, then try printing the file again. If the object prints, but with noticeable jaggedness on its curve segments, its output resolution is too low. Choose a higher resolution, and try printing again.

**TIP** To reset the output resolution for all future objects in the same document, choose File menu > Document Setup, then change the number in the output resolution field. 800 dpi is the default Output resolution for path objects.

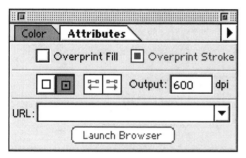

**1** *Change the **Output** resolution for an individual object using the **Attributes** palette.*

## Selection Info and Document Info

To display information about a selected object (or objects), choose File menu > Selection Info. With Objects chosen from the Info drop-down menu, the Selection Info dialog box lists the number of paths, masks, compounds, color objects, patterns, gradients, fonts, and linked and embedded images in the object. To view more detailed information about any of these elements, choose from the Info drop-down menu ■. Click Done when you're finished.

To display information about the entire illustration, make sure no objects are selected, then choose File menu > Document Info. The Document Info dialog box displays the current Document Setup dialog box settings ■. You can also choose to display information about all Objects, all Spot Colors, etc.

Click Save to save Document or Selection Info as a text document. Choose a location in which to save the text file, rename the file, if desired, then click Save. Use the system's default text editor to open the text document. You can print this file and refer to it when you prepare your document for imagesetting.

## Printing smooth color blends and a wide range of gray levels

When printing gradients and blends, you should consider the relationship between the printer's lines per inch setting and the number of printable levels of gray. The higher the lines per inch (also called the screen frequency), the lower the number of printable levels of gray. For the smoothest printing of gradients and blends, the printer should output 256 levels of gray.

If you—and not the print shop—are supervising the color separation process, first ask your print shop what screen frequency (lpi) you will need to specify when imagesetting your file and what resolution (dpi) to use for imagesetting. Some imagesetters can achieve resolutions above 3000 dpi.

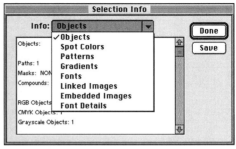

■ *The Selection Info dialog box opens when an object is selected in the illustration.*

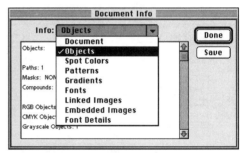

■ *The Document Info dialog box when no objects are selected.*

**Potential gray levels at various output resolutions and screen frequencies**

| | Output Resolution (DPI) | Screen Frequency (LPI) | | | | | |
|---|---|---|---|---|---|---|---|
| | | **60** | **85** | **100** | **133** | **150** | **180** |
| *Laser printers* | **300** | 26 | 13 | | | | |
| | **600** | 101 | 51 | 37 | 21 | | |
| *Image-setters* | **1270** | 256 | 224 | 162 | 92 | 72 | |
| | **2540** | | 256 | 256 | 256 | 256 | |
| | **3000** | | | 256 | 256 | 256 | 256 |

## The blend or gradient length

To ensure that a gradient fill or a blend does not band into visible color strips:

- Use the appropriate lines per inch setting for the printer to output with 256 levels of gray.

- Have at least one color component (R, G, or B or C, M, Y, or K) in the gradient or blend differ in percentage by at least 50% from the starting or ending color.

- Keep the blend length to a maximum of 7½ inches. If you need a longer blend, create the blend in Photoshop and place it into Illustrator.

Illustrator determines the number of steps in a gradient or a blend based on the largest difference in color percentage between the gradient color components. The greater the percentage difference, the greater the possible number of steps, and thus, the greater the length the blend can be. At 256 steps, the blend length can be up to 7½ inches. Here's the formula for calculating the optimal number of blend steps:

Number of steps = Number of gray levels from the printer × The largest color percentage difference.

Use the chart on page 303 of the Adobe Illustrator 7.0 User Guide to calculate the maximum blend length based on the number of blend steps entered in the Blend dialog box.

**Blend or Gradient Length**

An Illustrator file can be saved in a variety of file formats for export into other applications.

## To save (export) a file in a different format:

1. With the file open, choose File menu > Export.

2. Enter a new name in the Export This Document As field to retain the original file in its original version.

3. Choose from the Format pop-up menu (Mac) or Save as Type menu (Win).

4. Choose a location in which to save the new version. If you'd like to create a new folder, click New, enter a name, then click Create.

5. Click Save or press Return/Enter.

**TIP** The text formats (MS RTF, MS Word, Text, WordPerfect) only save text objects (text in a box, on a path, or point text). When imported, each text object will become a separate paragraph. Any original paragraph groupings, text styling, and color will be preserved.

**TIP** Windows users: When saving a file, Illustrator automatically appends the proper file extension to the name (i.e., .ai, .eps, .tif, etc.) based on the Save as Type format chosen.

**TIP** In the Save As or Export dialog box, if you don't alter the name of the file and you click Save, a warning prompt will appear. Click Replace to save over the original file or click Cancel to return to the Save As or Export dialog box.

## Choose from these formats to export an Illustrator file

### Amiga IFF
Use to transfer your Illustrator file to the Amiga format, which is supported by a few Macintosh graphics applications.

### BMP
Windows bitmap graphics format. You can choose the level of resolution, system format, and color depth.

### PCX
A popular DOS and Windows graphics file format.

### Pixar
Use for Macintosh 3-D modeling and rendering programs.

### PNG
Use to compress 24-bit color images for viewing in Web browsers. This format supports alpha channels of 256 levels of gray that can be used to define areas of graduated transparency.

### Targa
Use for high-end DOS-based graphics applications. This format includes options for choosing the color depth of the image.

### TIFF
A format widely used by graphics programs on Mac and Windows for saving bitmap images, particularly scanned images. Includes options for saving a color model, anti-aliased edges, and compressing an image file.

GIF 89a is discussed on page 281, and JPEG is discussed on pages 279–280.

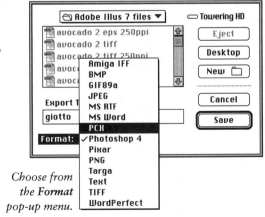

*Choose from the Format pop-up menu.*

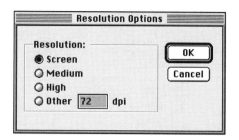

## Secondary export dialog boxes

### *Raster*

If you choose a raster (bitmap) file format like Amiga IFF, BMP, JPEG, PCX, Pixar, PNG, Targa or TIFF, the general Resolution Options dialog box will open. Choose Screen (72 dpi), Medium (150 dpi) or High (300 dpi) or enter a custom resolution value.

### *Photoshop 4*

If you choose the Photoshop 4 file format, the Photoshop Options dialog box will open. Choose a Color Model from the drop-down menu for the resulting file color. For file resolution, choose Screen (72 dpi), Medium (150 dpi) or High (300 dpi) or enter a custom resolution. Check the Anti-Alias box to smooth the edges of objects (shades of pixels will be added along an object's edge).

### *JPEG*

If you choose the JPEG file format, the compression dialog box will open after you click OK in the Resolution Options dialog box. Move the slider to adjust the amount of image compression. There is a tradeoff between the image quality and the amount of image compression. The greater the compression, the greater the loss of image data and the lower the image quality.

Experiment by exporting copies of the file using a different compression setting for each copy, and then view the results in the application you're importing into.

JPEG format is a good choice if you want to compress files that contain placed, continuous-tone, bitmap images or objects with gradient fills. JPEG is also used for viewing 24-bit images via the Web. Remember that the JPEG image decompresses when it's downloaded to a browser, which takes time. JPEG is also not a good choice for a file that contains flat-color images or type, because its compression methods tend to

*(Continued on the following page)*

*The JPEG compression dialog box. As of this writing, the box contains a simple slider. Adobe may, in the future, add the options like those found with Photoshop 4's JPEG options.*

**Raster; Photoshop 4; JPEG**

produce artifacts along the clearly defined edges of these types of images when viewed on an 8-bit (256 color) monitor.

### PNG

If you choose the PNG file format, the PNG Options dialog box will open after you click OK in the Resolution Options dialog box. Choose an Interlace method and a filter option to control the file compression method.

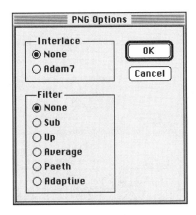

### Targa

If you choose the Targa file format, the Targa Options dialog box will open after you click OK in the Resolution Options dialog box. Choose a Resolution (bit depth), which is the amount of color/shade info each pixel is capable of storing.

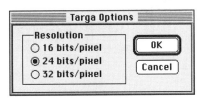

### TIFF

If you choose the TIFF file format, the TIFF Options dialog box will open. Choose a Color Model for the resulting file color. For the file's resolution, choose Screen (72 dpi), Medium (150 dpi) or High (300 dpi), or type in a custom resolution. Check the Anti-Alias box to smooth the edges of objects.

Check the Embed ICC Profile box to save monitor and printer profiles with the file. These profiles are used for RGB-to-CMYK conversion for print output or CMYK-to-RGB conversion for screen output. Including the profiles should help insure better color management.

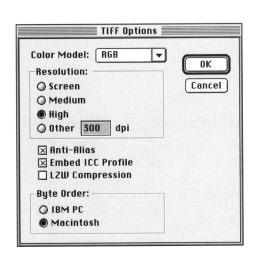

Check the LZW Compression box to compress the file. This type of compression is lossless, which means it doesn't cause loss or degradation of image data.

Choose a Byte Order to export the file to a different operating platform.

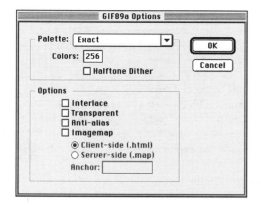

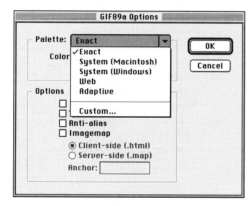

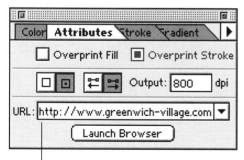

## Attach a URL link to an object

Select an object or objects in Illustrator, then type in a URL address in the URL field on the Attributes palette.

### GIF

GIF is an 8-bit format, capable of containing only a maximum of 256 colors. Since most people view the Web on an 8-bit monitor (which display a maximum of 256 colors), GIF is the standard format to use, and is a good choice for images that contain flat color areas and shapes with well-defined edges, like type. GIF format will compress a file's storage size, with a small reduction in image quality. The smaller file size will download faster and the drop in image quality usually won't be too obvious—an acceptable tradeoff.

### GIF89a

1. Choose a palette from the drop-down menu in the GIF89a Options dialog box:

   Exact if the image contains 256 or fewer colors. No colors will be eliminated.

   System (Macintosh or Windows) if you're going to export the file to an application that only accepts the Macintosh/Windows default palette. The color table (palette) for the exported file will derive from the chosen operating system.

   Web if the image is intended for Web viewing. This option limits the file's color table to only colors available in the most commonly used Web browsers. This is also a good choice if you want to display more than one image per page—all images will have the same default color palette.

   Adaptive for the best color substitution. Use this option when the Exact option is not available.

   Custom to choose an existing custom palette. Use the open dialog box to locate and open a custom palette file.

2. Check any of the following options:

   Halftone Dither for gradients and placed images to be dithered using a horizontal/vertical pattern scheme.

   Interlace if you want to display the image in progressively greater detail as it downloads onto the Web page.

GIF

Transparent to have unpainted areas in the file become transparent in a Web browser. This is a good choice for displaying an image with a non-uniform background pattern on a Web page.

Anti-aliased if you want the edges of shapes to be smoothed by having pixels added along their edges.

Imagemap to have objects, to which you have assigned URLs via the Attributes palette, become clickable buttons on a Web page to link a viewer to the specified URL. Choose Client-side when you will be placing the two resulting files into an HTML-code page or into a Web page design application like PageMill for the purpose of creating a Web page. Illustrator will save the objects to a GIF file and produce the appropriate HTML file with the link information for the imagemap.

The two resulting files must be saved in the same location to be read correctly by the HTML code and the Web browser. You must designate an Anchor name for the imagemap to differentiate it from other imagemaps within the same HTML code.

Choose Server side if the artwork file will be uploaded to a Web server. Consult with your internet service provider when using this option.

### Keep a path as a path?

You can use the Clipboard (Copy and Paste commands) to copy objects from Illustrator to any other Adobe program. If you paste into Photoshop 4, you'll be prompted to choose whether to paste the object as pixels or as a path.

If you drag-and-drop a path object from Illustrator into Photoshop, it will appear as pixels on its own layer. Hold down Command/Ctrl when dragging to keep the path object as a path in Photoshop 4.

**TIP** To match colors between Illustrator and other applications, see page 129.

### Illustrator to Macromedia Director

In Illustrator, hold down Option (Macintosh) or choose WMF (Windows) when choosing Edit menu > Copy to place the object on the Clipboard. The operating system will rasterize the object. In Director, click on a Cast Member window on the Cast palette and choose Edit menu > Paste Bitmap. You can copy an object containing a gradient or a pattern fill or a small Illustrator-rasterized object this way into Director.

**TIP** Create Illustrator objects in RGB color mode to prevent color substitution and dithering when they appears in Director.

**TIP** Illustrator type can be Option-copied or WMF copied into Director. If you find that type edges in Director have white halos around them, choose Preferences > Keyboard Increments, then uncheck Anti-alias type. If Illustrator type is copied first into Photoshop, use Edit menu > Paste and make sure to uncheck the Anti-Alias option in the Paste dialog box to prevent white halos from appearing in Director.

### Illustrator to Painter 4.0

Copy the object in Illustrator, then, in Painter 4, choose Edit menu > Paste > Normal. The objects will become editable Painter shapes. Or, in Painter, choose File menu > Acquire, then locate and open the Illustrator file. You will be given the option to have Illustrator gradient fills convert to Painter blends. The acquired objects will become editable Painter shapes.

## Tips for creating Web images

■ Let the image content—flat color or continuous-tone—determine which file format you use.

■ Use as small an illustration size as is practical, balancing the file size with aesthetics.

■ Remember this fail-safe option for coloring objects for viewing on both Mac and Windows browsers: Copy swatches from the Web Swatch library into the document's Swatches palette for your color choices.

■ Reduce a placed image's resolution to 72 ppi.

■ View the image through a Web browser on someone else's computer so you can see how quickly it actually downloads and how good (or bad) it looks.

## Illustrator to the World Wide Web

The basic formula for outputting an image for on-line viewing may seem straightforward: Design the image in RGB color mode and export it in GIF or JPEG format, the file format used by Web browsers (the applications that combine text, images, and HTML code into a viewable page on the World Wide Web). However, when you load and view an image via a Web browser, you may be disappointed to find that not all colors or blends display well on the Web, and an illustration with a large, placed image may take an unacceptably long time to download and render, due to its large storage size. If an image looks overly dithered (grainy and dotty), or was subject to unexpected color substitutions, or takes too long to view on a Web page, it means your design is not outputting well.

These key issues that you'll need to address for on-line output are discussed on the following pages: The size of the Web image, the color palette, and the file format (GIF or JPEG).

### Illustration size

In order to calculate the appropriate page size for your image, you must know beforehand what your intended viewers' monitor size and modem speed is. In most cases, you should design your image for a 13-inch monitor—the most common monitor size—and a 28.8 kbps modem.

The maximum size of an image that can be viewed on a 13-inch monitor is 480 pixels high by 640 pixels wide (roughly 6.6 x 8.8 inches). The Web browser window will display within these parameters, so your maximum illustration size will occupy only a portion of the browser window—about 6.5 inches high by 6.5 inches wide (470 x 470 pixels).

Saving the file in the GIF or JPEG file format will result in a smaller than normal file size due to the compression schemes built into these formats.

**World Wide Web**

The degree to which a GIF or JPEG file format compresses depends on how compressible the image is. Both formats cause a small reduction in image quality, but it's worth the size reduction tradeoff, because your image will download faster on the Web. A file size of about 50K will download in about 30 seconds on a 28.8 kbps modem.

A document with a flat background color and a few flat color shapes will compress a great deal (expect a file size in the range of 20 to 50K). A large document (over 100K) with many color areas, a placed bitmap image, or gradients won't compress nearly as much.

### Exporting gradients and placed images from Illustrator

Placed photographic-type images will become posterized and dithered when you use Illustrator's GIF89a format, regardless of whether you use the Adaptive or Web palette option. This posterized effect will be visible when you reopen the GIF file in Illustrator or in the browser. If you want to combine Illustrator object shapes with photographic-type images, we recommend you place the illustration into Photoshop and use Photoshop's Export > GIF89a Export command. The resulting Web image will be truer to the original bitmap image's colors.

If you want to export only object shapes, then Illustrator's Export > GIF89a command will work fine.

JPEG is the better format choice for an illustration containing a placed, photographic-type image exported from Illustrator.

### GIF: A compromise

GIF is an 8-bit file format, which means a GIF image can contain a maximum of 256 colors. Since a majority of Web users have 8-bit monitors, which can display a maximum of 256 colors, not the thousands or millions of colors that make images look pleasing to the eye, GIF is the standard format to use, and a good choice for images

### How big?

To determine a file's actual storage size (Macintosh), highlight the file name in the Finder, then choose File > Get Info. This is a more accurate measure of a file's storage size than the View by Name readout in the Finder.

To determine a file's actual storage size (Windows), highlight the file name in the Explorer, then right-click on the file name and choose Properties. This is a more accurate measure of a file's storage size than the View > Details readout in the Explorer.

that contain flat color areas and shapes with well-defined edges, like type.

To prepare an image for the GIF format and to see how the image will look when viewed via the browser, set your monitor's resolution to 256 colors (not Thousands or Millions).

Your color choices for a GIF image should be based on the display capabilities of the Web browser palette. Most browser palettes are 8-bit, which means they can display only 256 colors. Macintosh and Windows browsers share only 216 colors out of the possible 256 colors on an 8-bit palette, so working with a Web palette is essential. Colors that aren't on the palette are simulated by dithering, a display technique that intermixes color pixels to simulate other colors. To prevent unexpected color substitutions or dithering, make sure you use the Web palette when creating or exporting your illustration as a GIF. Color substitutions are particularly noticeable in flat color areas. *(See also pages 281–282.)*

### Illustrator's Web palette

Illustrator provides two places for accessing the Web palette. You can open the Web Swatch library and copy the color swatches into the document's Swatches palette. Or you can use the Export > GIF89a dialog box and choose the Web palette option. Use the Web Swatch library for coloring objects, and use the GIF89a Web palette for making colors in placed images conform to the standard Web browser palette. Bear in mind that using Illustrator's Web or Adaptive palette option for exporting a GIF will cause gradients and placed imagery to become posterized and dithered.

### JPEG: The sometimes solution

The JPEG format is a better choice for preserving color fidelity if your illustration contains gradients and placed images and if it's aimed toward viewers who have a 24-bit monitor, which can display millions of colors.

## Dressing down your bitmaps

Use an image editing program like Photoshop to reduce the number of pixels and color complexity in a bitmap image before placing it. Reduce the image resolution to 72 ppi.

You can also use Illustrator's Rasterize command to reduce the pixel resolution of a placed image (check the Anti-alias option).

To reduce color complexity, try posterizing a continuous-tone image down to somewhere between four and eight levels in the image editing program and then place the image. The resulting file size will be similar to that of a flat color image, but you will have lost the smooth, continuous-color transitions in the bargain.

*World Wide Web*

A JPEG plus: it can compress a 24-bit image to as small a file as the GIF format can compress an 8-bit image.

JPEG's shortcomings: First, a JPEG file has to be decompressed when it's downloaded for viewing on a Web page, which takes time. Secondly, JPEG is not a good choice for flat-color images or type, because its compression methods tend to produce artifacts along the well-defined edges of those kinds of images. And third, not all Web viewers use 24-bit monitors, and a JPEG image will be dithered on an 8-bit monitor. You can lower your monitor's setting to 256 Colors to preview what the image will look like in an 8-bit setting.

If you choose JPEG as your output format, you can experiment by creating and saving several versions of the illustration using varying degrees of compression. Open the JPEG versions of the illustration in Illustrator and view them at 100% or a more magnified view. Decide which degree of compression is acceptable by weighing the file size versus diminished image quality.

Each time an image is resaved as a JPEG, some original image data is destroyed, and the more the image is degraded. The greater the degree of compression, the greater the data loss. To prevent this data loss, edit your illustration in Illustrator format and then save a JPEG copy when the illustration is finalized.

# SEPARATIONS/TRAPPING 24

*You can produce color separations directly from Illustrator 7. This chapter contains a brief intro-duction to Illustrator's Separation Setup dialog box and an introduction to trapping, which helps to compensate for color misregistration on press.*

Trapping and color separations are usually han-dled by a prepress provider—either a service bureau or a print shop. Talk with your print shop before producing color separations or building traps. They're in the best position to tell you what settings to use. Don't guess—this isn't the time to "wing it."

## What are color separations?

To print an illustration on press, unless your print shop uses direct-to-plate technology, you need to supply them or have them produce paper or film output (color separations) from your Illustrator file—one sheet per process or spot color. If you give your print shop paper, they will have to pho-tograph it to produce film. If you output directly onto film, you will save an intermediary step, and the print quality will be better. Your print shop will use the film separations to produce plates to use on the press—one plate for each color.

In **process color** printing, four ink colors, Cyan (C), Magenta (M), Yellow (Y), and Black (K) are used to produce a multitude of colors. A docu-ment that contains color photographs or other continuous-tone images must be output as a four-color process job.

In **spot color** printing, a separate plate is produced for each spot color. Pantone inks are the most com-monly used spot color inks. Using Illustrator's Separation Setup, you can control which spot col-ors are converted into process colors and which will remain as spot colors, and you can specify which colors will output.

Monitors display colors on screen using red, green, and blue (RGB) light. Print shops use CMYK or spot color inks. Illustrator tries to simulate print color on screen using its own color management system which works in conjunction with ColorSync (Macintosh) or Kodak ICC-compliant color management engine (Windows). In order to produce consistent and predictable output, you must choose a monitor and printer profile to tailor the color management to your specific setup.

### To calibrate your color monitor with color management software installed:

1. (Macintosh) Use the ColorSync control panel under the Apple menu to set up the overall system profile.

2. Choose File menu > Color Settings **1**.

3. (Macintosh) The chosen ColorSync setting will automatically be inserted for the monitor profile.

   (Windows) Choose a monitor profile from the Monitor drop-down menu.

4. Choose a profile from the Printer drop-down menu. If you are unsure of the final output, choose the Illustrator Printer Default profile.

5. Choose a rendering intent from the Intent drop-down menu. The Description field will display brief descriptions of each selected intent option.

6. *Optional:* Check the "Simulate print colors on display" box if you want the on-screen display of colors in the illustration to simulate their output equivalents for the chosen CMYK device. Check all the color channel boxes, unless you have a particular reason for excluding a channel from the output simulation. (Check the Simulate print colors on display option, then check only one or two channels to preview and print only those specific color channels.)

7. Click OK or press Return/Enter.

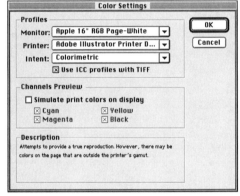

**1** *The Color Settings command uses this dialog box when color management system software is installed.*

Calibrate a Monitor

If you do not have color management system software installed, the Color Settings dialog box displays other options for calibrating on-screen color. Use a printed progressive color bar from your print shop for these instructions.

### To calibrate your color monitor with no color management software installed:

1. Choose File menu > Color Settings.

2. If you move files between Adobe Photoshop and Adobe Illustrator, check the "Use CIE calibration" box so Illustrator can match Photoshop's RGB-to-CMYK conversion settings 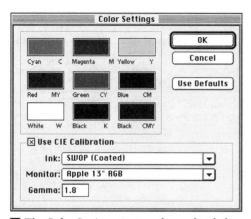.

*Follow steps 3–5 if you checked the use CIE Calibration box.*

3. Choose the ink and printer type your final printer will use from the Ink drop-down menu.

4. Choose your monitor type from the Monitor drop-down menu for better translation between on-screen color and printed color.

5. Macintosh users: Enter an amount in the Gamma field—the same amount as in Photoshop's Gamma Control Panel (usually 1.8).

*Follow steps 6–8 if you didn't check the Use CIE Calibration box.*

6. Compare the nine swatches with a printed progressive color bar from your print shop. If a swatch doesn't closely match the color on the printed bar, click on the bar.

7. In the system Color Picker, move the luminosity slider or change the Hue Angle, Saturation, or Lightness value to make the new color swatch match the color bar, then click OK 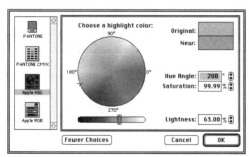.

8. Repeat steps 6–7 for any other swatches that don't match.

9. Click OK or press Return/Enter.

**1** *The Color Settings command uses this dialog box when there is no color management system software installed. If you have made changes and want to restore the original Color Settings dialog box settings and swatches, click Use Defaults.*

**2** *The Apple Color Picker.*

**Calibrate a Monitor**

## To prepare a file for Separation Setup:

1. Calibrate your monitor (*see pages 288–289*).

2. Decide which colors in the illustration you want to Overprint (*see the sidebar at right*).

3. Create traps, if needed (*see pages 295–296*).

4. *Optional:* Place any objects that you don't want to appear on the color separations on a separate layer and uncheck the Print option for that layer, or hide the layer altogether (*see chapter 12 and page 294*).

5. *Optional:* Create cropmarks (*see page 271*).

## What is overprinting?

Normally, Illustrator automatically knocks out any color under an object so the object color won't mix with the color beneath it. If you check the Overprint Fill or Stroke box on the Attributes palette, the fill or stroke color will overprint colors underneath it. Where colors overlap, a combination color will be produced. Turn on the Overprint option if you are building traps. Colors will overprint on a printing press, but not on a PostScript color composite printer.

You can simulate the mixing of overlapping colors by applying the Object menu > Pathfinder > Hard command (see page 100).

## To use Separation Setup:

1. Choose File menu > Separation Setup.

2. You'll see a file preview window on the left **1** and Separation settings on the right **2**.

3. To open or change the current PPD file, click the Open PPD button at the right of the dialog box.

4. Locate and highlight the PPD file specified by your service bureau for your target printer or imagesetter, then click Open **3**. The PPD files should be in the Printer Description folder (in the Macintosh Systems folder > Extensions folder) or the Windows subdirectory (Windows). If they're not there, check the Utilities folder in the Illustrator application folder.

5. *Optional:* The white area in the preview window represents the page size. Separation Setup will automatically choose the default page size for the chosen printer definition. Choose a new size from the Page Size drop-down menu if your print shop requests that you do so.

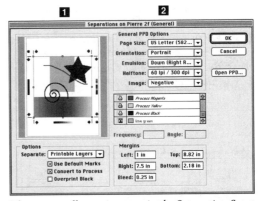

*The current illustration seen in the Separation Setup dialog box.*

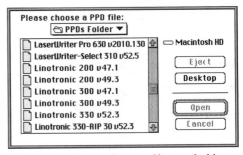

**3** *Locate and* **Open** *the PPD file specified by your service bureau.*

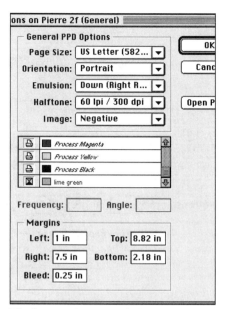

**1** *Choose settings specified by your print shop from the right side of the Setup dialog box.*

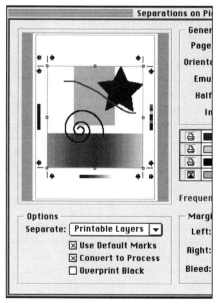

**2** *The illustration will preview on the left side of the Setup dialog box.*

*For steps 6–9, ask your print shop for advice.*

6. From the Orientation drop-down menu, choose Portrait to position the image vertically within the imageable area of the separation **1**–**2**.

   *or*

   Choose Landscape to position the image horizontally within the imageable area of the separation. The orientation of the image on the page will change, but the orientation of the page on the film will not.

7. Select Up (Right Reading) or Down (Right Reading) from the Emulsion drop-down menu.

8. Select a combined Halftone screen ruling (lpi)/Device resolution (dpi) from the Halftone drop-down menu.

9. Select Positive or Negative from the Image drop-down menu.

   You can click OK at any time to save the current Separation Setup settings and you can reopen the dialog box at a later time to make further changes. When you save your document, the separation settings will save with the document.

   Now follow the instructions on pages 292–294.

By default, Illustrator will create and print a separation for each process and spot color used in an illustration. Using the Separation Setup dialog box, you can turn printing on or off for individual colors or convert individual spot colors into process colors.

### To choose colors to print and/or convert to process:

1. Choose File menu > Separation Setup if that dialog box isn't already open.

2. In the process and spot colors scroll window, you will see a listing for each color used in the illustration **1**. For each process color you do not want to print, click the printer icon next to the color name to hide the icon. Click again to show the icon.

3. Check the Convert to Process box to convert all spot colors in the document. This is the default setting.

   *or*

   Uncheck the Convert to Process box, then:
   Click in the box next to the spot color name until a four-color process icon appears for each spot color you want to convert into a process color and print.
   *or*
   Click until a printer icon appears to keep the color as a spot color and print it.
   *or*
   Click until the printer icon disappears to prevent that spot color from printing.

**TIP** Don't change the settings in the Frequency and Angle columns unless you're advised to do so by your service bureau.

**TIP** Check the Overprint Black box if you want black fills and strokes to overprint background colors. You don't need to mix a process black (a black made from a mixture of C, M, Y, and K) to use this option.

*Four-color process icon: The spot color will convert to process and print.*  *Printer icon: The spot color will print as a separate plate.*  *A blank icon means the spot or process color will not print.*

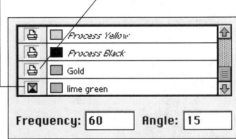

**1** *Uncheck the Convert to Process box in the Separation Setup dialog box, then click the icon next to the spot color name. In this example, the Gold spot color will print as a spot color, and the lime green spot color will convert to process and print.*

### Proof it

There are several reasons to proof your computer artwork before it's printed. First, the RGB colors that you see on your computer screen won't match the printed CMYK colors unless your monitor is properly calibrated. Obtaining a proof will give you an opportunity to correct the color balance or brightness of a picture, or to catch output problems like banding in a gradation. And most print shops need a proof to refer to so they know what the printed piece should look like. Digital (direct-from-disk) color proofs—like IRIS or 3M prints—are inexpensive color proofs, but they're not perfectly reliable. An advantage of using an IRIS print, though, is that you can color correct your original electronic file and run another IRIS print before you order film. A more accurate but more expensive proof is a Chromalin or Matchprint, which is produced from film (color separations). Matchprint colors may be slightly more saturated than final print colors, though. The most reliable color proof—and the most expensive—is a press proof, which is produced in the print shop from your film negatives on the final paper stock.

## To create crop marks for separations

If you haven't created crop marks for your document in Illustrator, the Separation Setup feature will, by default, create crop marks at the edge of the illustration's bounding box, which is the smallest rectangle that can encompass all the objects and direction lines in the illustration. It displays as a gray line rectangle in the preview window. Adobe recommends setting crop marks in Illustrator using the Make Cropmarks command rather than using Separation Setup to set crop marks, so you can control more precisely the exact printable area of your illustration.

Separation Setup regards crop marks created using the Trim Marks filter as artwork. If your document contains Trim Marks, you can uncheck Use Default Marks to remove the default cropmarks. Unfortunately, this will also remove all printer's marks (crop and registration marks and color bars).

The bounding box defines the printable area around which Separation Setup places crop marks. You can resize the bounding box in the preview window so it surrounds a different part of the illustration, though it usually does not need to be adjusted. If you move or resize the bounding box, Separation Setup crop marks will move with the bounding box. You might need to move the image and/or resize the bounding box if the illustration contains objects that are outside the Artboard and there are no Illustrator-generated crop marks, because Separation Setup will include off-the-page objects as part of the image to be printed. Follow these instructions if you want to resize the bounding box (and thus re-crop the illustration).

**Color Separations: Crop Marks**

## To re-crop the illustration in the bounding box:

To move the illustration relative to the bounding box, position the pointer over the image in the preview window, then press and drag **1**.

*or*

To move the gray line bounding box and the image, position the pointer over any non-handle part of the line and press and drag the box **2**.

*or*

To resize the gray line bounding box, press and drag any of its four corner or side handles **3**.

**TIP** To restore the default bounding box, reenter the original values into the Left, Right, Top, and Bottom boxes. You may want to note these values before you re-crop.

**TIP** To restore the default bounding box and the default printing marks, uncheck and then recheck Use Default Marks.

## To choose which layers in the illustration to separate:

Choose one of these options from the Separate drop-down menu in the Separation Setup dialog box to control which layers will be color separated **4**:

**Printable Layers** to separate only those layers for which the Print option was turned on. To use this option effectively, place non-printing objects on a special non-print layer; Separation Setup will place the crop marks correctly.

**Visible Layers** to separate only those layers that aren't hidden.

**All** to separate all layers.

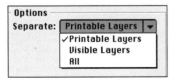

**4** *The Separate drop-down menu in the Separation Setup dialog box.*

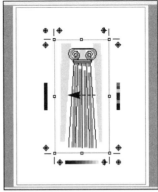

**1** *Move the image in its bounding box.*

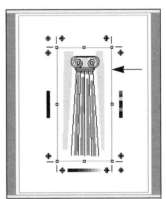

**2** *Drag any part of the dotted line except a handle to move the bounding box and the illustration together.*

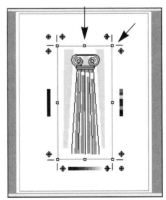

**3** *Drag a side or corner handle to reshape the bounding box.*

**1** *Spread a lighter color foreground object.*

**2** *Choke a darker color foreground object.*

*The arrows show the effect of reducing the area of the darker color object due to the trap.*

## What is trapping?

Trapping is the slight enlargement of a color area so it overlaps another color. The purpose of trapping is to compensate for gaps that might appear between colors due to misregistration on press.

There are two basic kinds of traps. A **Spread** trap extends a lighter color object over a darker background color **1**. A **Choke** trap extends a lighter background color over a darker color object **2**. In either case, the extending color overprints the object or background color, and a combination color is produced where they overlap.

In Illustrator, you can build traps automatically or manually by specifying your own stroke width percentage.

*Note:* Ask your print shop for advice before building traps into your illustration.

*Overprint Fill box.*    **3** *Overprint Stroke box.*

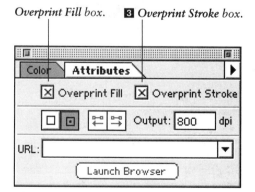

*The **Attributes** palette.*

## To create a spread trap:

1. Select the lighter color foreground object.

2. Apply a stroke in the same color as the object's fill. The stroke weight should be **twice** the trap width that your print shop recommends for this object.

3. Check the Overprint Stroke box **3**.

   The foreground object will overlap the background object by half the thickness of the new stroke. The new stroke will blend with the background color via the Overprint option, and will extend halfway inside and halfway outside the object's edge.

**Trapping: Spread Trap**

**295**

**To create a choke trap:**

1. Select the darker color foreground object.

2. Apply a stroke in the same color as the lighter background object's fill. Choose a stroke weight that is twice the trap width that your print shop recommends for this object.

3. Check the Overprint Stroke box on the Attributes palette.

   The lighter background color will now overlap the dark foreground object by half the width of the new stroke.

   **TIP** A choke trap reduces the area of the darker object by half the stroke weight. Be careful if you choke small type!

**To trap a line:**

1. Apply a stroke color and weight.

2. Choose Object menu > Path > Outline Path. The line will become a filled object, the same width as the original stroke.

3. Apply a stroke to the modified line. If the line is lighter than the background color, apply the same color as the fill of the line. Otherwise, apply the lighter background color. Choose a stroke weight that is twice the trap width that your print shop recommends for this object.

4. Check the Overprint Stroke box on the Attributes palette. The line will now overlap the background color by half the width of the new stroke **1**. The stroke will blend with the background color when it overprints.

### Trapping before scaling

If you apply automatic trapping and then change an object's size, the trap width will change, so it's best to apply trapping after you finalize the size of the objects.

### Strokes where you need them

Make a copy of the objects, put the copy on a new layer, apply the Pathfinder > Outline command to create strokes from selected objects, then set the resulting strokes to overprint. Finally, using the Direct Selection tool, select and then delete stroke segments that you don't need, such as any strokes on a blank, white background.

Choke Trap; Trap a Line

Normally, in PostScript color separations, objects on top knock out the color of objects underneath them so their ink colors don't intermix on press. When a color overprints, it prints right on top of the color beneath it and mixes with that color. Black is sometimes printed this way to eliminate the need for trapping. Using the Overprint Black filter, you can specify which black areas will overprint. Consult with your print shop before using this feature.

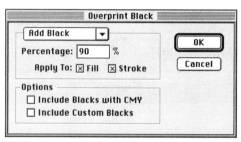

**1** *The* **Overprint Black** *dialog box.*

## To overprint a specified percentage of black:

1. Select an object or objects that contain black.

2. Choose Filter > Colors > Overprint Black.

3. Choose Add Black from the drop-down menu to turn the Overprint option on for the specified percentage you will enter **1**.

4. Enter an amount in the Percentage field. Objects containing this black percentage will overprint.

5. Check Apply To: Fill to overprint black fills; check Stroke to overprint black strokes.

6. Check the "Include Blacks with CMY" box to have any CMYK mixture containing the specified percentage of black overprint.

7. Check the "Include Custom Blacks" box to have any custom color containing the specified percentage of black overprint.

8. Click OK or press Return/Enter.

**TIP** If you select more than one black object and then apply the Overprint Black filter, the filter will affect only those objects containing the specified percentage of black. The objects affected will remain selected after using the filter.

**TIP** Use this filter to selectively color separate objects with specific percentages of black.

Overprint Black

The Trap filter creates traps automatically by determining which color object is lighter, and then spreads that color into the darker object. *Note:* The Trap filter won't trap an object containing a gradient or pattern fill or a placed image. It also may not trap an object with a stroke properly.

### To create traps automatically:

1. Select two or more objects.

2. Choose Object menu > Pathfinder > Trap.

3. Enter the Thickness amount that your print shop specifies for the trap 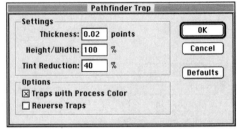.

*Ask your print shop about optional steps 4–7.*

4. Enter a value in the Height/width field to counter paper stretch on press.

5. Enter a value in the Tint reduction field to prevent trap areas between light colors from printing too darkly.

6. Check the "Traps with process color" box to convert spot color traps in the selected objects into process colors, and thus prevent the creation of a separate plate for traps.

7. Check Reverse traps to make darker colors trap into lighter colors.

8. Click OK or press Return/Enter.

The Trap filter doesn't always account for the stroke color of a selected object. To overcome this limitation, convert the stroke into a filled object.

### To create a trap on top of a fill and a stroke (a workaround):

1. Choose the Selection tool, then click on the object that contains a fill and stroke.

2. Choose Object menu > Path > Outline Path.

3. Deselect both objects, choose the Direct Selection tool, then click on the outermost object (the "stroke").

4. Choose Object menu > Pathfinder > Unite to remove any excess points from the outline path object (the "stroke").

5. Apply the Trap filter *(instructions above)*.

### Avoid trapping altogether?

Make sure all your colors share at least one component color in common (Cyan, Magenta, Yellow, or Black).

**1** *Choose trap Thickness and other options in the **Pathfinder Trap** dialog box.*

### Adjust trap height and width

Using the Trap filter, you can adjust the trap to compensate for horizontal or vertical stretching of the paper on press. Enter a Height/width percentage above 100% to widen the trap thickness for horizontal lines, or enter a Height/width percentage below 100% to narrow the trap thickness for horizontal lines. Leave the percentage at 100 to have the same trap width apply to both horizontals and verticals.

# KEYBOARD SHORTCUTS

| **Files** | **Macintosh** | **Windows** |
|---|---|---|
| New dialog box | Command-N | Ctrl-N |
| Open dialog box | Command-O | Ctrl-O |
| Close | Command-W | Ctrl-W |
| Save | Command-S | Ctrl-S |
| Save As | Command-Shift-S | Ctrl-Shift-S |
| Save a Copy | Command-Option-S | Ctrl-Alt-S |
| Separation Setup dialog box | Command-Option-P | Ctrl-Alt-P |
| Document Setup dialog box | Command-Shift-P | Ctrl-Shift-P |
| General Preferences dialog box | Command-K | Ctrl-K |
| Print dialog box | Command-P | Ctrl-P |
| Quit/Exit Illustrator | Command-Q | Ctrl-Q |

| **Dialog boxes** | | |
|---|---|---|
| Highlight next field/option | Tab | Tab |
| Highlight previous field/option | Shift Tab | Shift Tab |
| Cancel | Command . (period key) or Esc | Command . or Esc |
| OK | Return | Enter |

| *Open/Save dialog boxes* | | |
|---|---|---|
| Desktop | Command-D | Ctrl-D |
| Up one folder level | Command-up arrow | Ctrl-up arrow |
| Open file | Double-click file name | Double-click file name |

| **Palettes** | | |
|---|---|---|
| Show/hide all palettes | Tab | Tab |
| Show/hide all palettes except Toolbox | Shift-Tab | Shift-Tab |
| Reset Toolbox to default settings | Command-Shift double-click any tool | Ctrl-Shift double-click any tool |
| Show/hide Swatches | F-5 | F-5 |
| Show/hide Color | Command-I or F-6 | Ctrl-I or F-6 |
| Show/hide Layers | F-7 | F-7 |
| Show/hide Info | F-8 | F-8 |
| Show/hide Gradient | F-9 | F-9 |
| Show/Hide Stroke | F-10 | F-10 |
| Show/Hide Attributes | F-11 | F-11 |
| Show/Hide Character | Command-T | Ctrl-T |

**Keyboard Shortcuts**

Keyboard Shortcuts

|  | **Macintosh** | **Windows** |
|---|---|---|
| Show/Hide Paragraph | Command-M | Ctrl-M |
| Apply value in palette field | Return | Enter |
| Apply value in field, keep field selected | Shift-Return | Shift-Enter |
| Highlight next field | Tab | Tab |
| Highlight previous field | Shift Tab | Shift Tab |
| Highlight field used in last-used palette (if there are no fields, whole palette highlights) | Command-~ | Ctrl-~ |

*Layers palette*

|  | **Macintosh** | **Windows** |
|---|---|---|
| Hide/show all other layers | Option-click eye icon | Alt-click eye icon |
| View a layer in Artwork/Preview view | Command-click eye icon | Ctrl-click eye icon |
| View all other layers in Artwork/Preview view | Command-Option-click eye icon | Ctrl-Alt-click eye icon |
| Lock/unlock all other layers | Option-click blank box in second column | Alt-click blank box |
| Delete a layer (no alert box) | Option-click palette trash icon | Alt-click palette trash icon |

*Swatches palette*

|  | **Macintosh** | **Windows** |
|---|---|---|
| Quick-type to select a swatch name | Command-Option-click list, start typing name | Ctrl-Alt-click list, start typing name |

*Color palette*

|  | **Macintosh** | **Windows** |
|---|---|---|
| Change fill color if Stroke box on Toolbox is selected, or vice versa | Option-click or drag in color spectrum bar on Color palette | Alt-click or drag in color spectrum bar on Color palette |
| Cycle through color models | Shift-click color spectrum bar | Shift-click color spectrum bar |

**Undo/redo**

|  | **Macintosh** | **Windows** |
|---|---|---|
| Undo last operation | Command-Z | Ctrl-Z |
| Redo last undone operation | Command-Shift-Z | Ctrl-Shift-Z |

**Display**

|  | **Macintosh** | **Windows** |
|---|---|---|
| Preview/Artview View toggle | Command-Y | Ctrl-Y |
| Preview Selection | Command-Shift-Y | Ctrl-Shift-Y |
| Use crosshair pointer (drawing tools) | Caps lock | Caps lock |
| Show/Hide Rulers | Command-R | Ctrl-R |
| Show/Hide Edges | Command-H | Ctrl-H |
| Display entire Artboard | Double-click Hand tool | Double-click Hand tool |
| Fit in Window | Command-0 | Ctrl-0 |
| Actual size (100%) | Double-click Zoom tool or Command-1 | Double-click Zoom tool or Ctrl-1 |
| Zoom out (Zoom tool selected) | Option-click | Alt-click |
| Zoom in (any tool selected) | Command-Spacebar-click or Command -+ | Ctrl-Spacebar-click or Ctrl-+ |

| | **Macintosh** | **Windows** |
|---|---|---|
| Zoom out (any tool selected) | Command-Option-Spacebar-click or Command- – (minus) | Ctrl-Alt-Spacebar-click or Ctrl- – |
| Use Hand tool (any tool selected) | Spacebar | Spacebar |
| Hide a selected object | Command-U | Ctrl-U |
| Hide all unselected objects | Command-Option-U | Ctrl-Alt-U |
| Show All | Command-Shift-U | Ctrl-Shift-U |

## Create objects

| | | |
|---|---|---|
| Create object from center using Rectangle, Rounded Rectangle or Ellipse tool | Option-drag | Alt-drag |
| Create circle or square using Rectangle, Rounded Rectangle or Ellipse tool | Shift-drag | Shift-drag |

## Polygon, Star, Spiral tools

| | | |
|---|---|---|
| Move object as you draw with Polygon, Star, or Spiral tool | Space bar | Space bar |
| Constrain orientation as you draw with Polygon, Star, or Spiral tool | Shift | Shift |
| Add or subtract sides as you draw with Polygon tool, points as you draw with the Star tool, or segments as you draw with the Spiral tool | Up or down arrow | Up or down arrow |
| Align shoulders as you draw with Star tool | Option | Alt |
| Increase or decrease outer radius as you draw with Star tool or decay as you draw with Spiral tool | Command | Ctrl |

## Select

| | | |
|---|---|---|
| Use the last used selection tool | Command | Ctrl |
| Toggle between Selection or Group Selection tool and Direct Selection tool | Command-Tab | Ctrl-Tab |
| Toggle between Group Selection tool and Direct Selection tool | Option | Alt |
| Selection marquee (any selection tool) | Drag | Drag |
| Select All | Command-A | Ctrl-A |
| Deselect All | Command-Shift-A | Ctrl-Shift-A |

## Move

| | | |
|---|---|---|
| Move dialog box | Double-click Selection tool | Double-click Selection tool |
| Drag a copy of object | Option-drag | Alt-drag |
| Move selected object in current Cursor key increments (Preferences > General) | Arrow keys | Arrow keys |
| Constrain movement to 45°, 90°, 135°, or 180° | Shift | Shift |

|  | **Macintosh** | **Windows** |
|---|---|---|
| **Paths** | | |
| Toggle between Add-anchor-point tool and Delete-anchor-point tool (either selected) | Option | Alt |
| Use Add-anchor-point tool (Scissors tool selected) | Option | Alt |
| Use Convert-direction-point tool (Pen tool selected) | Option | Alt |
| Use Convert-direction-point tool (any selection tool selected) | Command-Option | Ctrl-Alt |
| Constrain angle of direction line to 45°, 90°, 135°, or 180° (Direct Selection tool or Convert-direction-point tool selected) | Shift-drag | Shift-drag |
| Convert a smooth point into a corner point using Direct Selection tool | Command-Option-click | Ctrl-Alt-click |
| Convert a smooth point into a corner point using Pen tool | Option-click | Alt-click |
| Erase while drawing with Freehand tool | Command-click new path | Ctrl-click new path |
| Join two selected endpoints | Command-J | Ctrl-J |
| Average two selected points | Command-Option-J | Ctrl-Alt-J |
| Average and Join two selected endpoints | Command-Option-Shift-J | Ctrl-Alt-Shift-J |
| **Paint** | | |
| Toggle between Eyedropper tool and Paint Bucket tool (either one selected) | Option | Alt |
| Fill/Stroke box toggle (Toolbox) | X | X |
| Apply last used solid color | , (comma) | , (comma) |
| Apply last used gradient | . (period) | . (period) |
| Apply fill/stroke of None | / | / |
| **Restack** | | |
| Bring To Front | Command-Shift-] | Ctrl-Shift-] |
| Send To Back | Command-Shift-[ | Ctrl-Shift-[ |
| Bring Forward | Command-] | Ctrl-] |
| Send Backward | Command-[ | Ctrl-[ |
| Paste In Front | Command-F | Ctrl-F |
| Paste In Back | Command-B | Ctrl-B |
| **Type** | | |
| Use Area Type tool (Type tool selected, over open path) | Option | Alt |
| Use Path Type tool (Type tool selected, over closed path) | Option | Alt |
| Select a word | Double-click | Double-click |

| | Macintosh | Windows |
|---|---|---|
| Select a paragraph | Triple-click | Triple-click |
| Select all type | Command-A | Ctrl-A |
| Hard Return | Return | Enter |
| Link Blocks | Command-Shift-G | Ctrl-Shift-G |
| Unlink Blocks | Command-Shift-U | Ctrl-Shift-U |
| Align left | Command-Shift-L | Ctrl-Shift-L |
| Align center | Command-Shift-C | Ctrl-Shift-C |
| Align right | Command-Shift-R | Ctrl-Shift-R |
| Justify | Command-Shift-J | Ctrl-Shift-J |
| Justify last line | Command-Shift-F | Ctrl-Shift-F |
| Increase point size | Command-Shift-> | Ctrl-Shift-> |
| Decrease point size | Command-Shift-< | Ctrl-Shift-< |
| Increase leading | Option-down arrow | Alt-down arrow |
| Decrease leading | Option-up arrow | Alt-up arrow |
| Reset horizontal scale to 100% | Command-Shift-X | Ctrl-Shift-X |
| Reset tracking to 0 | Command-Shift-Q | Ctrl-Shift-Q |
| Select Font field on Character palette | Command-Shift-M | Ctrl-Shift-M |
| Select Normal or Roman style for highlighted Font field name | Return | Enter |
| Increase kerning/tracking | Option-right arrow | Alt-right arrow |
| Decrease kerning/tracking | Option-left arrow | Alt-left arrow |
| Increase kerning/tracking 5x | Command-Option right arrow | Ctrl-Alt right arrow |
| Decrease kerning/tracking 5x | Command-Option left arrow | Ctrl-Alt left arrow |
| Increase baseline shift | Option-Shift-up arrow | Alt-Shift up arrow |
| Decrease baseline shift | Option-Shift down arrow | Alt-Shift down arrow |
| Increase baseline shift 5x | Command-Option-Shift up arrow | Ctrl-Alt-Shift up arrow |
| Decrease baseline shift 5x | Command-Option-Shift down arrow | Ctrl-Alt-Shift down arrow |
| Force hyphenate a word | Command-Shift – (hyphen key) | Ctrl-Shift – (hyphen key) |
| *Curly quotes* | | |
| ' | Option Shift-] | Alt-Shift-] |
| ' | Option-] | Alt-] |
| " | Option Shift-[ | Alt-Shift-[ |
| " | Option-[ | Alt-[ |

|  | **Macintosh** | **Windows** |
|---|---|---|
| **Transform** | | |
| Transform tool dialog box (any transform tool) | Option-click | Alt-click |
| Transform object along nearest 45° angle (Shear or Reflect tool) | Shift-drag | Shift-drag |
| Rotate object in 45° increments (Rotate tool) | Shift-drag | Shift-drag |
| Scale object uniformly (Scale tool) | Shift-drag | Shift-drag |
| Repeat transformation | Command-D | Ctrl-D |
| Transform pattern fill only (any transform tool) | ~ drag | ~ drag |
| Transform copy of object (any transform tool) | Option-drag | Alt-drag |
| Proportionally scale an object (Transform palette) | Modify W or H field, press Command-Return | Modify W or H field, press Ctrl-Enter |
| Transform copy of object (Transform palette) | Modify W or H field, press Option-Return | Modify W or H field, press Alt-Enter |
| **Compounds** | | |
| Make compound path | Command-8 | Ctrl-8 |
| Release compound path | Command-Option-8 | Ctrl-Option-8 |
| **Clipboard** | | |
| Cut | Command-X | Ctrl-X |
| Copy | Command-C | Ctrl-C |
| Paste | Command-V | Ctrl-V |
| **Precision tools** | | |
| Show/hide Guides | Command-; | Ctrl-; |
| Make Guides | Command-5 | Ctrl-5 |
| Release Guides | Command-Option-5 | Ctrl-Alt-5 |
| Lock/Unlock Guides | Command-Option-; | Ctrl-Alt-; |
| Show/hide Grid | Command-" | Ctrl-" |
| Snap to Grid | Command-Shift-" | Ctrl-Shift-" |
| Constrain Measure tool to nearest 45° angle | Shift-click or double-click | Shift-click or double-click |
| Lock (selected object) | Command-L | Ctrl-L |
| Lock all unselected objects | Command-Option-L | Ctrl-Alt-L |
| Unlock All | Command-Shift-L | Ctrl-Shift-L |
| **Misc.** | | |
| Group | Command-G | Ctrl-G |
| Ungroup | Command-Shift-G | Ctrl-Shift-G |
| Reapply last-used filter | Command-E | Ctrl-E |
| Open last-used filter dialog box | Command-Option-E | Ctrl-Alt-E |
| Reapply last-used Pathfinder command | Command-4 | Ctrl-4 |

# THE ARTISTS B

**Michael Bartalos**
30 Ramona No. 2
San Francisco, CA 94103-2292
Voice 415-863-4569
Fax 415-252-7252
*xiii, 269, color section*

**Peter Fahrni**
Voice 212-472-7126
*84*

**Louise Fili**
Louise Fili Ltd.
71 Fifth Avenue
New York, NY 10003
Voice 212-989-9153
Fax 212-989-1453
*163*

**John Hersey**
Voice 415-927-2091
Fax 415-927-2092
ultraduc@linex.com
thingbat@aol.com
*color section*

**Jonathan Hoefler**
The Hoefler Type Foundry
611 Broadway, Suite 815
New York, NY 10012-2608
Voice 212-777-6640
Fax 212-777-6684
info@typography.com
http://www.typography.com
*257*

**Diane Margolin**
41 Perry Street
New York, NY 10014
212-691-9537
DiMargolin@aol.com
*54, 56, 57, 59, 65, 80, 88, 94,*
*128, 129, 146, 147, 149, 214,*
*220, 230*

**Daniel Pelavin**
80 Varick Street
New York, NY 10013
Voice 212-941-7418
Fax 212-431-7138
daniel@pelavin.com
http://www.inch.com/~dpelavin
*51, 195, 215, 221*

**Chris Spollen**
Moonlight Press Studio
362 Cromwell Avenue
Ocean Breeze, NY 10305
Voice 718-979-9695
cjspollen@aol.com
http://www.inch.com/~cspollen/
*xii, 1, 52, 103, 111, 133, 134*
*color section*

**Nancy Stahl**
470 West End Avenue, 8G
New York, NY 10024
Voice 212-362-8779
Fax 212-362-7511
NStahl@aol.com
*color section*

## Special thanks to

All the artists listed on the previous page. Their contributions of artwork enliven this book, and they're certain to inspire our readers.

Sonya Schaefer, Veronica Duran, and Christie Cameron at Adobe Systems, Inc.

Nancy Aldrich-Ruenzel, publisher of Peachpit Press, and all the Peachpitters— always a pleasure to work with.

Lois Sottile, for her layout services.

Ian Klapper (New York City), for helping us beta test Illustrator 7.0.

Erle Grubb, of Grubb Graphics (New York City) for helping us revise half a dozen chapters.

Jane Taylor Starwood (Mattituck, New York), for her proofreading services.

**Our Thanks**

# INDEX

Index

Index

Index

Index

Index

Index

## W

Watercolor filter, 241
Water Paper filter, 246
Wavy line, 96
Web palette, 285
Window,
    menu, 14
    move illustration in, 49
    new, 50
WindowShade, 17
Word spacing, 176
World Wide Web, 30, 283–286
Wrap type, 202

## Z

Zig Zag filter, 96
Zoom In/Out, 29, 46
Zoom tool, 46

**Index**